$$\left[\text{THIS WAR AIN'T OVER}\right]$$

THIS WAR

[FIGHTING THE CIVIL WAR IN NEW DEAL AMERICA]

AIN'T OVER

Nina Silber

THE UNIVERSITY OF NORTH CAROLINA PRESS

CHAPEL HILL

Designed by April Leidig
Set in Arno by Copperline Book Services, Inc.

The University of North Carolina Press has been a
member of the Green Press Initiative since 2003.

Cover illustration: Singer Marian Anderson performing at
the Lincoln Memorial, 1939. Photo by Thomas D. McAvoy/
The LIFE Picture Collection/Getty Images.

Library of Congress Cataloging-in-Publication Data
Names: Silber, Nina, author.
Title: This war ain't over : fighting the Civil War in New Deal America / Nina Silber.
Description: Chapel Hill : University of North Carolina Press, [2018] | Includes
    bibliographical references and index.
Identifiers: LCCN 2018020839 | ISBN 9781469646541 (cloth : alk. paper) |
    ISBN 9781469646558 (ebook)
Subjects: LCSH: Politics and culture—United States—History—20th century. |
    New Deal, 1933–1939. | United States—History—Civil War, 1861–1865—Public
    opinion. | United States—History—Civil War, 1861–1865—Influence. | Memory—
    Political aspects—United States—History—20th century. | Memory—Social
    aspects—United States—History—20th century.
Classification: LCC E806 .S545 2018 | DDC 306.20973/0904—dc23
    LC record available at https://lccn.loc.gov/2018020839

Portions of chapters 3 and 4 originally appeared in Nina Silber,
"Abraham Lincoln and the Political Culture of New Deal America,"
Journal of the Civil War Era 5, no. 3 (September 2015): 348–71.

MIX
Paper from
responsible sources
FSC
www.fsc.org   FSC® C013483

This war ain't over.
Hit just started good.

———

WILLIAM FAULKNER,
The Unvanquished

CONTENTS

Acknowledgments xi

Abbreviations xiii

Introduction 1

1. The Civil War at the Dawn of the Great Depression 9

2. Stories Retold, Memories Remade 35

3. Slaves of the Depression 65

4. A Passionate Addiction to Lincoln 99

5. Look Away! Dixie's Landed! 123

6. You Must Remember This 155

Conclusion: This War Ain't Over 183

Notes 189

Bibliography 207

Index 223

[ILLUSTRATIONS]

Advertisement for a Fargo, North Dakota,
showing of *Birth of a Nation* 22

Poster for D. W. Griffith's 1930 film, *Abraham Lincoln* 24

Unveiling the Eternal Light Peace Memorial at Gettysburg, 1938 47

"A Union and Confederate Veteran Join Hands" at Gettysburg, 1938 50

Susan Myrick and Ann Rutherford on the set of *Gone with the Wind* 57

"Mr. Tony Thompson, an ex-slave who studied at
Atlanta University forty years ago" 84

"Ex-slave and wife who live in a decaying plantation house" 89

Scene from the 1936 film *The Prisoner of Shark Island* 96

Scene from the 1935 film *The Littlest Rebel* 101

Marian Anderson at the Lincoln Memorial, 1939 116

Poster for the Federal Theatre production of *Prologue to Glory* 119

Poster for the Federal Theatre production of *Jefferson Davis* 129

Ann Rutherford and Evelyn Keyes as Scarlett O'Hara's
sisters in *Gone with the Wind* 131

Raymond Massey, Elmer Rice, and Robert Sherwood
on the set of *Abe Lincoln in Illinois* 161

Lincoln consults with FDR about war and
slavery in a 1942 cartoon 165

$$\left[\ \textbf{ACKNOWLEDGMENTS}\ \right]$$

THIS BOOK'S ORIGINS date back to car trips with my father. In my memory, I'm about ten or twelve and he's belting out a chorus, often off-key, of "Marching through Georgia." I was never quite sure why he sang this song with so much gusto. Now I think I know.

The scholarly genesis of this book, of course, doesn't go back quite that far, although it still feels like much time has passed. About fifteen years ago, I had a conversation with David Blight about the fascinating ways the Civil War was remembered in the 1930s and how someone really should do a book about that. Since that initial conversation, David has been a staunch supporter of this project. So have other colleagues in Civil War—and Civil War memory—studies, including Bill Blair, Thomas Brown, Fitz Brundage, Eric Foner, Gary Gallagher, Caroline Janney, and John Stauffer. Early funding from the National Endowment for the Humanities and the Gilder Lehrman Foundation enabled me to make some initial forays into the archives and glimpse the rich possibilities for this research. A fellowship from the Boston University Center for the Humanities gave me a chance to test out some preliminary arguments with a congenial and helpfully interdisciplinary group of BU colleagues. I am grateful, too, for the additional funds I received from BU's Center for the Humanities to help defray publishing costs.

Some of the most rewarding aspects of this project occurred on the road, in travels to libraries in New York; Washington, DC; Athens, Georgia; Champaign-Urbana, Illinois; and Gettysburg, Pennsylvania. Since we don't say it enough, let me just say it here: the men and women who staff these archives and libraries deserve the undying gratitude of all of us who write history books as well as everyone who reads them. I am especially grateful to Chuck Barber and Mazie Bowen at the Hargrett Library in Athens; Chatham Ewing and Dennis Sears at the University of Illinois; and Greg Goodell at the Gettysburg National Military Park. Big thanks, too, must go to Nanci Edwards and Bryan Sieling for their hospitality during my trips to Washington, including their heroic assistance during the earthquake that in 2011 forced me to flee the shaking stacks of the Library of Congress.

Pete Carmichael's generous invitation to deliver the 2014 Fortenbaugh Lecture at Gettysburg College offered a much-needed stimulant to pull together my musings about Lincoln in the 1930s. Various members of my department at Boston University, both faculty and graduate students, also listened to a version of this Lincoln talk and made me think anew about the sixteenth president's ever-changing image. My good friend and colleague Jack Matthews provided numerous suggestions for thinking about the literary angle on the Civil War in the 1930s, especially (and obviously) William Faulkner.

A fellowship in 2017 at the Charles Warren Center at Harvard helped catapult this book to the finish line. Having this wonderful, uninterrupted time for writing, along with the thoughtful responses I received from fellow fellows, allowed me to finally turn the disparate threads of this project into a completed manuscript. An additional thank you must be offered here to Susan Ware, who gave particularly thoughtful feedback on the gendered dynamics of the 1930s slavery discourse. My final project would, ultimately, have been incomplete without the contributions of Susan and Rich Neckes, whose fortuitous combination of goodwill, recording technology, and cable access made it possible for me to watch a very bad movie.

Accompanying me throughout were my wonderful compatriots in Booksquad, a group of Boston-area writers all trying to produce readable historical prose. I am grateful to all of you—Megan Kate Nelson, Liz Covart, Sara Georgini, Kevin Levin, and Heather Cox Richardson—for careful dissections, good conversations, delicious meals, fine wine, and mint chip ice cream. If I managed to wrangle out even a few well-turned sentences and succinctly phrased arguments, I owe my debts to you. As the book inched closer to finished form, and as footnotes needed checking and illustrations had to be collected, I felt fortunate to have help from two top-notch grad students: Patrick Browne and Ryan Shaver. Nor can I forget my good-natured and always responsive editor at the University of North Carolina Press. Thank you, Mark Simpson-Vos, for talking and walking me through this journey.

My final and most heartfelt thanks go to Benjamin and Franny, who bring light and joy into my life, and to Louis for, well, everything.

[ABBREVIATIONS]

BMP	Bureau of Motion Pictures
CCC	Civilian Conservation Corps
CPUSA	Communist Party USA
CWA	Civil Works Administration
FTP	Federal Theatre Project
FWP	Federal Writers' Project
GAR	Grand Army of the Republic
GWTW	*Gone with the Wind*
HUAC	House Un-American Activities Committee
NAACP	National Association for the Advancement of Colored People
NPS	National Park Service
OWI	Office of War Information
SCV	Sons of Confederate Veterans
UDC	United Daughters of the Confederacy
WPA	Works Progress Administration

[THIS WAR AIN'T OVER]

$$\left[\ \textbf{INTRODUCTION}\ \right]$$

HIS BOOK EXPLORES how Americans used a troubled past to navigate a complicated present. The past, in this case, was the Civil War, a time viewed from sharply opposing perspectives depending on region, race, and political viewpoint. The present, subject to equally divergent interpretations, was the time of the Depression and New Deal, including the years of World War II. These various efforts to view the developments of the 1930s and '40s through the prism of the past revealed the sharply fractured political culture of the New Deal era and some of the complicated ways Americans confronted problems of race and civil rights, workers' rights and the economic crisis, fascism and communism, and the waging of a war on a scale never seen before.

In a far more modest way, this book has also been a kind of family journey. When I was a year old, my father, Irwin Silber, published a book called *Songs of the Civil War*. With sections on "Negro spirituals," "dialect" songs, sentimental songs, and Lincoln songs, this 1960 compilation merged two of my father's chief interests: the American folk music tradition and the Civil War. He had already spent years organizing folk music events, calling square dances, editing a folk music magazine called *Sing Out!*, and being hounded by the House Un-American Activities Committee for his radical folk-inspired politics. As for his historical interests, my father was neither a professional scholar nor a Civil War buff. He enjoyed visits to historic sites but had little time for what I'm sure he would have seen as arcane debates about military tactics and the countless "what ifs" of the battlefield. Rather, my father came to the American Civil War as a capital-C Communist, the inheritor of an intellectual legacy that saw in the Civil War period the roots of an indigenously American radical tradition. Like others in his cohort, my father, the grandson of European Jewish immigrants, felt a connection to this nineteenth-century US conflict, rejoicing in the struggle for emancipation and celebrating the seeds of interracial democracy planted during Reconstruction. Like other American radicals, he was not an exporter of something far-fetched and foreign, but an admirer of something he saw as deeply rooted in the American folk.[1]

This book is not about my father's Civil War, although it is partly about the people who created the kind of Civil War that my father came to love, as well as those who created the kind of Civil War he despised. For years I had pondered the curious intersection of my father's radical politics and his fervent interest in the era of the sectional conflict. As I researched this book, learning more about communists and Popular Fronters like the writers Mike Gold, Sterling Brown, and Howard Fast, black activist Hosea Hudson, and modern dancer Martha Graham, I better understood the new, left-wing dedication to this singular moment from the American past and could better appreciate how remembering the Civil War, and Reconstruction, served specific political objectives with regard to interracial alliances and the struggles against Jim Crow and fascism. In Mike Gold, a Jewish communist from New York City's Lower East Side, I found my father's spiritual ancestor, someone who wedded a radical Jewish sensibility to Civil War history. And I found others, too, who had captured his imagination, including Carl Sandburg, the author of the long 1936 poem *The People, Yes*, from which my father liked to quote. In Sandburg's verse I heard echoes—although really they were the anticipatory cries—of the hootenannies and "folk-say" groups that were so central to my parents' political activism in the 1950s. Further away from my family's left-wing perspective was another Civil War phenomenon of the New Deal era, surely the biggest Civil War phenomenon of those years: the omnipresent book and film *Gone with the Wind*, both of which earned my father's intense dislike. Indeed, as I came to see, Margaret Mitchell's book and the subsequent film were embroiled in the politics of the period, defended by southern conservatives and Lost Cause apologists, while savaged by radical critics. In the 1930s and '40s, the Civil War was infused with Scarlett, but in many circles it also came deeply tinged with Red.[2]

This book represents my attempt to understand how Americans across the social, political, and economic spectrum found a "usable past" in the US Civil War in the 1930s and '40s, how they shaped a history that often spoke directly to their present-day political concerns. By the 1920s, the Civil War was certainly slipping into what C. Vann Woodward once called "the twilight zone that always exists between living memory and written history," a moment when a small but rapidly diminishing group of survivors still roamed the earth but when memory was becoming increasingly untethered from the feelings of that first generation of actors. By the 1930s, the "memory" of the Civil War, if we can call it that, was wholeheartedly embraced by a new generation who had little or no connection to the war's events and found the war eminently adaptable to their current conditions, perhaps more adaptable than ever precisely because the old generation was passing from the scene. Pushed and shaped in new directions, the Civil War bore the stamp of new political and cultural concerns, becoming embroiled in what were, in effect, the "culture wars" of that earlier time. In these years, the Civil War wore the face of new political actors: conservative southern Democrats; anticommunists; New Dealers; civil rights activists; and the communists and Popular Fronters who were my father's intellectual predecessors. If, as the historian Jennifer Ritterhouse suggests, this was a moment when the "'irrepressible conflict' of the twentieth century emerged," especially regarding questions of race, then it seems appropriate that it would also be a time when the Civil War occupied such vital rhetorical space. In our own times, too, when we live with continuations of the fractured politics of the New Deal years, when white supremacists and neo-Nazis rally to preserve old monuments to a lost cause, the signs are abundant of the Civil War's enormous, even devastating, political and cultural power.[3]

Culturally and politically, the Civil War had a vibrant presence in the 1930s and '40s. With the war entering its seventy-fifth-anniversary season, there were ceremonies and commemorations, especially on Civil War battlefields. A scattering of old veterans attended, as did thousands of civilians, too young to know much about the war but anxious to see and feel some connection to a treasured national past. Spurred on by a remarkable infusion of federal money, federal arts programs also added to the Civil War's vitality in these years, helping to unleash old memories while also reshaping those memories to suit the current climate. Ultimately, the artists and writers associated with these programs produced thousands of oral histories, hundreds of historic guides, and a plethora of theater productions across the country. In the New Deal years, Civil War novelists likewise captured readers' imagination, especially those who told tales sympathetic to the Confederacy, perhaps none more so than Georgia author Margaret Mitchell. The film version of Mitchell's book became even more of a sensation, what with its long-term publicity campaign, a spectacular premiere, an extended search to cast the leading lady, and countless spin-offs and parodies. The book and film versions of *Gone with the Wind* stayed in the news not only because they generated Hollywood gossip, but also because they fomented heated controversy on both the left and the right. And of course no historical figure was more deeply etched into the fabric of these mid-twentieth-century years than Abraham Lincoln. Between Carl Sandburg's biographies, Robert Sherwood's plays, Aaron Copland's music, WPA festivals, Horace Pippin's folk paintings, and Marsden Hartley's modernist paintings, it's not hard to see how Americans had developed, in literary critic Alfred Kazin's words, "a passionate addiction to Lincoln."[4]

Why did Americans return to the Civil War again and again for artistic inspiration, emotional solace, political understanding, and moral counsel? That is the foremost question this book seeks to answer. Let me here suggest a few points for consideration. For one, during the cataclysm of the Depression, the Civil War offered some perspective on a national, domestic crisis, one that seemed to irreparably divide the country into bitter factions. In this way, the Civil War contained a story that many could agree on—New Dealers, southern conservatives, industrial workers, African American activists, and left-wing radicals. Many believed, too, that in dealing with the Civil War, Americans had learned valuable lessons—about survival, resiliency, struggling for justice and equality—that were eminently useful for the present day.

Still, it's not hard to see how different groups derived different lessons from this historical experience. The themes of survival and resiliency were particularly important for southern whites, who discovered in prior struggles with defeat and devastation a kind of spiritual reserve that could be drawn on for the current debacle. Notably, this type of Civil War story even held considerable appeal for nonsoutherners, and so lent added force to a long-standing Lost Cause narrative. Even more, the Civil War offered white southerners a story with powerful political impact, a kind of origin story in which they explained their 1930s circumstances by directing blame at a history of Yankee conquest. Particularly useful in this regard was the story of Reconstruction, told in the familiar form of corrupt and conniving carpetbaggers exploiting an "innocent" South. Southern whites often told this tale to rebut the New Deal tendency to make the South "a problem," a much-resented characterization that, as they saw it, failed to acknowledge northerners' role in creating the "problem" in the first place. Southern conservatives likewise used this Reconstruction story in political battles over federal civil rights legislation, including antilynching laws, which they decried as a kind of Reconstruction redux, a new form of federal overreach on matters related to race.[5]

In New Deal circles, the Civil War became a particularly potent frame of reference because it made the current economic crisis not just a question of atomized predicaments and individual suffering—which is how previous economic panics had been viewed—but as something of national scope, demanding national solutions. Thus, few worked harder than Franklin Roosevelt and his associates to hammer home the Civil War analogy and to use the precedent of Abraham Lincoln for insisting on strong federal intervention directed toward humanitarian ends. Yet gesturing toward Lincoln also raised the possibility of attending to long-neglected problems of racial oppression. While some New Dealers may have been ready to embrace this move, many others recognized how addressing racial justice issues could turn southern white Democrats against the central tenets of the New Deal agenda. As a result, Roosevelt and others tended to strip Lincoln, even the whole experience of slavery and emancipation, from any connections to race. A key argument in this book considers how slavery was increasingly portrayed, in speeches, novels, and films, as a problem with particular applicability to white suffering—in other words, how white Americans appropriated the legacy of black enslavement. Moreover, from a 1930s perspective, white slavery seemed troubling and urgent, while black slavery appeared to be a long-standing cultural development, an issue connected more to folkways than to economics.

Despite New Dealers' obfuscations, many Americans, black as well as white, recognized how much the Civil War hinged, in fundamental ways, around race. More than a few black southerners, in fact, saw a direct link between the efforts of abolitionists and radical Republicans of the 1850s and 1860s and civil rights workers of the 1930s. Indeed, as one black communist insisted, the latter had come to "finish the job" started by the former. In the 1930s, as moderate and left-wing protesters worked to make the fight for civil rights central to interwar politics, both black and white activists affirmed the importance of the Civil War for current struggles. Men and women, especially those in and around the broadly defined Popular Front, talked about slavery, fully cognizant of its connection to a racialized system of exploitation, and raised the possibility of a new antislavery struggle that would bring black and white together to combat common forms of oppression. Popular Front writers and artists likewise celebrated figures like John Brown for their relevance to an ongoing battle with slavery. They also turned to Lincoln, pushing back against the race-neutral interpretations of New Dealers, seeking to transform the sixteenth president into a civil rights figure whose legacy had significant bearing on current concerns about Jim Crow discrimination and racial violence. Notably, too, they recognized how much the 1930s craze for the Confederacy—*Gone with the Wind* in particular—represented a prop for the present-day politics of white supremacy. Their ability to challenge that craze, however, was stymied by a host of factors, including the rising tide of anticommunism, the new ways in which the Lost Cause was sold and packaged, and the lingering influence of Confederate sensibilities in American politics and culture.[6]

The heart of this book, then, explores how these various actors—New Dealers, Popular Fronters, civil rights activists, white southerners with pro-Confederate leanings, and anticommunists—came together and broke apart over various issues related to the Civil War, especially slavery and emancipation, Abraham Lincoln, and the Lost Cause. "Civil War memory," as I think of it throughout this study, is not confined to remembrances of wartime events. Rather, it is an expansive concept, encompassing a range of political and cultural reflections on slavery, emancipation, the life of Lincoln, Reconstruction, and the war itself, all of which intersected and impinged on one another, giving various groups an arsenal of memories that could serve different political agendas. Indeed, it seems important to note the wide-ranging historical reflections of these twentieth-century actors and how much their own memories wandered in and around the Civil War, picking up stray shards of information that became part of a broader kaleidoscope of historical thinking. Thus, it seems noteworthy that 1930s Americans were unusually obsessed with Abraham Lincoln, from tales about his boyhood and youthful romances to conspiracy theories regarding his assassination. In some ways, in fact, Lincoln became their touchstone figure for thinking about a wide range of issues related to the ultimate triumph of the Union cause. In this period his star eclipsed all other personalities or events that had once been present in Americans' memories of the Union war.

In considering these extensive ruminations about the past, I focus primarily on politics, culture, and the intersection of the two. Surveying a wide array of cultural offerings that came out of Hollywood and the federal arts programs as well as literary and theatrical circles, I explore these as cultural productions deeply embedded in a contentious political landscape. Even more, this political landscape, I maintain, was built on the unequal playing field of memory. The culture and politics of the 1930s drew, in significant ways, on memories related to the Civil War—memories celebrating the Lost Cause, or emancipation, or sometimes the triumph of reconciliation—but various factors conspired to give some memories greater power and influence than others. For example, the tendency to read "black slavery" as the product of culture and "white slavery" as the urgent economic problem of the moment had the effect of silencing the memory that highlighted antebellum slavery's oppressive consequences for black Americans. Likewise, the politics of anticommunism short-circuited artistic work that put the struggle for emancipation central to the memory of the Civil War while also giving greater weight to the Lost Cause.

When the United States entered the Second World War, the politics of memory experienced a significant realignment. With a new premium placed on unifying more Americans across both racial and regional divides behind the massive mobilization to fight a war against fascism, certain Civil War memories gained strength while others began to fade. Indeed, propagandists and artists often cast the struggle of the 1940s as a conflict with a similar moral imperative as the sectional conflict: to prevent the perpetuation of a world that was "half slave" and "half free." This narrative ultimately had important implications for domestic politics and culture and the symbols that might be marshaled in ongoing fights for racial justice. It also became just a little bit harder to overlook the brutal and exploitative nature of antebellum slavery. And it had the effect of elevating Lincoln to a still more influential position, not only in terms of domestic US politics, but also in a newly emerging culture of imperialism, as a figure of relevance for "freedom" struggles across the globe.

MY FATHER, seven years old when FDR took office, was, in his own way, a kid of the Depression. He experienced that decade's economic anxieties, as well as the era's social and political ferment. When he was a bit older, he drew inspiration from the kind of work being done—by John and Alan Lomax, Sterling Brown, Benjamin Botkin, and others—to unearth the songs and stories of the American folk, both black and white. After the war, he channeled that inspiration into his own, more intensely left-wing efforts in the 1940s with the founding of People's Songs, a group dedicated to publishing and publicizing contemporary folk music being written and performed by left-wing folk-singers. By then, however, such an obviously radical agenda flew in the face of the rising tide of anticommunism. Although my father was never sent to jail, in 1958 he was summoned before the House Un-American Activities Committee. Asked to explain what subversive subject he had taught when he worked for a communist-sponsored school in New York, his reply was truthful: "square-dancing." Thus, it made perfect sense for him to combine his folk interests, his historical curiosity, and perhaps a hope to fly below the political radar, in his 1960 Civil War song book. And while the reactionaries of the Cold War era may have had trouble seeing anything radical in the American Civil War, my father could look back to the 1930s and come to a very different conclusion.

[1]

THE CIVIL WAR
AT THE DAWN OF THE
GREAT DEPRESSION

ADMITTEDLY, the Civil War was not the first thing on the minds of the American people when the nation plunged into an economic abyss at the beginning of the 1930s. Sometimes, though, the connections presented themselves anyway. In 1932, Louis Rubin was eight years old and living in Richmond, Virginia, when the two events collided. Born into a Jewish family from Charleston, South Carolina, Rubin was not a typical Lost Cause devotee, but, like many other white southerners, he joined in the communal worship of the ancient Confederate heroes when they gathered for a last hurrah in the Virginia capital. Rubin attended the veterans' parade with his father, just then recovering from a serious illness and dealing with the impending bankruptcy of his electrical business. In Rubin's mind, the plight of the defeated veterans and his father's personal trials became intertwined. The story of one particular ex-soldier, a man who had lost everything in the war but then came to Richmond to build a bakery "in the burnt-out ruins of the downtown city," stood out with particular force. "In my eight-year-old imagination," Rubin recalled, "it must have addressed itself to my father's situation."[1]

Hindsight allowed Rubin to look back on 1932 and recognize a moment, not unlike the situation facing southern whites in 1865, that he called the "very nadir" of the Great Depression; yet, when stocks tumbled in 1929 and banks began to fail soon after, Americans certainly had no way of knowing what they were in for. Even as the situation worsened, most probably figured that the economy was experiencing a periodic, and momentary, downturn. Although Herbert Hoover took extraordinary measures to address the situation, he also urged people to think in temporary terms and to remain optimistic about the future. Encouraging Americans to say "depression" instead of "panic," Hoover hoped to make the current state of affairs seem more ephemeral than previous downturns.[2]

But even before Hoover's presidency had ended, things looked bleak. Statistics tend to be the preferred method of measuring just how bleak things were, but they are, of course, wholly inadequate at explaining the intangibles. So we can say, for example, that unemployment reached almost 25 percent by 1933, putting close to 13 million people—officially—out of work. Or that annual manufacturing wages declined from about $1,500 in 1929 to about $1,000 in 1933. But the numbers wouldn't tell us about the millions of people who worked but feared that soon they wouldn't. Or people who worked on a catch-as-catch-can basis, making well below the $1,000 mark. Or about millions of parents who worried that their children would never get jobs when they entered the workforce. Ed Paulsen, who scoured the California coast in search of work right after high school, remembered seeing "great queues of guys in soup lines" but also noted that he and his brothers "didn't know how to join a soup line": they had simply never seen themselves "that way." Mary Owsley, living in Oklahoma City in the 1930s, had a still bleaker recollection. "The majority of people were hit and hit hard," she remembered. "There was a lot of suicides that I know of. From nothin' else but just they couldn't see any hope for a better tomorrow."[3]

Those kinds of stories multiply when we turn to the massive suffering in rural America, where agricultural income plummeted and farm foreclosures numbered around two hundred thousand in the single year of 1933. Those still raising and selling crops in 1933 now took in two-thirds of what they had made before the Depression began, especially as prices for cotton, wheat, corn, and other staples began to plunge. The county elevator in South Dakota, as Oscar Heline recalled it, "listed corn as minus three cents. . . . If you wanted to sell 'em a bushel of corn, you had to bring in three cents." Numbers, although revealing, still can't tell us just how desperate life became for those forced to work the land that other people owned, how many people feared there wouldn't be enough food to feed their families. "When you took a man's horses and his plow away," recalled Iowa farmer Harry Terrell, "you denied him food, you just convicted his family to starvation." Statistics remind us that $140 billion in bank deposits had evaporated by 1933, but that figure alone can never really tell us about the things—a new home, a marriage, more time in school—that now would never come to pass for millions of Americans.[4]

Catastrophic as the situation was, it took some time for the full weight of these problems to register. Initial responses, at least for most people, tended to be individually focused: work harder; save more; and blame yourself for failure.

But when millions stand in breadlines and trusted institutions go bust, people will start to look beyond their own immediate circumstances and wonder what went wrong. Increasingly, the mood of self-blame competed with something else in the public imagination: a tendency to look at the crisis in broader, even epic terms. "In the Public Schools," wrote one of the discontented in December 1930, "our little children stand at salute and recite a 'rig ma role' in which is mentioned 'Justice to all' what a lie, what a naked lie." The source of the problem, many suspected, was systemic, not individual, and it would require structural, not individual, readjustments. With so many enduring a tremendous and desperate type of poverty—while receiving little support from national leaders and institutions—people began to raise some fundamental questions about those leaders and institutions, not to mention the basic tenets of "the American way of life." In July 1932, thousands of World War I veterans came to the nation's capital seeking an early bonus payment from Congress to help alleviate their economic suffering, only to be met by a vicious police assault. "I used to be a hundred-percenter," said one man in the aftermath of the "Bonus March." "I had an American flag, but the damned tin soldiers burned it. Now I don't ever want to see a flag again." By the time of FDR's first presidential victory, later that same year, few believed this was just another run-of-the-mill recession. Rather, there was a sense that Americans might have reached a crossroads, that a moment was at hand when fundamental beliefs might require reconsideration, when structures long believed integral to the nation's health might need to be transformed. As Roosevelt put it before his election, the nation now had to focus on "the killing of the bacteria in the system rather than . . . the treatment of external symptoms."[5]

By the mid-1930s, as the historian Wendy Wall explains, there was a notable uptick in discussions about "the American dream," or "the American way of life," brought on, in part, by the crisis of the Depression and the way it forced a reckoning with long-standing ideals and institutions. Certainly if men like Ed Paulsen and his brothers were suddenly confronted with the prospect of joining a soup line, it suggested that some fundamental notions about making a living were in the process of being undermined and transformed. Changing demographics, according to Wall, also made the conversation about "America" increasingly urgent. The hundreds of thousands of new immigrants who came to the United States before the 1924 immigration restrictions—with many arriving from seemingly more foreign points of origin, like Syria, Armenia, Russia, and Japan—had changed the face of American cities and manufacturing centers. Black southerners, too, had migrated in growing numbers to points north and west, thus raising questions about how, if at all, American ideals would be extended to people across the color line. As people encountered this altered landscape—the ethnic and racial diversity as well as the ubiquitous soup lines—they also grappled with the very essence of national identity.[6]

It shouldn't be surprising, then, to see many Americans also grappling with their history, attempting to assess the character of the American people from a long-range point of view. To be sure, historical contemplation had never been Americans' strong suit. The general mood had long been fixated on progress and improvement and was largely indifferent to backward reflection. The editors of the *Saturday Evening Post*, writing in 1930, chastised an American "public that always takes its past for granted," although exceptions might have been made for southerners. Both historians and contemporary commentators observed, however, that it didn't take long for Americans to feel an unusual longing for their past, perhaps for the nostalgic comfort it offered, perhaps for the chronologic vantage point it brought, and perhaps, too, for the sense of collectivity it provided, a sense of steering through trying times as "an American people." All of this, and more, would come into full bloom later in the decade when artists and writers and historians began plumbing the depths of the American psyche; documenting the folkways of various American subgroups; and taking a particularly hard and meaningful look at events from the American past, including the Civil War as well as the institution of slavery. In the early 1930s, a few tendrils of historical consideration were beginning to sprout, early signs of the contest over the historical soul of the modern United States.[7]

Once Americans began to measure more fully the depths of the Depression, they became less inclined to look forward toward the rosy future that, as Hoover still insisted in 1932, stood "just around the corner." Rather, historical comparisons offered a means of putting the crisis in perspective and measuring its magnitude. Military analogies proved particularly useful in conveying the enormity of suffering. Hoover, for his part, began to think in terms of wartime analogies because "in war times no one dreamed of balancing the budget," a concept that might be useful for the present crisis. Another observer compared the extent of the Depression's devastation in large industrial cities with casualty lists from the Somme. Franklin Roosevelt shaped his 1932 radio address on "the forgotten man" around military comparisons in order to emphasize the kind of mobilization that would be needed to address the crisis. He spoke about Napoleon but mostly focused on the war in 1917, which had generated a strong response but also, he thought, posed less of an emergency than 1932. Even more, the military analogy aroused a sense of nationalism, envisioning the crisis as something that drew Americans into a wide-ranging community, all facing a common foe. Increasingly, the military comparison that seemed more applicable was not the Great War—a conflict about which many Americans had mixed or negative feelings—but a war from the nineteenth century. That earlier war not only called up the sense of a national crisis for the American people but also addressed certain values and beliefs deemed critical to the American condition. The nation, wrote the historian Gerald Johnson in a February 1932 article, is "under the most terrific strain to which it has been subjected since Gettysburg." That same year, John Dewey believed the nation was "in the midst of the greatest crisis since the Civil War." And Rexford Tugwell, one of Franklin Roosevelt's chief advisers, recalled that FDR also began to see the Civil War comparison as uniquely revealing. "There had never been a time," Tugwell recalled FDR's thinking, "the Civil War alone excepted, when our institutions had been in such jeopardy."[8]

Over the course of the Depression, the Civil War analogies would be fleshed out in many ways and by many different groups of people: there would be ubiquitous references to "slavery" and "emancipation," comparisons between Lincoln's efforts and New Deal initiatives, even denunciations of anti–New Dealers as "Copperheads." Yet, at the most fundamental level, the invocation of the Civil War, especially in these early years, was meant to suggest that this was no ordinary predicament that could be neatly classified in bland economic statistics. They hinted at an internal conflict, not necessarily sectional but perhaps economic and social, that produced its own form of casualties and endangered the nation. The Civil War analogy also meant homing in on internal problems and implied, perhaps to the relief of many, less focus on foreign entanglements. What may have been most important, though, about the turn toward a Civil War–laden discourse, especially on the part of Roosevelt and other supporters of those legislative initiatives that would soon become known as "the New Deal," was the way it transformed an economic crisis, which Americans usually thought of in terms of individual suffering and privately based solutions, into something national in scope that demanded the kinds of public, government-driven initiatives used in wartime. Roosevelt seemed to be suggesting that the American people should endure this economic crisis not in their own private ways but rather under the watchful gaze of an active government.

Still, for all the power it could muster, the Civil War could be a problematic analogy, resting as it did on a tremendously contentious history that, even sixty-five years after Appomattox, remained the source of extreme bitterness and division. It would be hard to put the Civil War in the national spotlight without provoking long-standing and often widely divergent memorial traditions that had taken root among northerners, southern whites, and African Americans. For many white southerners, the Civil War came heavily filtered through the accumulated weight of a long-standing Confederate tradition, one that had encouraged exactly the kind of celebrations that eight-year-old Louis Rubin had attended in 1932. In the decades since the Civil War, and especially since the turn of the century, countless southern communities had built monuments to Confederate leaders and soldiers and had paid tribute to aging veterans on "Confederate Memorial Day," a springtime ritual in many southern states. More than these rites of remembrance, southern whites also drew from their own arsenal of memory, ideas many referred to as "the Lost Cause," that offered solace and justification for the disastrous Confederate war. Foremost among white southerners' Lost Cause principles was an insistence on the moral and constitutional legitimacy of secession—that it had been undertaken to uphold "states' rights" and not slavery and, if successful, would have perpetuated a vaguely defined yet still superior and more refined way of life. The Lost Cause likewise stressed the great courage displayed by Confederate soldiers and commanders and argued the Union triumph had only come about because of superior resources that could be hurled against brave southern troops. Increasingly, too, the Lost Cause took particular aim at the memory of Reconstruction, seen as a moment of untold northern outrages committed against white southerners, most notably in its attempt to give a measure of political and economic power to former slaves. The Lost Cause, in sum, allowed white southerners to preserve a memory of an honorable southern past while also justifying the continued commitment to white supremacy and black subordination.[9]

The rapidly approaching demise of soldiers who had fought seventy years earlier did not seem to loosen white southerners' Lost Cause attachments and might, in fact, have made them stronger, particularly when they feared Yankee aggression. Thus, when Albert Bushnell Hart, a Harvard historian, spoke in Richmond in the early 1930s, his audience denounced his "atrocious taste" in concluding his address with a quote from Abraham Lincoln. The very notion that the sectional conflict of the nineteenth century might be termed "Civil War" incited the wrath of Confederate defenders everywhere. At their 1930 convention, the United Daughters of the Confederacy (UDC), perhaps responding to the proliferation of Civil War references in the national discourse, created a committee to petition the United States Congress to officially adopt the name "War between the States" when referring to the conflict. The latter, they argued, legitimated the Confederate quest for national independence by disavowing the idea of a war fought within the confines of a single nation. No one pointed out the irony of demanding that the principal legislative body of the United States adopt a term that would essentially challenge its own credibility. Indeed, in yet another tone-deaf gesture, the 1930 UDC meeting urged their members to redouble their efforts to identify various southern roads as part of the "Jefferson Davis National Highway." By 1930, the Atlanta journalist Margaret Mitchell had already completed most of a still-untitled Civil War novel, one that emerged out of the years of stories she had heard about Confederate bravery and heroism from relatives and family friends in Georgia. Later she would jokingly recall her shock on finally learning, at age ten, that "General Lee had been defeated." Unlike many earlier examples of Civil War fiction, Mitchell's novel would chronicle only the Confederate side of the conflict and would reveal an obvious bias and sentimental sympathy for the values and principles of white southern slaveholders.[10]

Over time, the Lost Cause had grown and flourished in the hothouse of southern politics. "States' rights" became a potent political tool, used most notably by the southern wing of the Democratic Party, to rally both rich and poor southern whites against any intrusions of federal power into state affairs, especially when those intrusions threatened to upset white domination. The commitment to "states' rights" and the Confederate past offered a means for rallying behind the system of segregation, disenfranchisement, and racial terror that shaped the racial status quo of the early twentieth-century South. Indeed, it was surely no coincidence that so many southern communities raised monuments to Confederate leaders in the first decade of the twentieth century when Jim Crow was legalized. By solidifying white southern identity as a "Confederate" identity, the Democratic Party in the South managed to build a powerful cross-class coalition of white southerners, united in their fealty to their Confederate past and their ongoing commitment to white supremacy.[11]

Southern white elites added something else to this veneration of the Confederate past with their insidious homages to the "loyal slaves" of the Civil War era. Devoted "mammies" and faithful black servants were, of course, mainstays of much plantation fiction, perhaps nowhere more so than in Margaret Mitchell's writings. UDC women, too, wallowed in "mammy" recollections, recounting stories of black women who put their ties to the "white family" above all else. Having already tried, unsuccessfully, to construct a "mammy" monument in Washington, DC, the organization still kept up the work through its "Faithful Slave Memorial Committee." These were, of course, fantasy stories meant to comfort southern whites with the illusion of a system that was, at root, neither cruel nor punishing, but kindly and paternalistic. They could be used, too, as cautionary tales, designed to distinguish the "good negroes" of the past, schooled in slavery's racial etiquette, from the disgruntled ones of the present. But these were also stories that did important political work for the South's ruling class: they implied that southern blacks knew to cast their lot with southern whites and would not be deterred by radicals or outside agitators. Oscar Johnson, a wealthy Mississippi cotton planter, liked to tell himself a version of this story as it related to Lincoln and the Emancipation Proclamation. Calling Lincoln's pronouncement "one of the cruelest and most diabolical acts ever taken by an American President" and "an invitation to the Negroes to rise up in the South," Johnson had convinced himself that "there was not a single instance in which the Negroes took advantage" of that proclamation—that they had remained loyal to their white masters. "I think," he remarked, "that is a great tribute to the Negro race." Living amid the chaos of the Depression on a vast plantation where four thousand black sharecroppers worked and suffered the ongoing indignities of southern racism, Johnson probably had to tell himself this story every day of his life. And when the 1930s brought a new wave of agitation—in the form of sharecroppers' strikes, communist organizing, and heightened civil rights activity—the story acquired more weight than ever before.[12]

Before the Depression began, several southern white writers and intellectuals had breathed new life into the Confederate tradition during the 1920s. A group of poets and writers gathered at Vanderbilt University, where for a time they published a journal called *The Fugitive*. Dedicated to celebrating regional characteristics, the magazine also aimed to challenge the Yankees and the liberals who imagined Dixie as a Bible-thumping, Scopes-attacking place of backwardness and narrow-mindedness. By the end of the 1920s, many in this group would begin referring to themselves as Agrarians; in 1930, they published a manifesto titled *I'll Take My Stand: The South and the Agrarian Tradition*. Allen Tate, Robert Penn Warren, Stark Young, Donald Davidson, and others used this volume to criticize what had become known as "the New South creed" and its unquestioning celebration of science and industrialization. By contrast, they longed for a return to Old South traditions that, in their mind, placed a premium on individualism, honest labor, religion, and family. They mourned the South's defeat in the Civil War because it represented a loss of those values and the triumph of northern materialistic and industrial principles, which logically concluded, or so they believed, with Soviet-style communism. Despite their backward glances, though, the Agrarian writers also imbibed a modernist sensibility in recognizing the alienation that separated twentieth-century Americans from the heroic values of the past. Finally, their celebration of southern Agrarianism, even when tempered by a somewhat pessimistic modernism, rested on a firm commitment to white supremacy in its failure to acknowledge the destructive, dehumanizing system of racial slavery that lay at the foundation of southern agriculture. Perhaps the most famous literary offering that sprouted from the Agrarian mind-set was Allen Tate's "Ode to the Confederate Dead," a 1926 poem that paid tribute to the heroic soldiers of the southern past ("the inscrutable infantry rising / Demons out of the earth they will not last") yet recognized, and mourned, the modern-day poet's distance from the sensibilities of that long-ago time. The Agrarians' fondness for a simpler, rural way of life and their rejection of the dehumanizing aspects of industrialization resonated even more forcefully after the economic collapse when the wreckage wrought by modern-day capitalism showed itself in more dramatic and noticeable ways. In 1934, the Agrarian writer Stark Young published a best-selling novel titled *So Red the Rose*, a portrait of noble southern plantation families during the Civil War that was remade as a Hollywood picture the following year.[13]

The Unionist Civil War tradition was, in contrast, a more muted, not to mention less aestheticized, affair in the years before the Depression. White northerners had heard stories, too, about the heroic war for the Union, although they had a less active memorial tradition than southern whites did. True, there were still chapters and gatherings of Union veterans and their kin who continued to honor the soldiers of the North and who also challenged any Confederate incursions in the national memory of the Civil War. In 1935, two sisters, daughters of a Union officer, started the "Society for Correct Civil War Information" and published a bulletin designed to counter UDC propaganda. Northern whites could also draw on a well of traditions of their own such as "schoolroom thrills in singing 'Tenting Tonight,' 'John Brown's Body' and other Civil War songs" and also "vaguely remember[ed] stories of ancestors who died or were wounded in the War." These were the things the Yale psychologist John Dollard recalled, memories that, to him, were part of "an abolitionist tradition which has soaked into our frame of social perception." Yet Civil War remembrance was more diffused in the northern population and had a weaker hold on the millions of foreign-born who inhabited the states north of the Mason-Dixon line. An even more pointed challenge to the Unionist memory came from those northerners, including ex-Union soldiers, who had made their own tributes to Confederate bravery and extolled the virtues of Confederate commanders like Robert E. Lee. As early as 1902, Charles Francis Adams, Union veteran and scion of the New England elite, did his bit to make Robert E. Lee a hero of national stature, a man he lauded as "humane, self-restrained and strictly observant of the most advanced rules of civilized warfare." In 1914, a thirty-two-foot-high Confederate memorial was dedicated at Arlington National Cemetery, initially established as a burial ground for Union dead at the close of the Civil War.[14]

If white northerners wavered on their Unionist principles, African Americans remained the nation's most steadfast defenders of the Union cause and vigilant critics of the Confederate legacy. The *Chicago Defender*, for example, took particular pleasure in chastising Confederates who claimed to be patriotic Americans yet insisted that southern schoolchildren should not be forced to pay tribute to Lincoln. They also cheered on the Grand Army men, white and black, who refused to hold joint ceremonies with their Confederate counterparts. In 1931 they reminded their readers of this crucial distinction: that the Grand Army of the Republic "meets to commemorate UNION AND LIBERTY" while "the Confederate Veterans meet to commemorate SLAVERY AND TREASON. Think of what this country would be, what YOU would be, if Lee and not Grant had won the War of the Rebellion." Not surprisingly, the *Defender* also gave prominent attention to the historic struggle for emancipation and kept its readers apprised of various Emancipation Day celebrations. These events persisted in black communities around the country, sometimes as a parade-and-picnic kind of holiday, sometimes as a more solemn and religious event. Black Texans generally commemorated their freedom on June 19 (the day the end of the war, and emancipation, was announced in Galveston, Texas) while others observed either January 1 or September 22 (the dates associated with the final and preliminary versions of the Emancipation Proclamation). Some orators paid their respects to long-standing African traditions of culture and civilization, while others turned their attention more toward current events.[15]

Yet building a vibrant emancipationist tradition posed serious obstacles for black Americans. Black communities lacked the resources to hold sizable events, and their commemorative activities seldom attracted the kind of attention given to white veterans' reunions. Commemoration, too, collided uncomfortably with present-day realities, since so many black Americans were presented, on a daily basis, not with reminders of emancipation but with the ongoing legacy of antebellum slavery. With many still indebted to white landholders, working on cotton plantations, and even living in slave cabins, it was hard not to see the likeness with antebellum days. No surprise, then, that when interviewers began, in the late 1920s, systematically talking to ex-slaves throughout the South, many had vivid recollections of the old days and poignant reflections about similarities with their current circumstances. But those, for the most part, were memories that lay dormant until prodded by a particular line of questions. Even when pressed, Elizabeth Sparks, an ex-slave, said she didn't want to talk about slavery because it was "too awful to tell anyway." Those who had prospered since emancipation may have also preferred to keep their thoughts focused on the present rather than dredge up difficult memories about the past.[16]

Thus, by 1930, and especially as the economic crisis began to seep into African American communities, there was a decided waning of interest, especially on the part of black youth, in the old ways of commemorating the past. "There are quite a number of people of our group who feel embarrassed at emancipation celebrations," observed journalist and NAACP leader Max Barber in a 1932 speech in Pittsburgh. And while the black press covered Emancipation Day activities, they also felt some ambivalence about a memorial tradition that seemed to demand gratitude for white people, who took the preponderance of credit for emancipation. Some even wondered whether the historical record, in terms of black participation in the antislavery struggle, was worth commemorating. "The sad part of history," opined the editors of the *Pittsburgh Courier,* "is that there were Negroes, and plenty of them, who actually fought in the Southern army and fought against freedom." Apparently, even in the African American press, a white southern version of history, with its veneration of the so-called loyal slaves of the Confederacy, exerted considerable influence. Some black leaders even found the notion of "slave loyalty" a useful political tool when it came to getting white people to give aid to African Americans suffering in the early days of the Depression. The black representative Oscar DePriest, for example, urged in 1932 that Congress enact pensions for ex-slaves with the argument that "these of my racial group were never known to be disloyal, not only to America but to the individual slave masters."[17]

Thus, among those who gave their attention to Civil War memories, multiple stories reverberated, among whites and blacks, in family gatherings and small-town ceremonies, where people told tales that reflected their individual circumstances and individual prejudices. On a larger scale, though, Americans also required a more unifying story about their past, one that would allow them to make sense of their national identity and that could undergird a sense of patriotic belonging, without inciting a sectional squabble. This was the kind of fantasy story that had been pieced together in the years after Reconstruction, in novels, theater, popular histories, and eventually in film; a Civil War narrative that had, albeit imperfectly, attempted to twist together the divided reflections on the conflict, at least in a way that might cement loyalties across sectional lines, although not necessarily across the racial divide. The basic elements of that narrative went something like this: the Civil War had been a tragic break in the American family, a moment of division that resulted from a vague mix of constitutional and cultural differences. Slavery had played a part, but certainly not a decisive one, since both sections had contributed to the emergence and growth of that institution. The slaves themselves weren't truly members of the family, only its stepchildren, or distant relatives. In the war itself, both Union and Confederate soldiers fought bravely and with distinction, although most accounts tended to see a bit more bravery and distinction on the part of Confederates, who, after all, had to battle against some pretty tough odds. In the end, all could agree that the war brought about the happy consolidation of a stronger United States, along with slave emancipation. There was, of course, the unfortunate aftermath of the war, when extremists in Lincoln's Republican Party pushed a vengeful and punishing agenda—which in no way conformed to what Lincoln himself would have done—but once southern whites were allowed to return to "home rule," bringing with them an unquestioned victory for "white supremacy," national reunion was complete.[18]

This version of the Civil War story was, not surprisingly, well suited to an expanding, increasingly powerful nation, just beginning to take its place on a global stage. Indeed, it was hardly coincidental that some of the most compelling tributes to this reunion story came during the Spanish-American War, when the ex-soldiers of the Union and Confederacy joined together to defeat a foreign foe. By healing the old wounds and recognizing each other's heroism, the United States became a mighty power, ready to take on the world. The story likewise heralded the strength and wisdom of elite white men and took comfort in the economic "progress" that came from their joint stewardship of national affairs. It was a story, too, that justified the continued economic exploitation of African Americans in the rural South and implied that black folk did best under the oversight of those who had supervised them for generations. Some even made explicit connections between the internal subjugation of black folk at home and the oversight of nonwhite peoples abroad.[19]

This "reunion over race" story did not, of course, wipe out the individual and regional prejudices that might be heard at Union or Confederate gatherings, in small-town political meetings, at Emancipation Day events, or even around family dinner tables. But it did have a powerful hold on the American imagination, especially as various forms of popular culture—magazines, radio, movies—permeated a national audience. Indeed, the pressures of selling a national product weighed heavily on magazine editors and film distributors who understood the problem of making a story that wouldn't ruffle either northern or southern (white) sensibilities. As far back as the 1880s, the editors of the *Century* magazine helped devise the formula that could build on people's interest in the Civil War while still allowing them to sell magazines to a nationwide audience. In soliciting articles for their hugely popular "Battles and Leaders of the Civil War" series, they stressed battlefield movements over political causation and hoped to "soften controversy" through the "exclusion of political questions." Later, as veterans died off, they took some of their more troublesome personal recollections with them, giving even greater latitude to the tale of harmony and conciliation.[20]

All of which meant that the story of the white family feud, now healed in defense of sectional reconciliation and white supremacy, had a strong presence in American culture, continuing into the early years of the Depression. Its most extreme expression appeared in the novels of Thomas Dixon, in books like *The Leopard's Spots* and *The Clansman*, and then in D. W. Griffith's 1915 film, *The Birth of a Nation*, based on one of Dixon's novels. Both Dixon and Griffith were southerners, although Griffith's film, considered the first truly epic motion picture, played widely to a national audience. Still, the filmmaker attended to southern sensibilities by melding critical aspects of the Lost Cause story to an inflammatory white supremacist agenda and to what he regarded as a genuinely historical presentation of factual events. He reminded viewers of the beauty and romance of the Old South, particularly the harmony between slave and slaveholder. He demonstrated the tragedy of the sectional division as it drove a wedge between lovers across sectional lines. And he culminated his story with the triumph of white men, North and South, over the unruly freed blacks who had been pressed into rape and rebelliousness by misguided white Republican allies. Moreover, he gave all of it the stamp of historical legitimacy, drawing freely on quotes and texts as well as photographic re-creations of certain "historical" scenes. Finally, in Griffith's imagining, Lincoln was an important but by no means central character: he appeared most notably as a benevolent leader who patiently heard the pleas of the Confederate mother begging for her son's pardon. Still, there was an oddly ambiguous quality in Griffith's Lincoln— perhaps a subtle reflection of regional prejudice—that made him good but not necessarily heroic. Indeed, in a number of scenes Lincoln seemed downright girlish, giving free rein to his emotions and pulling a shawl closely around his shoulders right before that fatal shot at the theater.[21]

Although the film certainly hewed closely to traditional versions of the Civil War story, it nonetheless wore its badge of white supremacy in a way that other accounts had not. Outraged at degrading portraits of blacks—usually

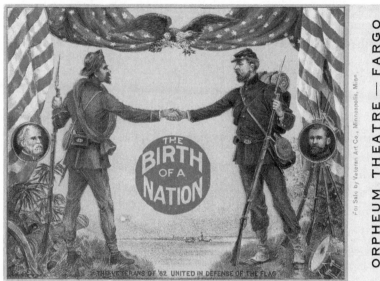

Advertisement for a Fargo, North Dakota, showing of *Birth of a Nation*. Although promotional materials for D. W. Griffith's film often highlighted the role of the Ku Klux Klan, this advertisement called attention to the theme of reconciliation between the Blue and the Gray "united in defense of the flag." Institute for Regional Studies, Fargo, North Dakota (North Dakota State University Archives).

white actors in blackface—the newly organized National Association for the Advancement of Colored People protested film showings around the country. Even some whites were alarmed by the way a newly resurgent Ku Klux Klan had drawn on the good publicity it got from Griffith's film. Hoping to avoid the controversy that had plagued *Birth*, most films and books during the 1920s were less explicit about race and portrayed black characters in less vicious, though still demeaning, ways. By 1926 *Birth of a Nation* was itself no longer the popular draw it once was and plans to rerelease the film with sound, at the end of the decade, met with a decided lack of enthusiasm.[22]

But even when the virulent racism of Griffith's film began to fall out of favor, the reconciliation theme continued to take center stage, and calls for Confederate appreciation seemed, if anything, to get a bit louder. Perhaps with fewer actual Confederates around, Americans got a bit nostalgic about the old rebels. "The country," said a speaker honoring southern veterans at a 1929 Memorial Day ceremony in Westchester, New York, "is slowly turning toward a middle course embodying the principles of both the Confederates and the Unionists."

Rather than just accepting reunion for what it was—that is, confirmation that the Union objective had triumphed—those who made the case for reconciliation often felt compelled to acknowledge Confederate achievements: praising the bravery and nobility of southern soldiers and keeping questions of race on the sidelines so as not to tarnish Confederate objectives. Certainly this seemed to be a guiding principle in the construction and unveiling of the Lincoln Memorial in Washington, DC. This 1922 monument did not ignore emancipation— Jules Guerin's mural portrays the Angel of Truth liberating slaves—but the overriding theme focuses primarily on union. "By emphasizing his saving the union," explained the art critic who composed the words above the statue of the seated Lincoln, "you appeal to both sections. By saying nothing about slavery you avoid the rubbing of old sores." At the unveiling ceremony, former president William Howard Taft praised the "brotherly love" of North and South, while black attendees were forced into sidelined Jim Crow seating.[23]

Indeed, despite the massive stone memorial that immortalized the Civil War president, the reconciliation narrative had the effect of making Lincoln a rather underwhelming figure. In *Birth of a Nation*, the sixteenth president had little to do with the nation's "birth," as Griffith portrayed that deed as largely accomplished by the unified strength of white men in the North and the South. When Griffith again took Lincoln as his subject matter, in a biopic that appeared in August 1930, he still hesitated to make him a vital and commanding leader. *Abraham Lincoln*, Griffith's first talking picture, cast Walter Huston as Honest Abe and opened with scenes of the future president as a carefree young man, hopelessly in love with his sweetheart, Ann Rutledge. When Ann dies, Lincoln struggles to overcome his first real adversity. As Griffith's producer put it, he "loses the one woman from his heart but grows on until he can take a whole people into his heart." Thus, like Griffith's earlier Lincoln, this new Lincoln continues to lead from the heart and his emotions. As he moves toward the presidency, Lincoln is motivated by one singular objective, declared repeatedly, even monotonously, by Huston: "The Union must be preserved." What Griffith gives us, then, is a Lincoln who loves all the American people and believes that winning the war is, in fact, "a duty we owe the South as well as the North." Some slaves are freed along the way, but as a tangent to the main business at hand.[24]

As reviewers noted with approval, Griffith never allowed the focus on Lincoln to deter him from making a movie that would "be fair to the two halves of our nation." Thus viewers learn of "Northern profit in slave importation" as well as of the great humanity of Lincoln and "the equal generosity of that other great man, Gen. Lee." Even more, reviewers appreciated Lincoln's ability to provide

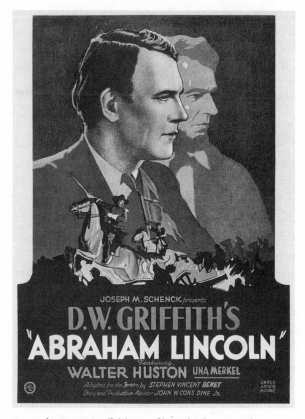

Poster for D. W. Griffith's 1930 film, *Abraham Lincoln*.
Reflecting his long-standing interest in reimagining the
Civil War, D. W. Griffith's first talking film was a biopic
of Civil War president Abraham Lincoln. Photofest.

a calm and moderating role model in trying circumstances, although they may
have responded more to the Lincoln they desired than to the Lincoln Griffith
had given them. "In these days of stress," wrote reviewer David Belasco, "what
a magnificent object-lesson this picture of Abraham Lincoln gives in faith . . . in
sanity of judgment . . . in courage. Courage to face the crisis." Here was a story—
a fantasy, of course—designed for a national crisis: turn to a leader of courage
and sanity who could pull the nation together, especially the white people of the
North and the South.[25]

Audiences, however, seemed largely uninterested. Much as reviewers praised
Griffith's work, they recognized that "the public does not 'flock' to such a

picture." Perhaps people didn't want to watch a history lesson in the fall of 1930. Perhaps, too, they weren't keen on the same old story of tragic sectional division and healing leadership that seemed of dubious value in the current crisis. Nor did Griffith really help to make Lincoln a figure of inspiring authority: he was a kind and sentimental figure, perhaps, but really given more to platitudes than to meaningful governance, and in 1930 few people were interested in platitudes.[26]

Coming into the Depression decade, there was also another artistic trend that would have an important effect on the way Americans approached the Civil War narrative and may have contributed to audiences' lackluster response to Griffith's film. Particularly in the 1920s, more writers and artists showed an inclination to challenge bulwarks of history, to inject some iconoclastic skepticism onto a traditional hero-driven account of the past. In a decade that celebrated youth and innovation while questioning earlier "puritanical" values and highly cherished historical myths, it was perhaps inevitable that Civil War heroes would get knocked down a few pegs. Plus, the leaders who had dragged the American people into the recent European war prompted a cynicism that could be retroactively applied to the men responsible for an earlier military conflict. "Abraham Lincoln," explains Bill Gorton in Ernest Hemingway's *The Sun Also Rises*, "was a faggot. He was in love with General Grant. So was Jefferson Davis. Lincoln just freed the slaves on a bet." In his 1922 "Poem, or Beauty Hurts Mr. Vinal," e. e. cummings drew on the phrasings of "My Country 'Tis of Thee" to speak of "land of Abraham Lincoln and Lydia E. Pinkham, land above all of Just Add Hot Water And Serve—from every B.V.D." Other writers still wanted the heroic deeds, and even the heroes, although they made those heroes more human and less refined. Carl Sandburg, for example, didn't call Lincoln a "faggot," but he did have quite a bit to say about the wild ways of Abe's maternal grandmother, who gave birth to Lincoln's mother out of wedlock. Indeed, in a decade that seemed more willing to accept the prevalence of physical intimacy—at least of the heterosexual variety—those who chronicled the Civil War likewise discovered that even nineteenth-century women and men had sex. Certainly Margaret Mitchell must have been channeling some of the flapper spirit of the 1920s in her own Civil War chronicle, most of which she composed between 1926 and 1929, detailing the often-torrid love affair between Rhett Butler and a character she called "Pansy Hamilton." Amazingly, even Griffith's producer on the *Abraham Lincoln* film hoped to "capture the interest of the flappers" by selling them "on the fact that if they come to see this picture they will find out some startling truths about Lincoln's private life that few people have known in the past."[27]

Sexual innuendo, along with a spicier writing style, also helped spur reader-ship for Claude Bowers's *The Tragic Era*, the revamped history of the Recon-struction period that became an enormous bestseller on its publication in 1929. Bowers, an Indiana journalist active in Democratic Party politics, had long used history writing to vindicate current partisan feuds. He had already written in praise of Jefferson's principles of states' rights democracy against the aristo-cratic federalism of Alexander Hamilton. Indeed, his extreme defense of Jef-ferson won him, in 1928, a place as keynote speaker for the Democratic Party convention, along with support from the party's rising star, Franklin Roosevelt. *The Tragic Era* further reflected Bowers's Democratic allegiances, particularly his concern that southerners had fled from the 1928 Democratic nominee, Al Smith, because of his Catholicism and had embraced the Republican, Herbert Hoover. "I have written a book," Bowers told a friend, "which will be the most powerful single factor bringing the South back into line. . . . If I do not have the appreciation of the Democratic Party for this work on which I near broke my-self down by day and night labor for five years I have written my last line in an attempt to serve it." Above all, Bowers wanted to reveal the venal and degraded corruption that overtook the Republican Party in the aftermath of the Civil War and how it led them to savagely punish southern whites while elevating an ignorant class of blacks. In this, Bowers did not depart all that much from previous accounts of the Reconstruction era, including the dominant scholar-ship produced by the so-called Dunning school, although he was more explicit about directing his story toward a popular audience and a partisan objective.[28]

Indeed, Bowers's familiarity with the popular mood no doubt encouraged him to pepper his tale of Reconstruction with personal stories of debauchery and feminine intrigue. Perhaps in a bid for female readers, Bowers highlighted "the unprecedented prominence of women throughout these struggles" and projected a kind of sexual politics onto the Reconstruction era. *The Tragic Era* is laced with accounts of social gatherings where "ladies of indifferent morality" displayed their "seductive charms" in the hope of getting obliging politicians to bow to their nefarious ambitions. Political leaders like Thaddeus Stevens and Charles Sumner have illicit sexual proclivities, one a fondness for black women, the other a less-than-enthusiastic embrace of heterosexuality. In Columbia, South Carolina, Bowers explained, Radical Republican strategies were plotted in salons where "white men . . . bowed low over the hands of colored women."[29]

Bowers had still another objective, beyond sexing up the Reconstruction era and besides making a bid for southern Democratic allegiances. He hoped to make Lincoln a Democratic standard-bearer for both northerners and southerners in the party. "There are a few fools in the South," Bowers explained in a letter to a political colleague, "who want us to attack Lincoln." Bowers intended not to bad-mouth Lincoln but to show how much the Radical Republicans had broken with the Lincoln tradition. Much as Bowers wished to appeal to the southern wing of the Democratic Party, he had no intention of appealing to southerners' anti-Lincoln bias. He hoped, instead, to show that the present-day Democrats were the true descendants of the sixteenth president: that these were the men who truly respected the rights of the states against the overbearing federalism practiced by modern Republicans. And while it might be hard to make Lincoln a "states-rights" man, Bowers insisted that Lincoln represented the continuation of Jefferson's popular democratic principles, while the Republican Party had abandoned Lincolnian democracy in favor of Alexander Hamilton's aristocratic inclinations. In this, Bowers anticipated some of the fractures and realignments that would shape Civil War memories in the 1930s. In particular, he contributed to a political trend that would come to fruition under FDR in the 1930s, although by the time FDR got his hands on Lincoln, he would look very different from the kind of Democrat Bowers had in mind.[30]

Like Bowers, Stephen Vincent Benét was interested in telling a more popular tale about the Civil War; and like Sandburg, he was drawn to the myths and legends of the past yet wanted to "exhume" human beings from long-standing legends. Pennsylvania-born and raised in a military family, Benét spent time in California and Georgia before studying at Yale. Following a brief stint of service in World War I, Benét completed his literary studies and began writing poetry. A Guggenheim Fellowship brought him to Paris, where he became interested in understanding "America," or "at least some of the America I knew," a quest he contrasted with those writers of his era—the more fervent iconoclasts—who had little interest in ideas like "America" or national "heritage." In 1928 Benét published *John Brown's Body*, a fifteen-thousand-line blank verse poem that followed the stories of numerous individuals, including John Brown himself, in the years leading up to and during the Civil War. The poem, which went on to win the Pulitzer Prize, offered Benét a way to reclaim his idea of American heritage, partly by returning to some of the standard story lines about the Civil War: he reflects on Lincoln's anguish over how to save the union; on the tragic fortitude of the aristocratic Clay Wingate, who fights for the South; and on the loyalty of Cudjo, the slave who has a bond with his master that "would hold / On either side until both were cold." Typical of the reunionist narrative, *John Brown's Body* even begins with a vignette about a Yankee slave ship, commanded by a New England captain who shows little regard for his human chattel. A well-worn convention, this tendency to fix responsibility for the slave trade on northern shoulders could also undercut the notion that Confederates had insisted on fighting for slavery, since now it could be argued that everyone had an interest in the peculiar institution. As for John Brown himself, his single-minded quest blinds him to the havoc he wreaks, whether it's the death of his own son, or of a "free negro, baggage-master of the small station" at Harpers Ferry who failed to halt under the orders of Brown's men. When a slave in Brown's brigade is killed, it leads, ironically, to the selling of the man's wife and children from their plantation. In Benét's telling, there is clearly no preponderance of moral virtue in the northern cause.[31]

But the southern cause is also tainted, especially in the murky waters of interracial sex. Cudjo, for example, "could trace with unerring ease / A hundred devious pedigrees" and knew that white blood coursed through the veins of "yellow babies down by the Slough." Even the woman who wins Clay Wingate's heart has a mysterious genealogy, a "French" father who passes "an alien grace" onto his daughter, as well as a penchant for lively dancing. Lively and lovely as she may be, Sally Dupree remains an outcast in southern society and can never be a suitable partner for the aristocratic Wingate.[32]

Both sides possess moral failings, but Benét ultimately sympathizes more with the Union cause than the Confederate. As he told his mother, he really was "more interested in [the northerner] Ellyat's story than in Wingate's" [the southern story] and that "as for the politics of the time" he was really "a Union man or a Lincoln man." Lincoln, in particular, earned Benét's respect for the way he used his "huge, patient, laborious hands" to "start kneading the stuff of the Union together again." Ultimately, Benét cast his lot with the Union side and even, in a begrudging way, with John Brown himself, because he, along with the soldiers who sang his dirge, unleashed America's destiny, albeit in ways that could scarcely be known or seen at the time. In short, the moral triumph of the Union cause emerges, in Benét's telling, almost as an unintended consequence. And because it is unintended, Benét manages to maintain a conciliatory and even-handed perspective, celebrating the heroism of both sides while also bemoaning the moral shortcomings of northerners and southerners who lived in the 1850s and '60s. In Benét's hands, the reconciliation theme becomes a kind of temporal reunion: the North's gestures toward the future united with the South's gestures toward the past. Perhaps John Brown's body did lie amoldering, but out of that body, claims Benét, "the tall skyscrapers grow / Out of his heart the chanting buildings rise / Rivet and girder, motor and dynamo / Pillar of smoke by day and fire by night / The steel-faced cities reaching at the skies."[33]

Despite what he may have set out to do, Benét hewed closely enough to traditional stories about northern and southern triumphs—and failings—that those
who were attached to those traditions could take comfort in what he wrote. In
1928, a friend of D. W. Griffith's urged him to read Benét's work because it would
"bring back to you some of the romance of the South, especially the great ideal-
ism of Lee." When he began working on his Lincoln film, Griffith brought Benét
to Hollywood and enlisted his help in countless rewrites of the film's screenplay.
Greatly impressed with Benét's work, Margaret Mitchell also found considerable resonance between *John Brown's Body* and her own reflections on the Civil
War. Two southern historians, writing in the 1930s about the South on the eve
of the sectional conflict and waxing rhapsodic about the lives of southern white
women, referred readers to Benét's fictional portrait of the mistress of Wingate
Hall as a fine substitute for history.[34]

In their own ways, Sandburg, Bowers, and Benét reinforced many of the traditional narratives about Lincoln, Reconstruction, and the Civil War. A more
sustained blow to myth-making came from African American artists and writers of the 1920s. The new generation of African Americans was leaving the rural
South and making a life in urban settings, and many of them felt the impulse to
cast off "history" and embrace new experiences. Literary scholar Alain Locke
saw this trend, in fact, as a critical component of the Harlem Renaissance.
Whether or not the old stock characters had ever conformed to historical reality, Locke believed their influence must be shaken off so that what was new
about negro life—urbanization, class differentiation, the mixing of African and
New World cultures—could be embraced. "While the minds of most of us,"
Locke wrote in 1925, "black and white, have thus burrowed in the trenches of
the Civil War and Reconstruction, the actual march of development has simply flanked these positions, necessitating a sudden reorientation of view." The
Civil War myths, Locke implied, had borne down with particular fierceness
on African Americans, keeping the national imagination locked into age-old
thinking about loyal "aunties," "uncles," and "mammies" and ignorant of young
black poets, West Indian immigrants, and rising black professionals.[35]

Which isn't to say that "New Negro" thinking and the culture of the Harlem
Renaissance shut out the African American past altogether. Rather, many black
writers and artists now looked toward a less well-known black history, one that
seethed with protest and rebellion. As the Depression intensified, those themes
resonated even more deeply. Black historian Carter Woodson had already established his *Journal of Negro History* and continued to pursue explorations of
slave life and slave rebellion. In his 1913 Star of Ethiopia pageant, W. E. B. Du

Bois showcased important black historical figures including the slave insur-
rectionist Nat Turner, whom he called one of "the twelve apostles of Negro
Christianity." A 1931 article in the *Crisis* likewise took encouragement from Nat
Turner's example in that it showed "a typical Negro willing to seal his covenant
of beliefs with his own blood." Around the same time, the black writer Arna
Bontemps moved to northern Alabama and became entranced by the stories
of slave rebels like Denmark Vesey, Turner, and Gabriel Prosser; he eventually
wrote a novel, *Black Thunder*, that profiled Prosser's revolt.[36]

What started then, with the Harlem Renaissance, as a challenge to backward and simplistic myths, rode into the 1930s as a hunger for a history of black
protest. That hunger, in turn, was fueled by current events: especially by the
heightened militancy of both black and white activists, ready and willing to
protest racial injustice, whether it took the form of film showings of *Birth of a
Nation* or the lynching of a black man by a southern mob. The event that especially caught the attention of African American activists and artists was the
arrest, trial, and imprisonment of the nine "Scottsboro Boys." In March 1931
nine black men and boys, riding a train carrying white and black folk in search
of work, were arrested in Scottsboro, Alabama, after two white women riding
the same train accused them of a gang rape. By July, eight of the nine had been
convicted and sentenced to die. But the case had also caught the attention of
activists, particularly communists, who publicized the case and moved quickly
to challenge and appeal the court's verdict. In doing so, the Communist Party
showcased the corruption at the heart of the southern legal system and mobi-
lized a broad-based protest movement that made the region's Jim Crow practices the focus of attention and condemnation. Scottsboro was, in many ways,
a turning point, a key event that would help spark a new era of political protest
and agitation in Dixie.[37]

Little wonder, then, that African Americans were growing impatient with
age-old stories of black submissiveness, whether they came in the form of
present-day admonitions to abide by the "etiquette" of the Jim Crow South or
historical tales about the faithfulness of antebellum slaves to their slaveholding
masters. When a number of southern lawmakers in the 1920s proposed, at the
urging of the UDC, constructing a monument in Washington, DC, to the faithful "black mammy," one black publication offered up its own version of what
the monument should look like: an old black woman on an up-ended washtub
with a plaque remarking on the wages she never received over the course of her
lifetime. Soon after the Depression began, the stalwart forces of Confederate

tradition would come face-to-face with this newly energized spirit of black resistance in a showdown at Harpers Ferry.[38]

AS EARLY AS 1920, the UDC had made plans to unveil a marker to Heyward
Shepherd, a free African American killed during John Brown's raid in 1859.
Wishing to pay tribute to their imagined notion of black fealty, the Daughters
also hoped to cast aspersions on those who might find inspiration in the abolitionist leader's courageous assault against slavery. Certainly it wasn't coincidental that the UDC took this unusual interest in Shepherd right when black
activists began organizing more visible tributes to John Brown. Storer College,
a black institution with a white president located in Harpers Ferry, commemorated Brown's heroism with a tablet in 1918, prompting local whites to demand
a countermemorial for Shepherd. In 1922, the NAACP had initiated regular pil-
grimages to Brown's gravesite in North Elba, New York, eventually forming a
Memorial Association that held regular meetings and raised funds for a statue
to Brown, unveiled in 1935. Interest in Brown was apparently on the rise, part of
the 1920s impulse to rediscover the more radical features of the African American past. The fiery white abolitionist thus was recalled for striking the blow
against slavery that would culminate in wartime emancipation. But he spoke,
too, to the resurgent activism among civil rights workers in the 1920s and 1930s,
to men and women building interracial coalitions and making the fight against
black oppression not just a race struggle but a broader crusade for human justice
and equality. Back in 1909, W. E. B. Du Bois had praised Brown for recognizing
that "the cost of liberty is less than the price of repression"—that when one race
suffered, no people could ever really be free. Even more, in applauding his willingness to use violence, blacks who honored Brown likewise made telling links
to African American manhood, making heroes of those who had aggressively
challenged the racial status quo.[39]

From the UDC's perspective, it would be hard to imagine a more threaten-
ing agenda than this one, so different from their picture of the emasculated
and always deferential loyal slave. As an organization that delighted in telling
old "mammy stories" and praising old-time "darkies" who gladly helped their
white superiors, the Confederate Daughters hoped to fit this cloak of racial submissiveness on the body of Heyward Shepherd, "the faithful slave who stood
between Southern womanhood and a renegade adventurer." Plans for the memorial, though, were held up when town leaders, reflecting some of the concerns voiced by administrators at Storer College, asked for a revised, and less

inflammatory, inscription than the one the UDC originally proposed. When the Daughters convened at their annual meeting in 1931, they observed that new interest had emerged in John Brown and Heyward Shepherd following the publication of Benét's work, although, as they noted, Benét had mistakenly identified the fallen black man as Shepherd Heyward and had (correctly) described him as a freed man. Further research allowed the UDC to correct their original inscription so that they now called Shepherd "an industrious and respected colored freedman," no longer using their conventional terminology of the "faithful slave." They also removed an offending phrase about "pikes and staves for bloody massacre," no doubt hoping to make John Brown's whole enterprise sound a bit less inflammatory, particularly in the ears of restless African American college students.

On October 10, 1931, an interracial group composed of black and white representatives from Storer College, a descendant of Heyward Shepherd, and various members and supporters of the UDC gathered in Harpers Ferry for the unveiling of the revised Shepherd memorial. They listened to UDC president Elizabeth Bashinsky sing the praises of Shepherd while decrying the perfidy of Brown. She also introduced her own veneration of "the old negro 'Mammy,' who with her humility and sweet decorum has become a real institution." After she completed her remarks, something unexpected occurred: the black music director of Storer College, Pearl Tatten, stood up and told a different story. "I am the daughter of a Connecticut volunteer," said Tatten, "who wore the blue and fought for the freedom of my people, for which John Brown struck the first blow. Today we are . . . pushing forward to a larger freedom, not in the spirit of the black mammy but in the spirit of freedom and rising youth." Awkward silence followed.[40]

The black press and black political leaders hailed Tatten's outburst. Max Barber, president of the John Brown Memorial Association, wrote in the *Pittsburgh Courier* that Tatten had "startled the 'daughters' almost as much as John Brown's raid" had alarmed slaveholders back in 1859. She signaled, in effect, a warning to southern whites that their version of Civil War history would not go uncontested, that younger blacks were prepared to cast aside the "aunties" and "uncles" and "mammies" so precious to the southern (and even northern) white imagination. And they wouldn't do this simply in the kinds of poems and short stories lauded by Alain Locke, but right on the ground where southern whites hoped to memorialize the landscape. Nor did Barber miss the opportunity to score a point for African American patriotism while demeaning Confederate treason, now being defended by a woman, Bashinsky, whose name,

Barber observed, sounded a lot like "Bolsheviki." Indeed, to make clear their intention to reclaim the commemorative landscape, the NAACP organized a follow-up meeting at Harpers Ferry where they planned to unveil their own plaque to John Brown's memory. Composed by Du Bois, the NAACP tablet lauded not only Brown's work against slavery but also the efforts of the black soldiers and millions of wartime slaves who made Brown's goal a reality. When the white president of Storer College rejected the tablet, the NAACP agreed they would hold a ceremony in May 1932 in Harpers Ferry but then move the tablet to the organization's New York offices. Du Bois, the speaker for the ceremony, no doubt hoped to draw a lesson from John Brown's work that might be applied to current NAACP campaigns when he chose as his theme "The Use of Force in Reform."[41]

Perhaps, then, it made perfect sense for men like John Dewey and Guy Johnson to talk about the nation, in 1932, facing its greatest crisis since the days of the Civil War. They probably knew little about the latest confrontation at Harpers Ferry, but they certainly knew about Scottsboro and could see that racial tensions, especially in the context of people's economic miseries, had heightened. They no doubt also understood how the economic crisis had compounded southern poverty, thus potentially exacerbating sectional tensions as well. And they certainly knew that a strong undercurrent of discontent flowed in the streets and rural byways of the United States, already manifesting itself in marches of the unemployed and down-and-out veterans and soon to take the form of labor organizing and nationwide strikes. Dewey, Johnson, and Roosevelt himself called up the Civil War analogy to convey a sense of crisis; but the depth of this crisis would force a revision of the old ways in which Americans had once derived comfort from their story of the Civil War. The fight over the Harpers Ferry memorial pointed to some of the battle lines that would emerge in the coming years: a growing appreciation for black protest on the part of a new generation of African American civil rights activists, along with their white allies, versus a long-standing Confederate traditionalism that hoped to render black defiance mute. Going forward, those opposing positions would bump into, and be transformed by, the emerging political culture of the 1930s, especially in the form of a left-leaning Popular Front and its vibrant cultural celebration of laborers, democracy, and interracialism.

[2]

STORIES RETOLD,
MEMORIES REMADE

D URING THE DEPRESSION, Americans tried to remember an event that
hardly anyone alive had experienced. There were, of course, many descendants of the Civil War generation still active in the 1920s and '30s, including many who defined themselves based on their kinship connections, as
the "Sons" and "Daughters" of those who came before. And many Americans
wrote books, or took political positions, mindful of the stories they had heard
from their nineteenth-century forebears. Yet the Civil War no longer presented
itself to 1930s Americans—as it once had—as personal experience or family
lore. Now, in interesting and often self-conscious ways, Americans of the 1930s
faced the problem of how to remember an earth-shattering event when the
participants were few and far between and the whole purpose of remembering
seemed to shift.[1]

For the first several decades after the Civil War, the principal keepers and
purveyors of the nation's Civil War memories were the men and women who had
experienced the war and who—in writing, sculpture, and public ceremonies—
found various ways to bring their stories to the American people. By the time
of World War I, and then in the 1920s and '30s, a decisive shift was under way,
especially with the passing of the men and women of the Civil War generation.
In 1932, the long-running *Confederate Veteran* magazine, an organ produced by
and for veterans, stopped publication. Once-vibrant Grand Army of the Republic chapters shuttered their doors. Descendant organizations, most notably
the United Daughters of the Confederacy (UDC), remained active in the field
of memorialization, but their position as keepers of the memory flame became
more tenuous, the result of the ever-greater thinning of family ties to that long-
ago conflict. New wars and new military accomplishments—in the Spanish-
American War and then the Great War—crowded out the personal reflections
from the Civil War era.[2]

In the first few decades of the twentieth century, and especially in the 1930s, the memory of the Civil War was remade. More removed than ever from first-person remembrances, the war came to Americans in new settings, through new types of narratives, and with new types of messages. Increasingly, those messages were less tethered to events and emotions of the 1860s and far more to the concerns, sensibilities, and structural imperatives of twentieth-century life. True, Civil War memories had always been manipulated to suit contemporary needs, but by the 1930s, the veteran experience became far less pertinent to the new narratives being spun. Additionally, Civil War stories now had new sponsors who aimed their tales at broad, national audiences. In supporting various arts programs, FDR's New Deal entered decisively into the arena of creative memory-making, with numerous plays, essays, books, and murals offering reflections on American history. Federal officials, too, invested in historic sites, like Civil War battlefields, and imparted new types of lessons about the conflict. Yet even more influential in the memory game were Hollywood movies, perhaps the most popular form of mass culture in America. Although most films ignored the Civil War, several extremely popular movies from these years spotlighted the sectional conflict—among them Shirley Temple films like *The Littlest Rebel* and *The Little Colonel*, as well as the top-grossing film of the decade, *Gone with the Wind*—while dozens of other films indirectly incorporated Civil War–related themes. In these years, Hollywood became what novelist Viet Thanh Nguyen calls a "memory industry . . . ready to capitalize on history by selling memory to consumers hooked on nostalgia." Over the course of the Depression decade, Hollywood's "memory industry" drew Americans ever more tightly into its web of longing and fantasy with respect to the Civil War.[3]

During the 1930s, traditional storytellers had to reckon with new memory-makers. Confederate memorial groups now had to work with, and sometimes clash with, federal agencies and administrators over how the Civil War story should be told. Ordinary Americans, both black and white, found opportunities to engage with interviewers and writers employed by the federal government and sometimes relinquished private recollections into the hands of New Deal administrators. And throughout the 1930s a subtle back-and-forth between Hollywood producers, with their own complex mix of commercial and ideological concerns, and American moviegoers also put its stamp on the memory of the Civil War.

THE 1930S OFFERED a unique opportunity for recording the Civil War stories of old because the federal government demonstrated a new interest in art and culture—and backed that interest up with cash. Particularly important in this regard were the federal programs created late in Franklin Roosevelt's first term, specifically under the rubric of the Works Progress Administration. Known as "Federal One," these WPA arts-related programs, including the Federal Theatre Project (FTP), the Federal Writers' Project (FWP), and the Federal Art Project, were launched in 1935 with the specific intent of providing employment opportunities to out-of-work writers, artists, actors, and musicians around the country. Spawning thousands of artistic, dramatic, and written productions, and employing tens of thousands of creative workers, these Federal One programs produced and developed artistic material covering an incredibly wide range of subject matter: from massive murals showcasing American industrial workers to classical music concerts in small-town squares to theater productions on controversial current events topics. Invariably, Federal One programs also dealt with historical themes, including the Civil War.[4]

Indeed, history, not to mention memory, had a particularly strong appeal among New Deal artists and administrators. For many, the difficulties of the Depression encouraged retrospection: to recall a time when the democratic tendencies of the American people were more fully on display. Going back to a romanticized past meant seeing Americans in an idealized preindustrial, precommercialized era, a time when folk culture and folk traditions presented a more "authentic" view of people's honorable and noble impulses. Viewing Americans through this mythical lens, in short, meant viewing them before corporate greed and political corruption had driven the nation into crisis; it meant unearthing the silver lining of native intelligence and popular integrity that might rescue the country from further peril. Additionally, as many artists and writers came to realize, looking back to the past could also make their art seem safer to the American public since it did not intrude, at least not explicitly, on contemporary controversies. True, not every town rejoiced over the artwork they got, including many in Kansas who were shocked to find a bloodied, fanatical John Brown gracing the walls of their state capitol. But in most cases, the historical perspective did give local people a sense of their communal past and a feeling of pride about their place in history.[5]

Historical inclinations in the 1930s blended with ideological leanings toward cultural pluralism as well as contemporary sociological thinking about "regionalism," tendencies that further encouraged the safeguarding of memory. Many intellectuals and administrators with New Deal affiliations spoke openly of tolerance and acceptance for a range of ethnic and immigrant cultures, emphasizing how much diversity and variety stood as hallmarks of American culture.

Whereas 1920s culture had been marked by extreme xenophobia, 1930s culture showed strong tendencies toward acknowledging, although not necessarily perpetuating, non-Anglo-Saxon differences. New Deal culture also took a page from the new work on "regionalism," particularly work being done by southern sociologists like Howard Odum. According to Odum, deep-rooted and long-standing factors, including climate, agriculture, and slavery, had established well-entrenched "folkways" across the South, traditions that both united and separated whites and blacks. Neither nostalgic Agrarian nor ardent New South proponent, Odum believed older regional folkways must be respected and ac-commodated before the South could progress. Thus, in many ways, New Deal arts programs came primed for the job of seeking out and enshrining cultural memories, whether in the form of ethnic traditions or the historical practices of different regions. Such efforts included the cataloging and creating of Native American artwork, murals showcasing the Hispanic presence in the American Southwest, and plays devoted to African American historical figures, as well as written and artistic material that considered the specific "folkways" of black and white southerners.[6]

In short, the federal arts programs broadcast a multiplicity of voices and, somewhat remarkably, created the space for competing conversations about the American past. Federal programs accommodated writers and artists with Lost Cause sympathies—indeed, sometimes employing and working directly with members of the United Daughters of the Confederacy—as well as black intellectuals committed to showing the harsh realities of African American history. These programs also gave jobs to a rising crop of left-wingers, many in the broad sphere of cultural workers participating in the loosely configured "Popular Front." Writers and artists like Mike Gold, Michael Blankfort, How-ard Koch, and Richard Wright—some of whom were in the Communist Party and some in its orbit—contributed historically themed work to Federal One and often used history as a window onto contemporary problems of racial op-pression, workers' rights, or economic inequality. By opening the doors to what administrators saw as the regional and cultural pluralism of the American folk, and by giving a wide range of struggling artists a platform for their views, these programs inevitably set the stage for a competition between distinct political perspectives and opposing interpretations of the history of the Civil War, the Reconstruction era, and antebellum slavery.

Consider, for example, the mix of offerings that came out of the Federal Theatre Project. At its height, the FTP employed close to thirteen thousand people—both black and white—including writers, designers, actors, and directors, and produced thousands of plays in cities and towns across the United States. It also invited scores of amateur and professional playwrights to submit their work for evaluation by a board of readers who would judge whether it was suitable for production. Civil War themes appeared frequently in these submissions, although many were rejected for their heavy reliance on "negro dialect" and minstrelsy. *Daughters of Dixie*, a play about the son of a Confederate veteran who fights in the World War, struck one reader as "a very banal, and amateurish, treatment of a trite and shopworn theme." Yet pro-Confederate themes were hardly dismissed out of hand. *Jefferson Davis National Highway*, a play submitted by a North Carolina chapter of the UDC, earned praise for the musical tributes made to all the states on the highway's route, convincing the reader that while it was "regional in quality it possesses a national touch" and might be "suitable for school and community presentations." An even more successful contender was *Jefferson Davis*, written by John McGee, the FTP's Southeast District director. In February 1936, seventy-five years to the day after Davis's inauguration, the play became the first Federal Theatre production to be performed in New York's Times Square. Strongly affirming the South's right to "decide the question [of slavery] for ourselves as the constitution promises we may," the play gave Lost Cause adherents something to cheer about. The play, already vetted by the UDC, scheduled a tour across the South that would include welcoming celebrations by local UDC chapters. Surely McGee and the FTP believed they were making good on the New Deal pledge to sustain the stories told by the traditional caretakers of the Civil War past and to give voice to regional "folkways."[7]

Still, the Federal Theatre's commitment to pluralism meant the Project also supported plays that dealt with topics like abolition, slavery, Union soldiers, and the early life of Abraham Lincoln. This included a play recounting Frederick Douglass's toils under slavery and his quest for freedom as well as one of the Federal Theatre's more successful offerings, *Battle Hymn*, a 1936 play by left-wing playwrights Mike Gold and Michael Blankfort about John Brown's war in Kansas. Showcasing Brown as "a model of revolutionary action on behalf of all oppressed people," Gold and Blankfort connected a nineteenth-century struggle against slavery to the Depression-era fight for workers' rights. *Battle Hymn*'s producers also hoped their play would speak to "Negro organizations" and their constituents, given the play's focus on this singular moment in black history. And, in the interest of speaking to average citizens, promoters even devised a plan "to invite all the John Browns in the telephone directory to a performance of the play," apparently to drive home the point that John Brown of the 1850s had something to say to the John Browns of the 1930s, at least the ones that had phones.[8]

Perhaps the most successful of the Federal Theatre's Civil War plays was E. P. Conkle's *Prologue to Glory*, a story of Lincoln's rise to political prominence. In many ways, Lincoln was the ideal subject for the federal stage. By the mid-1930s, biographers like Carl Sandburg had helped turn the sixteenth president into a "folk hero," a man uniquely in touch with the commonsense beliefs of ordinary Americans. Often drawing directly on Sandburg's work, Federal One programs helped promote what ultimately became a Lincoln cult in the New Deal years: plays about Lincoln's early life in the hardscrabble towns of the Illinois frontier, a favorite theme, provided an opportunity to show Lincoln's rough, grassroots origins. Not surprisingly, Conkle's play was also far less aggressive than *Battle Hymn* about celebrating the fight for racial justice. By looking at the antebellum Lincoln, *Prologue* was able to evade the thorny business of fighting a war against fellow Americans and the military emancipation of the slaves.[9]

Cultural pluralism and regional diversity were also on display in the Federal Writers' Project, although in ways that also produced sharper conflicts, within the agency, about memory and historical interpretation, and about how to use and assess firsthand observations. Unlike the theater productions, the FWP's work involved a more intensive vetting process whereby authors in the state-level agencies submitted material to editors and reviewers in the national office. Among those working in the state-level offices, especially in the South, were writers affiliated with the UDC, including the director of the Alabama state writers' program. As an organization devoted to memory-keeping, the UDC must have seemed like a natural partner for such FWP projects as the *American Guide*, a multivolume compilation chronicling the history, culture, and geography of the forty-eight states and the District of Columbia, as well as the numerous oral history projects conducted with ordinary black and white folk around the country. Yet UDC workers did not always get the final say on what got published: writings produced at the state level, many filled with racial caricature and Lost Cause sentiments, received editorial scrutiny in the national office, including thorough inspections from one of the most prominent black intellectuals in the New Deal administration, the poet and critic Sterling Brown. Thus, Civil War memory in the FWP went through a complex series of twists and turns, involving the storytelling of numerous firsthand observers, the packaging of those observations by a veritable army of FWP writers (mostly white but some black), and the editorial vetting of those observations at the national level, including careful screening by a forceful black editor determined to root out prejudicial and stereotyped depictions of the African American past.[10]

Consistent with its mission and philosophy, the Federal Writers' Project was interested, from the outset, in securing firsthand testimony about historical events. They sent employees into the field to collect stories, giving particular emphasis to "ordinary" folk, black and white, especially in the South and the West. The Writers' Project thus recognized this moment when memories were fading and worked to record voices, presumed to be rich with historical wisdom, for posterity. Invariably, those interviewers came upon informants who had tales to tell about the Civil War. "Parson Bill" Holmes, age ninety, told project workers James Aswell and Ruth Clark that he remembered his Confederate Army experience "like it was yesterday," having emerged with a sense of being chosen by God to survive the war so he could do the Lord's work. "Yankee balls," he explained, "jist buzzed me past and done me no harm at all." Ernestine Faudie of McLennan County, Texas, was born in Germany in 1853 but moved to Texas with her family that same year. She had uncles fighting for the Confederacy, but recalled hard treatment from both armies. "When any of the soldiers on either side came thro our place," she explained, "they took anything they could find, the rebels felt that they had a right to it for they were fighting for us." And H. C. Wright in Austin, Texas, recalled going west for the Confederacy to fight in New Mexico, Arizona, and California: in his journeys, the only clothes he ever received were the ones he got from enemy soldiers.[11]

Thus in the 1930s the federal government became a kind of liberator of historical memory, releasing and sometimes publishing recollections of both white folk and black. Since they gathered more interviews in southern states than northern ones, they probably liberated more Confederate stories than Union ones. The government was also mindful of a different strain of memory in the states of the "Old South" and dispatched dozens of FWP writers and interviewers to document the stories of thousands of elderly black men and women who had once been slaves. Mindfulness, however, did not necessarily result in consistency or clarity in how to handle these ex-slave reminiscences. As scholars have long noted, the slave interviews had a troubled genesis and produced problematic results: poor and aging men and women were asked questions about long-ago past experiences, including their time as slaves, by mostly white interrogators who openly revealed their prejudices in the way they formulated their questions and wrote up the responses. Nostalgic accounts of games played, quaint customs observed, and good deeds done by kindly masters, all expressed in contorted "negro dialect," abounded. Given the dearth of accessible firsthand testimony up to this point, as well as deeply prejudicial histories of slavery, writers and interviewers often fell back on tropes and stereotypes to present what they heard, adding their own embellishments in terms of speech patterns or even editorializing about racial traits and characteristics. One Arkansas interviewer, for example, submitted a narrative done "in a sort of vaudeville parody of colloquial speech." Yet some interviews—those conducted by black writers or by particularly diligent whites—surely revealed some truths about the way ex-slaves understood the past. In a few states, Negro Writers' Units were established as part of the state project, yielding reflections that highlighted slaveowners' brutality and looked more at freedom than at slavery. William Sherman Jr., for example, was interviewed by a worker with the Florida Negro Writers' Unit and described his own version of "Sherman's March": toward the end of the war, he gathered a large group of slaves and urged them to leave their plantations and follow him to "meet the Yankees."[12]

Still, white interviewers predominated in the FWP ranks, and many in the southern states had strong pro-Confederate sympathies that invariably shaped the way they approached their task. In a number of cases, southern writers with ties to the UDC posed questions or reframed the narratives to conform with their own views about the kindly relations between masters and slaves and slave loyalty to plantation owners. The WPA in Florida even circulated many of these Lost Cause–leaning slave narratives in the state's public schools. But white writers and interviewers did not always get the last word and generally had to send their work to a team of national editors and directors. The most telling exchange occurred between some of the southern state project directors and New Deal appointee Sterling Brown. Born in Washington, DC, Brown got some historical schooling from Carter Woodson when he taught in Lynchburg, Virginia, where he embraced Woodson's injunction to learn the history of the Negro people, to seek out the documents and the folk material that black people themselves had produced, and to push back against white mythologizing about blacks. In a speech before the National Negro Congress in 1937, Brown urged black writers to alter "stereotypes of Negro life and character, whose growth extends from the beginning of the American novel in Cooper to the latest best seller, 'Gone With the Wind.'" Appointed to lead the FWP's Office of Negro Affairs, Brown gave careful attention to copy dealing with African American culture and history. He often challenged historical biases and racial caricatures. When the writers for the Texas guide, part of the *American Guide* series, wrote about Reconstruction-era blacks as a "lazy-good-for-nothing lot," Brown's objections produced this revision: "Black individuals had been 'cast adrift' by an indifferent government." Brown and his team of editors were successful in steering through other revisions to demeaning depictions of black southerners. With respect to the ex-slave interviews, he urged writers to avoid prejudicial language and to be mindful of "the language of the ex-slave." In these ways, Brown tried to cut through the biased frame of white interviewers and get closer to first-person memories.[13]

Just by forcing this dialogue between a national black editor and local southern white writers, the Federal Writers' Project set in motion an unusual cultural dynamic, one perhaps wholly new to the American scene, and certainly one that tempered some of the more egregious manifestations of Confederate and anti-black prejudices. By and large, however, Brown's revisions and suggestions never really surmounted the Lost Cause portrayal of the antebellum and Civil War–era South that pervaded both the *American Guide* series and most of the ex-slave interviews. Since writers tended to think of the *American Guides* primarily as tourist tracts, state directors wanted a free hand to play up romanticized portrayals of the South, replete with references to "mammies in bandanas" and picturesque Negroes who sang mournfully about "King Cotton." With the slave narratives, Brown may have had some effect on the presentation of "Negro dialect," but Brown also operated under some serious constraints. One, surely, was a basic lack of documentation about the slave experience that had not already come filtered through Lost Cause biases, forcing him to work in a field described by W. E. B. Du Bois as "devastated by passion and belief." An additional problem was the increasing weight historians were placing on "objectivity," on producing work that reflected balance and lack of bias. Thus, when those in the national office read an interview containing a horrific story about a "nigger box" in which slaves were imprisoned and practically starved, they concluded that it must be full of "exaggerations." Apparently administrators had trouble imagining the full extent of slavery's depravities. Finally, Brown had to operate in a larger New Deal framework that preferred folk wisdom and popular tradition to historical accounts of suffering. Hence, there was little he could do to change the stories obtained from ex-slaves if local white interviewers followed the directives they received from the national office, which explicitly asked them to look more at quaint folk traditions under slavery than at ruthless exploitation.[14]

In the end, the Writers' Project and the Theatre Project hit yet another wall that further narrowed the range of voices, especially from African Americans. By 1937, Federal One programs began attracting the political scrutiny of congressional representatives who were wary of using federal money for artistic purposes. The following year, Martin Dies's House Un-American Activities Committee took aim at both the FTP and FWP to expose disloyal political influences in the arts programs. And while the definition of "disloyal" could certainly be far-reaching, the committee made communist, not pro-Confederate, influence its principal target. Plays with prominent racial themes and with mixed-race casts came under particular scrutiny, since many conservative congressmen saw these as markers of communist influence. The Federal Theatre play about John Brown, *Battle Hymn*, was an obvious target given the left-wingers who worked on it and promoted it. Senator Rush Holt of West Virginia saw communist infiltration all over the production, evident in the affiliations of the writers, advisers, and promoters, and even in the miniaturized window display at the Workers' Bookshop in New York. Budget cuts, government scrutiny, and the threat of future cuts and future scrutiny had a chilling effect on the development and production of creative work that advanced critical interpretations of racial slavery, black exploitation, or interracial activism. The congressional investigations apparently encouraged Negro Units in the FTP to shy away from controversial material and lean more toward music and dance numbers. A hard-hitting show that focused on black history and included scenes of slavery was scratched, some alleged, because of the hostile political climate. Indeed, not even E. P. Conkle's extremely popular and relatively uncontroversial Lincoln play was safe: HUAC member Parnell Thomas called it a "propaganda play" with "communist leanings." And it seems likely that a Washington, DC, performance of Conkle's play was canceled because of the unusual attention coming from Congress. John McGee's *Jefferson Davis*, by contrast, got some bad reviews but never suffered political censorship. In the FWP, material documenting racial conflict and prejudice, including Sterling Brown's essay "The Negro in Washington," likewise drew congressional conservatives' ire. Brown's essay was part of a longer guidebook for the city, and its focus on discrimination led congressmen to call it "insidious propaganda" authored by "communistically inspired agitators." In an attempt to stymie Richard Wright's contributions, HUAC investigators forced the black writer to produce a notarized statement certifying that he was a US citizen.[15]

More than any other cultural force on the American scene, Federal One programs had the potential to give Americans a full airing of the broad range of competing Civil War memories. With plays celebrating both Jefferson Davis and Frederick Douglass, oral interviews documenting the experience of Confederate soldiers as well as ex-slaves, and the numerous theatrical and artistic tributes to Abraham Lincoln, there were certainly possibilities for loosening the grip of Lost Cause accounts when it came to national reflections about the war. Yet even in this most favorable of climates, the pro-Confederate interpretation maintained considerable staying power, partly because its advocates were situated in important sites of cultural influence, but also because artistic material with a pro-Confederate bent never drew attention from political scrutinizers for its "un-American" point of view.

FEDERAL OFFICIALS became even more directly involved in presenting Civil War stories through their new role as custodians of Civil War battlefields. But on the terrain where the war had been fought, firsthand actors were increasingly pushed to the sidelines, and Lost Cause interpretations emerged more prominently here than in the Federal One programs. In the immediate aftermath of the war, places like Gettysburg, Vicksburg, Antietam, and Manassas bore the stamp of veteran efforts to preserve and memorialize their own wartime experiences. Working with private groups and government bodies, veterans and their organizations worked actively to mark and preserve battle sites, seeking to re-create their presence on the battlefield with scores of tablets, markers, and statues. During the 1890s, these predominantly white veteran groups collaborated with the federal government, now a more active partner in the business of battlefield preservation, to create and maintain five military parks—Gettysburg, Antietam, Shiloh, Vicksburg, and Chickamauga/Chattanooga—that would be overseen by the War Department. In 1933, the federal government emerged as a still more significant player in battlefield interpretation when the National Park Service (NPS), created seventeen years earlier as a bureau within the Department of the Interior, assumed the management of numerous historic monuments, cemeteries, and battlefields. Under the terms of FDR's Executive Order, this included those Civil War parks previously supervised by the War Department. Over the course of the 1930s, several more Civil War sites came under Park Service oversight.[16]

The transfer from the War Department to the Park Service was far more than a simple bureaucratic reassignment. Rather, it reflected a new way of thinking about what Civil War battle sites would mean for the general public. Under the War Department's supervision, Civil War battlefields had welcomed mainly veterans, soldiers, and students of military history, offering space where ex-soldiers could recall and commemorate their military deeds and where army units could train for twentieth-century warfare. Markers explained the placement and movements of specific regiments but did little to enlighten a tourist about the overall flow of events. Civilian travelers relied on private guides, not the government, if they wanted to learn some history. As the Park Service entered the field of historic preservation, interest grew in the NPS acquiring Civil War battlefields that could be incorporated into broader, more sweeping efforts to tell the nation's history. With FDR's Executive Order, the federal government moved more actively into the work of maintaining and interpreting Civil War battlefields, while veterans and their organizations receded into the background. During the 1930s, when Americans visited Civil War sites, they saw a landscape and learned a story that had passed through the complex web of the nation's growing federal bureaucracy.[17]

Money, of course, greased the wheels of that growing bureaucracy. While individuals and private organizations were strapped for cash during the Depression, New Deal administrators spent considerable sums to build roads, manage landscapes, improve public works, and put people to work. At the National Parks, including the new Civil War parks, government money took human form through the Civilian Conservation Corps (CCC), initiated in 1933 with the aim of employing mainly young men to work on outdoor conservation projects. Tasked with building roads, repairing fences, and constructing visitor stations and restrooms, CCC camps—including a number of all-black units—were established at several Civil War battlefields. Two all-black CCC camps operated at Gettysburg during the 1930s. Through CCC labors, Civil War battlefields were physically transformed from the veteran-oriented shrines of old to modern-day tourist sites. In part, this meant turning these places into recreational sites where American travelers could enjoy a "natural" setting, albeit one with parking areas, smoother roads, and picnic spaces scattered on the landscape to accommodate larger numbers of visitors with cars. Park administrators also acknowledged the historical component of these sites and sought to provide educational material that recognized the modern tourist's lack of knowledge about the past.[18]

Park personnel consciously worked to accommodate new visitors more than old veterans. In the past, explained Gettysburg superintendent James McConaghie, "an emotional stage," one that reflected the longings of the veterans, had led to "the erection of monument after monument." In 1936, however, the goal was "to preserve an area of great historical value in such a manner as to permit the visitor to visualize conditions of the day" while also recognizing that new visitors required an "educational program . . . to replace the personal knowledge of yesterday." At Gettysburg, this meant taking a much more measured approach to monument construction, as well as placing trees and shrubs so that "the numerous monuments will appear to fit and be screened so as not to unduly

Unveiling the Eternal Light Peace Memorial at Gettysburg, 1938. Designed for the
seventy-fifth-anniversary ceremony at Gettysburg, the Eternal Light Peace Memorial,
unveiled in a ceremony that brought together Union and Confederate veterans, once
again drew attention to reconciliation. Contemporary concerns about global warfare,
however, tended to shift attention away from military efforts and toward peaceful uni-
fication. Records of National Park Service, Gettysburg National Military Park, General
Historical Photographic Prints (GETT 41135_5E-5118)

affect the landscape." It also meant the placement of an occasional picnic table
or "comfort station," and the expansion of roads to accommodate heavy auto
traffic, even if these new thoroughfares disrupted the original lines of battle.
In short, new visitors were meant to see an educational landscape, a place that
told a piece of the national story, not a commemorative landscape that honored
specific men for specific actions.[19]

All of which makes it instructive to consider the monuments built at Gettysburg during the New Deal years. Although hundreds of monuments had sprung
up on this Pennsylvania ground prior to Roosevelt's administration, only two
monuments were erected between 1933 and 1945: an Alabama state monument that had been in the works since 1927 and was completed in 1933; and the
Eternal Light Peace Memorial, completed in 1938 in time for the seventy-fifth

anniversary of the July battle. Of the more than thirteen hundred monuments that currently sit on the Gettysburg field, the Eternal Light monument is the only one that highlights peace and, perhaps more than any other structure, relegates the battlefield endeavors of Civil War actors to a relatively minor point of consideration. In this regard, the monument marks a startling break with the concerns of firsthand participants and demonstrates the new generation's agenda.

First conceived during the fiftieth anniversary in 1913, momentum for the peace monument began to build as the 1938 commemoration approached. Designed by the French-born Philadelphian Paul Cret, the structure, costing $60,000, was paid for by contributions from the federal government and seven state governments, fewer than initially expected because several states were strapped for cash. Not surprisingly, the sculpture strongly highlights the theme of peaceful reunification: two embracing figures on the bas-relief, carved by artist Lee Lawrie, symbolize the reunited sections, while the central slogan proclaims: "Peace Eternal in a Nation United." The materials used for construction—Maine granite and Alabama limestone—also signaled an intentional gesture toward North-South reunion. The monument's unveiling came amid a massive ceremony in early July, billed as the "final reunion" for the men of the blue and the gray, which brought together thousands of civilians, close to two thousand veterans, and the president of the United States. A former soldier of the Union and one from the Confederacy pulled the ropes in a July 3 observance that revealed the forty-seven-foot-tall structure. In these respects, the monument and the ceremony echoed countless occasions that came before, events in which Union and Confederate veterans had united to voice the mantra of reconciliation, sometimes genuinely and sometimes strategically.[20]

In other ways, however, this new Gettysburg memorial, and the events surrounding its unveiling, gesture toward a new message, one that suited the sensibilities of the interwar years, and especially contemporary anxiety about future military entanglements. The Eternal Light Peace Memorial focused less on soldiers' bravery in battle and instead raised questions about perpetuating war, any war, in a world surrounded by horrific conflict. The monument's bas-relief sculpture portrayed no male warriors, just entwined female figures holding a laurel branch and a wreath. A gas peace light was ignited, designed to run in perpetuity. In order to construct the monument, the Park Service agreed to demolish historic property where soldiers had fought and some Confederates had been buried, at the Forney farm. The 1938 structure, in sum, had a closer emotional connection to the nation's most recent conflict, the European war of 1917–18, than to the Civil War, and so was shaped and interpreted by those emotions. The profound ambivalence many Americans felt about that war inevitably affected the feelings people had about this ceremony honoring the last remaining veterans of the Civil War.[21]

Not that these aging ex-soldiers were entirely overlooked. Thanks to government funds that covered the travel and lodging costs for each soldier, about two thousand veterans, one-quarter of the eight thousand still living, came to the Pennsylvania fields for the four ceremonial days marking the seventy-fifth anniversary of the battle in July 1938. Those able to attend were enthusiastic about making the trip. "I am able to strike the back of my hands behind my back," wrote William Kimberly from Los Angeles in response to a government survey, "and 'skin a cat' yet." J. K. Moore of Tennessee was also determined to make the trip, although he admitted he was "praying that we will all keep sober during the whole time of that great important occasion." Black veterans, too, were eligible for the government travel benefits, including Josiah Waddle of Omaha, Nebraska, who judged his Gettysburg sojourn "the most enjoyable trip" of his life. Another African American vet, John Young of Pine Bluff, Arkansas, affirmed his intention to make the journey: "I'll be there if I have to crawl."[22]

The presence of black vets did not mean the ceremonies included much, if any, awareness of the distinctive factors that shaped the African American soldiers' experience, in terms of either slavery or emancipation. The scant reflections about slavery and abolition came from black CCC men, assigned to work the Gettysburg property, including one enrollee who had even been moved, a few years earlier, to write a poem about Gettysburg's Union dead: "The soldiers fought to set us free / And we, the boys of the C.C.C. / Pay our respect to the boys in blue / Who nobly fell for a cause so true." In the 1938 ceremony, however, silence about slavery and abolition were overwhelming. Speakers assiduously avoided points of conflict and praised what Secretary of War Harry Woodring called "the miracle of reconciliation." Pennsylvania governor George Earle did praise the "high and inspired ideal of liberty and justice" that motivated Gettysburg's soldiers, but his speech, tellingly, cast all the veterans as the upholders of those principles. More typical were the remarks of the commander of the American Legion, who marveled at this unique American experience of reunion, noting how "men who fought on one battlefield have met again and clasped hands in friendship."[23]

Of course, many of the men who attended the 1938 reunion had not actually fought on this "one battlefield." The veterans at the seventy-fifth-anniversary ceremony were not simply Gettysburg veterans: all Civil War veterans, from

"A Union and Confederate Veteran Join Hands" at Gettysburg, 1938. Echoing the iconic imagery from the 1913 Gettysburg Reunion, aging vets, although not necessarily men who had fought at Gettysburg, once again shook hands at the final joint gathering in 1938 at the seventy-fifth anniversary of the famous battle. Special Collections & College Archives, Musselman Library, Gettysburg College.

both North and South, who were still alive in 1938 were invited to attend. Since the fiftieth anniversary gathering in 1913, Gettysburg had loomed large on the Civil War landscape and so could conveniently serve as the gathering spot for all the former soldiers. Then, as more veterans passed away, Gettysburg increasingly became the battlefield that came to stand in for the whole, a synecdoche carrying all the weight and symbolism associated with the entire Civil War conflict. Yet the more Gettysburg carried that larger symbolic weight, the more specific memories associated with that precise scene of struggle—particularly the memory of the Union's success on those Pennsylvania fields—were eclipsed. As early as 1932, Chamber of Commerce secretary Paul Roy found that battlefield guides at Gettysburg showed a decided indifference "regarding the outcome of the struggle." "The victory of the Northern army," he explained, "is not broadcast." A place that might have been remembered with a keener appreciation of the Union cause was now being recalled for both Union and Confederate acts of bravery, and especially for both Union and Confederate willingness to reunite.[24]

In a way, then, the 1938 gathering suggested again how much further Americans' cultural memory of the Civil War was moving away from the experience of actual veterans. Even more telling was the way observers tended to view the former soldiers as increasingly irrelevant to contemporary America. For one, these men, many well into their nineties, were unquestionably old: "feeble of frame, dim of eye, gray of hair," "march[ing] together into the twilight of time and the morning of eternity." Even more, these men had made their mark by fighting, yet modern Americans showed a decided disinclination to celebrate military hostilities. Indeed, the preoccupation with the horrors of modern warfare encouraged observers to minimize the bloodshed at Gettysburg. "Measured by the physical magnitudes of the conflicts in the World War," opined the *Hartford Courant* editors, "the forces engaged and casualties suffered at Gettysburg seem not so great." The *Tucson Star* agreed: "Gettysburg was a sporting proposition compared to modern warfare." Surely veterans themselves would have strenuously disagreed with this apparent diminishment of their martial efforts. But the Civil War in 1938 came heavily filtered through a war of more recent vintage, as well as the intensifying conflicts of the present, all of which contributed to a more skeptical view of the fighting done by men of the Civil War generation. At a Memorial Day ceremony at Antietam a Maryland senator acknowledged that the bravery of the Union and Confederate soldiers had long been celebrated but lamented that "too little attention has been paid to ... the patient, cooperative and no-less-courageous attitude of many people ... to avert the impending conflict." The take-away point for many was this: that war, whether in the nineteenth century or the twentieth, represented politicians' spectacular failure to enact peace.[25]

Historians of the time lent scholarly credence to these observations. Scholars such as Avery Craven, George Milton, and James Randall viewed the Civil War as a needless, preventable conflict brought on by irresponsible politicking. Generally adhering to a prosouthern bias, these historians singled out abolitionists as extreme fanatics who made efforts to compromise over slavery impossible. Slavery, argued Avery Craven, was "but a passing incident," fanned into conflagration by alarmist agitation, exploded into war by the work of "pious cranks." By 1938, such views had gained a strong following, influencing other observers and intellectuals who saw in the horrors of the Great War, as well as in the emerging hostilities of their own time, a crucial historical lesson about the necessity, and ultimately the possibility, of avoiding conflict. Inevitably, this thinking worked against an earlier narrative that lauded Civil War veterans for their military fortitude, as well as their willingness to sacrifice for principles.

Current views held that these tenets were "born of misunderstanding" and that by unifying in the postwar era soldiers demonstrated "all too plainly," in the words of the *Fort Worth Morning Star*, "the shallowness of the prejudice which brought on the Civil War." Surely this did not reflect well on soldiers' dedication to their "cause," and cast those committed to the fight against slavery as little more than the victims of narrow-minded "prejudice." To the editors of the *Kansas City Star*, the lesson of Gettysburg was that conflict was not inevitable and that the issues dividing the country could have "been worked out by peaceful methods." The same, they insisted, was true at the present time: "Nowhere is it possible today to discern a difference among the nations that would justify war." These yearnings for peace clustered around the 1938 proceedings, as well as around the Peace Memorial itself, with many viewing the monument's tribute to "the peace and good will existing between the North and South today" as a statement with relevance for both domestic and international affairs.[26]

Gettysburg continued to stand at the apex of the Civil War conflict and therefore was the park that, anniversary or no, garnered the most attention. But Gettysburg also occupied an unusual position on the Civil War landscape. The vast majority of Civil War sites were not in Pennsylvania but in spots where most of the war had been fought: below the Mason-Dixon line. In these places, park supervisors and veterans forged a distinct relationship, one that pushed interpretation in a more explicitly pro-Confederate direction. To a great extent, this reflected the way Confederate veterans and their descendants had already established a presence at these sites, having acquired plots of land and constructed their own memorials to fallen soldiers. On a section of the Bull Run battlefield, for example, the Sons of Confederate Veterans (SCV) created a Confederate park in 1921 with the stated intention of telling the "distinct, wonderful, equally thrilling, all-important story" of the South and its fight for states' rights. By the 1930s, when Confederate sons were feeling the pinch of the Depression, they looked to the Park Service for assistance in the hope that their legacy might live on through the federal government's largesse. Seeking to establish a new site at Manassas, park officials entered into negotiations with the SCV, ultimately taking over the old Confederate park while still pledging to honor a number of Confederate memorial traditions. "No development, markers, monuments or inscriptions on this property," stated the official deed of conveyance, "will detract in any way from the glory due the Confederate heroes."[27]

Manassas supervisors, like their Gettysburg counterparts, embraced the goal of reaching a new generation of visitors to give them a larger picture of the "military operations of the War between the States" and to offer a way for the modern-day "motorist" to visit the various Virginia battlefields in a logical order. Also like Gettysburg's administrators, they lamented the trend toward "excessive monumentation," which would "interfere with the ability to visualize the original spot." In order to meet their pledge to the SCV, though, the NPS also made their landscape more hospitable to a Confederate point of view, demonstrated most clearly with the 1940 unveiling of a monument to Confederate General Stonewall Jackson to commemorate his defensive actions at the first Bull Run battle. At the Fredricksburg battlefield, the Park Service purchased the site of Jackson's death from the Richmond, Fredericksburg, and Potomac Railroad, which had named the site the "Stonewall Jackson Shrine." In 1937 they held a formal ceremony to mark the conveyance of this holy "shrine"—keeping the name by which it had long been known—to the federal government. The NPS even fostered Confederate commemoration at Gettysburg: despite a desire to control the proliferation of monuments, they dedicated the site for a future statue to General James Longstreet in a 1941 ceremony attended by Longstreet's widow and the movie actress Mary Pickford. And, as I have already suggested, the tendency to make Gettysburg the ultimate symbol for the war encouraged an erasure of what might have been a more pointedly Unionist memory of the conflict. In short, even as the National Park Service's Civil War sites pushed Civil War storytelling into a new era—one focused less on veterans and more on tourists—many sites encouraged a new appreciation for the symbols of Confederate heroism and sacrifice.[28]

IF, AS THE WRITER Viet Thahn Nguyen argues, "industrializing memory proceeds in parallel with how warfare is industrialized," Hollywood in the 1930s was ready to become an industrial dynamo, primed to unleash a more potent version of Civil War memory than anything Americans had previously seen. In marshaling its full arsenal of spectacular effects and images, movie studios had little interest in a simple retelling of first-person stories, seeking instead a more visually and aurally compelling way to speak to the emotions of American audiences. Of course, for the movies, unlike for the federal government, turning a profit remained the all-important touchstone, and even in economically desperate times, movies made money. Despite the hardships of the Depression, between one-third and one-half of the American people went to the movies on a regular basis during the 1930s. Studio officials recognized that stories that tapped into fantasies and desires yielded more revenue than historical accounts that lacked the tinge of romance or melodrama or other established genres that had proven profitable with American audiences. Even in the South, hardly the nation's most profitable moviegoing region, Hollywood officials worried about producing films that might not sell well with predominantly white audiences. As a result, filmmakers had a strong impulse to go with tried and tested formulas, in this case quaint plantation romances filled with stock portrayals of white masters and happy black slaves. The desire to win at least some of the southern market may have also dampened interest in the Civil War, a topic that could easily wound sectional feelings. However, when the stars aligned, the Civil War could be big business, especially when a film (a) was based on a best-selling book; (b) told a story that could appeal to the predominantly female portion of the moviegoing audience; or (c) gave Shirley Temple top billing.[29]

There was an additional challenge in producing Civil War–themed films, or really any kind of films, in the 1930s: what people then and since have referred to as "the Code." Formulated by the Motion Picture Producers and Distributors of America and its president, Will Hays, Hollywood's "Production Code" consisted of guidelines aimed at keeping a moral check on potentially inflammatory material, especially anything dealing with sex, race, profanity, religion, and alcohol. Although film portrayals of the South and the Civil War were obviously not its main target, the Code could affect them in various ways. It might be invoked on racially sensitive matters, not so much to curtail offensive stereotypes as to remove objectionable language (e.g., "nigger") that could spark the kind of black protest that had been aimed at the pre-Code blockbuster *Birth of a Nation*. The Code's enforcers were equally mindful not to offend southern white racial sensibilities with depictions of either too much intimacy, or too much hostility, between the races. Ultimately, the Code worked to push the movies toward a more benign portrayal of the Old South, as well as the postwar South, and to show mostly contentment and submissiveness on the part of African Americans.[30]

The first big Civil War movie of the 1930s was an adaptation of Stark Young's commercially successful novel *So Red the Rose* (1934; film, 1935). With this novel, Young, a writer with the Agrarian movement, made a nod back to family and tradition. An elderly Mississippi uncle, he explained, who "used to own more slaves than anybody in the South, with one exception, and had endless plantations" was the memory behind his tale. Steeped in Young's fervent belief in the cultured ways of the Old South, his book recounted the prewar pleasantries, wartime anguish, and complicated love affairs of two related and neighboring plantation families. After the book sold surprisingly well, Paramount studios bought the rights and put a well-established southern-born director, King Vidor, at the helm. Vidor made some, although not extensive, departures from

Young's novel to produce a film that hewed closely to the Hollywood formula: a movie filled with graceful plantation homes, julep-drinking masters rocking on porches, tortured declarations of love, and singing slaves. The studio apparently saw yet more profit to be made by playing on the memory angle, at least in terms of linking their work to "official" preservers of Confederate memory. In 1935, the best way to do that, or so they thought, was to win the support of the Confederate war's female caretakers.[31]

As a group that, even seventy years after Appomattox, retained some clout and a relatively sizable membership (one hundred thousand in 1924), the United Daughters of the Confederacy offered a convenient means by which Hollywood might win a Confederate stamp of approval. Over the course of the 1920s and early '30s, they had undertaken campaigns to make Confederate memory yet more visible—through the erection of monuments and markers as well as the construction of the "Jefferson Davis Highway"—and certainly helped keep the Confederate legacy in the news. They were also a well-organized band whose resources might be deployed by a movie industry still somewhat in its infancy. When *So Red the Rose* was in production, publicity director Robert Gilham took a tour of the southern states, appealed to UDC women, offered them scripts to review, and ultimately got them to send out sixty thousand promotional letters. Using his UDC connections, Gilham then arranged for the picture to have a well-publicized premiere in all eleven state capitals of the old Confederacy. At least one daughter of a Union soldier was outraged to see how much influence her female counterparts in the South had in Hollywood. "It makes one sick at one's stomach to have Union soldiers presented so unjustly," insisted Mrs. Helen S. Claassen. "I hope none of them who are still living see the picture."[32]

To some extent, *So Red the Rose* became enmeshed in an old-fashioned memory debate, promoted and assessed in terms of how well it matched the recollections of Civil War descendants. Yet despite all the planning and the appeals, *So Red the Rose* worked neither with audiences nor with most critics, and its failure may well have sent a warning message about the future of the Lost Cause in cinema. The *New York Times'* reviewer, for example, found it difficult to sympathize with the film's "rage against the uncouth legions of Mr. Lincoln as they dash about the lovely Southern landscape putting crazy notions in the heads of plantation slaves." He further objected to the depiction of enemy [Union] forces "as cruel and vulgar intrusions instead of inevitable realities." To *Variety's* film critic, *So Red the Rose* didn't "rest well" in the way it pitched "its sympathies with the kindly southern planter." Many reviewers, it seems, had trouble with the overt, even propagandistic nature of the film and its unquestioning endorsement of the plantation owners' morality, including their thorough repugnance toward abolition. In short, northern critics showed a decided unwillingness to accept a wholly uncritical and idealized version of the Lost Cause, one that seemed tailor-made for the United Daughters of the Confederacy. Rather, they preferred something with a bit more irony, a little more modern in its depiction of characters and their imperfections, and not nearly so vituperative toward the Union war effort. As filmmakers discovered, this did not mean abandoning pro-Confederate attitudes, and certainly not white supremacy, although it did mean striking a less strident and perhaps slightly less serious tone. Moviemakers still wanted to show southern white audiences that they were mindful of particular "southern" characteristics—whether those had to do with accents, mannerisms, or, most of all, racial sensibilities. But none of that required the input of the UDC.[33]

To deal with this situation, studios sought out advisers and artists for consultation and collaboration, men and women who served, in effect, as Hollywood's "professional southerners." Significantly, "professional southerners" in the 1930s were not the same Lost Cause storytellers of old. Stark Young, for example, was out. After rumors circulated that he might be asked to advise on the film version of Margaret Mitchell's novel, Young's invitation was, if not gone with the wind, at least lost in the mail. Brushing off Young's plea that she help him get the job, Mitchell instead promoted her longtime friend Susan Myrick, a journalist with the *Macon (Georgia) Telegraph* who was admired, at least by Mitchell, for her "utter lack of sentimentality about what is tearfully known as 'The Old South.'" Myrick arrived on the *Gone with the Wind* set not as an old-school Lost Causer but as one who carefully discerned style and presentation, making sure certain markers of southern culture, especially regarding accents, costumes, and settings, conformed to her idea of something acceptably "southern." She insisted, too, that black actors look, sound, and act like her idea of servile Negroes. Along with her coadviser Wilbur Kurtz, Myrick recommended against an overly romanticized picture of the antebellum South, adopting Mitchell's view that not all plantation homes were grandiose and not all plantation denizens high-toned aristocrats. But though Myrick cared about presentation, she had little interest in changing the historical substance. She raised no objections to the film's central historical tenets, which were basically restatements of fundamental Lost Cause creeds: that southern slaves were treated kindly by benevolent masters, that white southerners did not go to war over slavery, and that Reconstruction was an era of corrupt black and carpetbagger rule that tried to crush the spirit of southern whites. In the end, the film did include the opulent, aristocratic plantation homes of

Susan Myrick and Ann Rutherford on the set of *Gone with the Wind*. Hired to coach the cast of David O. Selznick's epic film on matters of southern etiquette and pronunciation, Susan Myrick, a friend of Margaret Mitchell's, played the part of a "professional southerner" for Hollywood. Photofest.

legend. It even won official approval from the UDC. And yet, unlike the UDC's support for *So Red the Rose*, their endorsement of *Gone with the Wind* seemed more like a cry of surrender—a capitulation to a Hollywood juggernaut—rather than an enthusiastic embrace. The Confederate Daughters had never really warmed to Mitchell's rambunctious and overly flirtatious heroine. They had also pressured filmmakers to cast southerners in the lead roles; one Florida chapter even considered boycotting because an English woman got the female lead. The Tulsa chapter of the UDC was also apparently concerned enough about possible missteps being taken in the making of the film that they passed a resolution insisting that the film give "a true interpretation of the spirit of the old South." The UDC, one suspects, had a different notion of "spirit" than either Mitchell or Myrick did.[34]

By setting films in the postwar era, filmmakers found another way to address southern sympathies but escape the kind of criticism that had plagued *So Red the Rose*: they could avoid showing Union troops, or Lincoln, in a bad light. Since few Americans would have disputed the pro-Confederate interpretation of Reconstruction, setting a film in the "tragic era" made good sense. Thus *The Prisoner of Shark Island* (1936), with Georgian Nunnally Johnson on board as screenwriter, focused on the dark deeds of the Reconstruction Republicans and their unjust prosecution of Dr. Samuel Mudd as one of the Lincoln assassins. Lamar Trotti, another Georgia-born screenwriter and "professional southerner," took an even lighter touch and pushed even further away from the war period, with the two southern films he made with director John Ford. Starting his movie career with the Hays Office, Trotti advised about various films with a southern angle in the early days of the industry. In 1927 he counseled against showing a new film version of *Uncle Tom's Cabin* in the South, arguing that southern whites would find the film's brutal depiction of chattel slavery offensive. But Trotti, not unlike Myrick, was no fan of the United Daughters of the Confederacy school of filmmaking. Indeed, one of Trotti's early successes, John Ford's 1934 film *Judge Priest*, takes aim precisely at organizations like the UDC, who are portrayed as loud champions of the Confederacy even as they shunt aside the poor and neglected veterans in their communities. Like Myrick, Trotti did not want to abandon Confederate sensibilities—*Judge Priest* has more than its fair share of singing "Dixie," Confederate flag-waving, and cheering for Jefferson Davis—but, as befits this twilight moment of memory, Trotti understood the intangible and fungible nature of remembrance. In the 1935 film *Steamboat Round the Bend*, also directed by Ford and with a screenplay by Trotti, the principal character, played by Will Rogers, takes over an old wax museum and, knowing he will need to market the museum to southerners, promptly turns the figure of Ulysses Grant into one of Robert E. Lee. *Steamboat* showcased precisely what Hollywood, and Trotti himself, could do with memory: manipulate images and emotions, confirming certain traditional historical sensibilities but in ways that suited a more modern temperament. One of the high points of Trotti's work on *Judge Priest* came when Henry Walthall, the "Little Colonel" actor of *Birth of a Nation* fame, appeared in a dramatic courtroom scene testifying in defense of a falsely accused veteran. For Trotti, this confirmed how movie memory, more than anything actually connected to the Confederate past, might become the new means for securing an attachment to the Lost Cause. "When you see him [Walthall] in his Confederate uniform," Trotti explained to a southern colleague, "you will rise and shout."[35]

Trotti's instincts seem to have been spot on. Reviews of *Judge Priest* praised Walthall's appearance as one of the most memorable features of the film.

Similarly, when *Gone with the Wind* was in production and Margaret Mitchell fans wrote to Selznick demanding authentic and credible renderings of the southern experience, they often referenced movies that got it wrong (*Jezebel* was often singled out for criticism) as well as films that got it right. "Do you realize," wrote Mary Elmore of Washington, DC, to Selznick, "that we have NOT had a REAL southern picture since *The Birth of a Nation.* . . . We want to see *Gone with the Wind* as big as fine as real as *Birth of a Nation.*" In other words, for many the criteria for determining how well a movie conformed to the "true" southern experience was not how many plaudits it earned from the UDC, but how much it followed in the steps of other successful Hollywood films.[36]

Using earlier movies to evaluate other movies certainly fit Hollywood's emerging frame of reality. Yet in one crucial respect Hollywood did have to break some new ground in 1930s moviemaking. In these years, filmmakers confronted a totally new and somewhat unexpected problem. Whereas earlier motion pictures, including *Birth of a Nation*, had mostly cast white men and women to play leading black roles, by the 1930s, film audiences now wanted to see actual black actors cast in these parts. But doing so meant that white producers, directors, actors, and audiences now had to deal with real-life black men and women, people far removed from a slave past, playing parts that clearly conformed to white supremacist fantasies about "slave-like" behavior. Much as southern white audiences insisted on "authenticity" in these black film performances, what they really wanted was *their* fantasy of the southern past as opposed to Hollywood's adaptation. In their version of Old South make-believe, southern white fans insisted that professionally trained actors could never do these parts justice. Minnie Richardson of Alabama wrote to one of Selznick's *Gone with the Wind* staffers in 1938 to press this point. "Give us some Real ones," she wrote about "the Negroes." "Why not use some honest to God old slaves?"[37]

It was, of course, an outlandish request, but Richardson did touch on a sore point that some in Hollywood had already been confronting. After all, having professional black actors on motion picture sets struck many in the movie industry as a potentially disturbing development. Producers for *So Red the Rose* even referred to this situation as a "sociological experiment." With *So Red the Rose* the problem was further compounded by the film's story line, which called for depicting a plantation rebellion led by disgruntled slaves. The publicity surrounding the film hinted at apprehensions that whites in Hollywood, as well as in theaters, may have had about seeing angry blacks enact a version of the southern past that, at least on the surface, contradicted their expectations about slave loyalty. To address this concern, Paramount created a story about the film's director, King Vidor, playing up his background as a southern white man who could control a racially driven uprising. "Familiar with the colored mind and sympathetic as well," Vidor was said to have spent fifteen minutes speaking to the black "mob" and presenting "a simple word picture of negro life during the period of slavery, stressing too the significance of the event which gave them their freedom." Thus, Vidor's southern roots, it was assumed, gave him unusual access to a historical record, and a racial sensibility, that he could convey to his black actors. Yet, while it was important that Vidor's storytelling, and not actual black anger, produce the desired emotion that would lead to a rebellion, publicists also wanted to assure their viewers that the "real" slave past would never have produced such a frightening display of disloyalty. Instead, Vidor made "a somewhat maudlin presentation of the evils which their ancestors were supposed to have suffered" in order to make it easier to direct them in these volatile scenes.[38]

The fact that black actors, instead of blacked-up white men, occupied these roles no doubt heightened the concern about whose historical record would inform the film. Filmmakers may have been particularly anxious to seize control of the narrative because of another problem they faced: when black men and women were cast in these deeply caricatured roles, they also gained a bit of leverage, allowing them to impede, even in minor ways, the white fantasy about slavery. Much as publicists and producers may have tried to convince their audiences that the black figures they saw on the screen were not far removed from slavery, the realities of black performance intervened. This happened most dramatically in *So Red the Rose* in a scene when Margaret Sullavan, playing the part of the plantation mistress, was expected to slap the leader of the slave uprising during the height of the revolt. Clarence Muse, the black actor playing this part, objected and proceeded to hold up "the studio two days and a half," knowing they would have to reach some kind of compromise because so much money had been invested in the film. According to a Beverly Hills newspaper, Sullavan "apologized to ... Muse for three sound slaps a script scene called for," and producers agreed that a minor participant in the mob would receive Sullavan's blow. The showdown between Muse and Sullavan foreshadowed the fight surrounding another, and even more notorious, master-slave confrontation: the one that called for Vivien Leigh's Scarlett to strike Butterfly McQueen's Prissy in *Gone with the Wind*. According to Sidney Howard's screenplay, the frustrated Scarlett "slaps the black face with all the force of her tired arm." In rehearsals, Leigh seems to have taken the direction to heart, leading McQueen to object strongly to the punishing blows. "I can't do it, she's hurting me," McQueen remarked.

"I'm no stunt man, I'm an actress." It may not have been a decisive confrontation over the memory of slavery, yet McQueen's complaint registered. Much as Hollywood may have wanted to capture something "real" and "authentic" about the slave experience, black actors would impose limits, at least small ones.[39]

Still, a paucity of black directors, screenwriters, and other behind-the-scenes creative artists severely constricted the possibility of black pushback to a cinematic Lost Cause, even the more "modern" version of the Lost Cause that was gaining ground. And on the rare occasion when African American artists did occupy important positions in structuring a film or shaping its story, their influence was often undermined by Hollywood's insistence on catering to southern white prejudices, or at least Hollywood's idea of what those prejudices were. When Clarence Muse and poet Langston Hughes teamed up to write a screenplay for a film, the little-known 1939 movie *Way Down South*, one goal was to show some of the troubling and exploitative aspects of slavery. But final word on *Way Down South* rested with neither Muse nor Hughes but with the white director, Sol Lesser, who made sure that the film contained no material white southerners might find offensive. In the end, only Yankees were shown to be responsible for acts of exploitation because, Lesser insisted, they do "not understand . . . the sentimental and emotional relationship that exists" under slavery.[40]

ON DECEMBER 15, 1939, the long-awaited Civil War movie of the decade had its world premiere in Atlanta, Georgia. In many ways, the making of *Gone with the Wind* provides a master class in how Hollywood remade Civil War memory. On the one hand, Selznick and his team acknowledged at least some of the fantasies white southerners had about the past, and about who might best be the arbiters of that long-ago time. Hence, they launched their much-publicized tour—really a highly orchestrated publicity stunt—to scour the South for an unknown actress to play the part of Scarlett. Likewise, when publicists made even limited attempts to curry favor with the United Daughters of the Confederacy, or when they arranged to hold the premiere in Atlanta, they again tried to appease a popular yearning, to get back in touch with a "history" that was slipping away. Although they had, of course, employed a significant number of professional black actors for the film, they nonetheless barred those men and women from attending the premiere, a move that placated Jim Crow demands and simultaneously fed the fantasy that "authentic" southern black folk, not the professional colleagues of Clark Gable or Vivien Leigh, appeared on the screen. Still, much as they appeased these racist sensibilities, Selznick and company had no intention of being swallowed up by a nineteenth-century version of the

Lost Cause. They got their historical counsel not from the UDC but from a woman who was both a white supremacist and a fierce opponent of Old South sentimentality. Much as they gestured toward southern actors, they went, instead, with known stars and English performers.[41]

And when all was said and done, *Gone with the Wind* paid little attention to the veterans who had fought the war. Union men, not surprisingly, condemned the film for its unsavory depiction of Federal soldiers as "hideous marauder(s) attacking women." Although they tried to enlist the aid of official movie censors to take steps against the film, their efforts were rebuffed in the name of "history," as well as entertainment. "I was not particularly happy [with the film]," explained the chairwoman of the Pennsylvania Board of Motion Picture Censors, "because it was a reflection on the north. But that's history. . . . I still think the picture will be a treat." Selznick, too, acknowledged receiving these complaints but insisted that the film's "historical facts [had been] checked thoroughly by a historian." As for Confederate soldiers, while their exploits were honored on film, actual Confederate veterans were, in the end, overlooked. When the premiere came to Atlanta, it apparently slipped everyone's mind that there were some ancient Confederate veterans still living in the Atlanta veterans' home. A car was quickly dispatched to bring them to the theater, where the crowd "greeted the bowed remnants of the proud, tattered armies of the Confederacy with spontaneous applause." Nonetheless, as a local reporter explained, "the applause was light in comparison with that given Hollywood's glamorous boys and girls."[42]

During the 1930s the Civil War got a makeover, thanks in large part to a new set of actors who felt compelled to tell new types of Civil War stories. National Park Service supervisors, Federal Arts administrators, Hollywood filmmakers— all of these groups, and more, would be vital to the reshaping of Civil War memory during the New Deal decade. All of them, as well, found themselves negotiating between traditional ways of telling the story and new political, aesthetic, and economic imperatives. In the quest to make movies profitable and broadly appealing, those in the film industry pushed the Civil War story further away from traditional Lost Cause accounts yet still conformed to a pro-Confederate story line. On Civil War battlefields, government supervisors responded to tourist needs, as well as contemporary political anxieties, as they made the Civil War landscape more modern and less focused on veterans' concerns. And in the Federal Arts program, writers and artists made an attempt to gather and shape traditional memories but also discovered how New Deal–era politics could end up privileging certain stories over others. Over the course of the decade, the contest over memory would become particularly wide-ranging and politically charged, especially when it came to three specific subject areas: the memory of slavery; the depiction of Abraham Lincoln; and the changing narrative of the Lost Cause, all of which will be examined in the chapters that follow.

[3]

SLAVES OF THE DEPRESSION

I N THE SUMMER OF 1933, just a few months after Franklin Roosevelt took office, Lorena Hickok set off on a cross-country journey to document the state of misery and want across America. Charged with observing and conveying the economic deprivation in urban and rural areas, in the South, the West, and the East, Hickok saw untold cases of staggering and unalleviated want, a want she found particularly poignant when it came so unexpectedly. Writing to her boss, Harry Hopkins, the head of the new Federal Emergency Relief Administration, Hickok described the want she saw in the faces of the Williston, North Dakota, farmers, once reasonably well off but now so chilled to the bone they crowded into Hickok's car as soon as she stepped away. She saw want in the face of the farmer who made his first visit to the local relief office, wearing an odd mix of clothes that he explained "belonged to his eldest son." "'They're all we've got now,' he said. 'We take turns wearing 'em.'" Hickok heard the tale of want, too, in her visits to New York City, where a social worker explained the dire circumstances of unmarried females. "'Single women? Why, they're just discards . . . huddled together in small apartments, three or four of them living on the earnings of one, who may have a job.'" In Houston, Hickok found want edging toward hopelessness when she met a twenty-eight-year-old woman, a one-time schoolteacher, now working for "an old woman in a convalescent home" for three dollars a week. The woman shrugged off her caseworker's advice to find a silver lining in her circumstances. "If, with all the advantages I've had, I can't make a living, I'm just no good. . . . I've given up ever amounting to anything."[1]

Sometimes Depression-era want compelled people, southerners most of all, to try to understand their misery by thinking about hard times past. A mule trader in Raleigh, North Carolina, compared his economic woes of 1930 with "the Reconstruction of the Slave War," a time when "a man simply couldn't make a nickel." The reform-minded playwright Paul Green remembered feeling the hard times of the Depression as "a continued statement of the poverty that

I knew as a child," a long-term problem he connected to "the effect of the Civil War." "There were a lot of old soldiers around," Green recalled, "and I would hear their stories." Living in what he called "the shadow of that great foolish tragedy," Green came to understand "the reasons for our condition." Paul Green here offered his own version of a tale heard repeatedly in the South in these troubled times: an origin story that looked back to the Civil War to explain the roots of southern poverty. Not everyone agreed, however, on *why* the war had made the region poor. Green's remarks about a "foolish tragedy" suggested some degree of Confederate culpability. Many other southern whites, however, tended to fix blame on northern rapaciousness during Reconstruction. "Most of the people I've talked to," Hickok learned during the southern part of her trip, "tell me the South is suffering, economically and socially, not from the Civil war, but from the Reconstruction period."[2]

Hickok no doubt heard this complaint mostly from white folks. But she also heard another type of historical reference, one that mainly surfaced when black and white laborers encountered grueling, difficult, and arbitrary conditions. She heard it in conversations about coal miners who worked the soft coal mines of West Virginia, where the few miners lucky enough to get jobs were forced to work on their knees, their backs constantly rubbing against the top of the vein above them. "No Negro on a Southern plantation before the Civil War," the relief workers explained to Hickok, "was ever more enslaved than thousands of those miners have been." A worker employed in the Appalachian Cotton Mill in Knoxville, Tennessee, described conditions there as "worse than miserable—they are no less than slavery." And when Hickok herself offered a broad assessment of the state of southern agriculture she, too, depicted what she saw in terms of previous conditions of servitude. "The truth is," she wrote from North Carolina in February 1934, "that the rural South never has progressed beyond slave labor. Their whole system has been built upon labor that could be obtained for nothing or for next to nothing. When their slaves were taken away, they proceeded to establish a system of peonage that was as close to slavery as it possibly could be and included Whites as well as Blacks." Indeed, as Hickok suggested, maybe this wasn't a metaphor at all, but the product of long-standing historical conditions.[3]

These accounts suggest just a few of the ways in which the Depression, and the economic dislocations that came in its wake, could prompt Americans to reflect not only on the Civil War era but also, more specifically, on the problem of slavery. Indeed, the language of slavery reverberated throughout the years of the Depression, finding its way into politics, history, and culture, and cutting across partisan and ideological affiliations. It was a potent language that fit well with many of the era's events and developments, and its frequent invocations suggested how much people saw the American system itself as caught in an economic, moral, and spiritual bind. Among black Americans, talk of slavery called attention to deep-rooted and severely oppressive historical and economic circumstances, conditions that showed no sign of abating in the 1930s. Increasingly, black activists and intellectuals used the notion of slavery's continuing grip of oppression to protest southern labor practices and the flawed nature of New Deal policies. Poor white southerners, in factories and on farms, also reflected on being "slaves," sometimes to the sharecropping system and sometimes to the stretch-out. Even middle-class southern whites claimed to be the true victims of slavery, crushed in both the past and present by the heel of Yankee oppression. Here, as Hickok observed, Reconstruction bore particular responsibility for initiating a new regime of "enslavement."

Slavery, though, was hardly a regional preoccupation, embedded in the language of southerners both white and black. By the middle years of the Depression, northern industrial workers, especially those seeking to challenge the intensified grind of capitalist exploitation, were also speaking the language of slavery. Over time, slavery also became a predominant metaphor in New Deal politicking, a noticeable element in Popular Front culture, and a pervasive trope in popular novels and Hollywood films. Thinking about slavery—a system with a long and troubled history in North America—of course meant reflecting on more than just the Civil War era. Yet the patterns and tropes employed in discussions of slavery greatly impinged on Civil War (and Reconstruction) memories, which in turn shaped the political outlook of New Deal Americans. And in this regard, one of the most remarkable things about the frequent depictions of slavery in 1930s American culture was the way white people appeared as the most prominent sufferers from enslavement. New Deal culture, whether it took the form of a political speech, a Federal Theatre production, or an epic motion picture, demanded a resolution to the crisis of white enslavement. In this regard, the decisive blow for emancipation came, time after time, not from the efforts of individual "slaves," or even their collective protests, but through the dispensation of government assistance. If white people had become slaves, 1930s culture taught them to see in government the instrument of their liberation.

WHEN THE DEPRESSION BEGAN, an older generation of southern whites remained wedded to a fable regarding a mild plantation system that inspired loyalty and faithfulness from enslaved black men and women. This old story offered them a fantasy of black love, made all the more touching by black men's and women's willingness to occupy positions of servitude and subordination. The Daughters of the Confederacy were frequent tellers of this tale of Negro fealty, celebrating it in monuments, performances, and ceremonies. Douglas Southall Freeman, the Virginia journalist who composed an epic, multivolume series on the life of Robert E. Lee and was a favorite author of the Daughters, viewed this system of affectionate enslavement as "typical" of the plantation world Lee inhabited: a place where slaves "helped to rear the children" and "served long and loyally" for kindly masters. Other scholars, even those based in the North, often drew on this southern white narrative in imagining a humane connection between owner and enslaved. In this, they assumed that plantation holders' musings about their leniency came closer to the truth than the harsh laws written "on paper." The esteemed historian James Randall explained: "There was truth in the common declaration that Southern abuse of the slave was often a matter of mistreatment through leniency." A Macmillan Company textbook confirmed: "The Negro of plantation days was usually happy" despite being "in a state of slavery."[4]

Yet even among white southerners, it was getting just a little bit harder to give the same full-throated endorsements of chattel slavery. Growing skepticism about historical myths of the past encouraged some to question the old story of leniency and contentment. Now, too, with the Depression providing ample evidence of the ugly side of economic exploitation, some southerners expressed greater uncertainty about slavery's unqualified benefits. The authors who penned the *Alabama State Guide*, part of the mammoth *American Guide* series undertaken by the Federal Writers' Project, hardly condemned the institution yet seemed less committed to notions of mutual love and loyalty. "Living conditions of Negroes during slave days were dependent on white owners," they wrote, "who for the most part considered their Negroes as property and therefore tried to keep them healthy for economic as well as humanitarian reasons." Taking a decidedly more negative view was a whole new crop of southern white writers who gave more explicit indications of the brutal and degrading circumstances slaves endured. William Faulkner, in his description of Thomas Sutpen's ruthless plantation quest in *Absalom, Absalom!*, may have been the most brilliant delineator of the cold and calculating disregard for slave life. Other writers, including those connected with the Agrarian movement, also did not shy away from describing self-centered slaveholders and miserably treated slaves. In *None Shall Look Back*, Caroline Gordon's 1937 Civil War novel, the book's Scarlett O'Hara–like heroine, Lucy Churchill, has little interest in her family's slaves and is mortified when asked to examine a slave woman who has been savagely beaten by the overseer. Lucy had heard about slaves being whipped, but until that moment "she had never before seen human flesh torn by a lash and the sight sickened her." Gordon observes slavery's brutality, as well as slaveholders' callousness: though initially Lucy is distressed by this scene of violence, her mood brightens abruptly when she anticipates an upcoming dance.[5]

Over the years white southerners had developed yet another way of talking about slavery. In this version, they tended to cast themselves as the "slaves" who suffered, both historically and in the present day, under the weight of Yankee oppression. "The North," explained the head of the Mississippi State Planning Commission to a southern journalist, "set our slaves free but the North made the whole South slave." Here was yet another iteration on the oft-repeated origin story of southern poverty, a tale that made "the whole South slave" but really accentuated the victimhood of southern whites, the ones who bore the brunt of Yankee brutality, "carpetbagger" excesses, and (so it followed) the oppressive relation imposed on the region by northern industrialists. It was, conveniently, a story that gave southern whites a pass as practitioners of exploitation, portraying as it did the whole southern population as a unified band suffering under the heel of northern domination. It was also a story that surfaced repeatedly during the Depression because it joined in a wider denunciation of northern capitalist greed, now vilified as the cause for southern economic woes. But the focus on "the South's" enslavement also tended to push the history of racial slavery to the sidelines: an unfortunate practice, many agreed, but surely not as devastating as the shoving down of an entire region. Those who told this version of the story used all the tropes and markers associated with slavery—whips and chains, auction blocks, fugitives running from bloodhounds—to drive home the tale of oppression. But now those symbols documented the "enslavement" of southern white men and women by their northern enemies. The southern author Clifford Dowdey, for example, who authored the best-selling 1937 Civil War novel *Bugles Blow No More*, peppered his account with descriptions of auctions and auction houses, although never as it related to the buying and selling of black slaves and only as it related to the scarcity of consumer goods for white people in wartime Richmond. These types of references became the building blocks for many stories composed about the South and the Civil War during the 1930s, with none more striking than the one told by Margaret Mitchell, who often imagined Scarlett O'Hara working or sleeping like a "field hand." Scarlett even tries to find comfort by humming the slave's lament, "Just a few more days for to tote the weary load." Meanwhile, the enslaved people in Mitchell's novel have virtually no knowledge of the work—raising cotton, delivering newborn babies—that would have been expected of black men and women in the antebellum South.[6]

White southerners were hardly the only ones talking about slavery in these times of economic distress. Those with a deep and painful past of chattel slavery also had much to say about the problem of American slavery, although, not surprisingly, their discussion was grounded more in history and law than in metaphors. During the 1930s, African American scholars publicized important historical accounts that pushed back against long-held racist myths about slavery and Reconstruction. This included the monumental efforts of W. E. B. Du Bois, especially his critical achievement in *Black Reconstruction* (1935). It also included the vital work of Carter Woodson, who in 1915 founded the Association for the Study of Negro Life and History (ASNLH), which gave new and sustained attention to launching the careers of numerous black historians while also undertaking concerted efforts to publicize that work in black communities and black public schools. Although the Depression might seem an inopportune moment for teaching black history in impoverished and segregated public schools, the ASNLH in these years put considerable effort into fundraising and community work and had some moderate success in popularizing "Negro History Week" in black schools throughout the South. Through these efforts, a new generation of black schoolchildren and their parents learned about the brutality of the slave trade, the militancy of slave rebels like Nat Turner, and the achievements of black legislators during Reconstruction. This historical work, moreover, provided ammunition for black intellectuals pushing back against the Old South mythology. The black poet Sterling Brown drew on this work when he oversaw the Negro affairs division in the Federal Writers' Project. And when he reviewed the novel *Gone with the Wind* in 1937, the critic George Schuyler explained that Mitchell's distorted picture of black incompetence during Reconstruction was "contrary to the facts as Du Bois has shown in 'Black Reconstruction.'" Schuyler's point: Mitchell traded in fantasy, while Du Bois had produced well-documented history.[7]

This reexamination of the historical record gave added force to black Americans' modern-day protests. Mindful of the way historical circumstances informed present-day realities, African Americans frequently called attention to ongoing patterns of race oppression, of the continued plight of "enslavement" to which black people, long after emancipation, were subjected. Sometimes it just seemed obvious southern blacks remained bound to conditions that differed little from slavery. "The colored people," remarked Parker Pool, an ex-slave interviewed as part of North Carolina's slave interview project, "are slaves now more than they was then." Black journalists, intellectuals, and civil rights activists made a similar point, although with a more polemical intent, describing specific cases where black men's and women's lives and economic opportunities had been constricted, sometimes by incarceration, sometimes by white conniving, but almost always by a system that took advantage of African American powerlessness. The *Chicago Defender*, for example, described the "slavery" practiced on a Mississippi plantation where men had been kept at work to pay off arbitrarily imposed fines. They wrote, too, about the four boys in Kentucky unlawfully kept at work at a sawmill until they finally "grew tired of this slavery" and escaped. What journalists wrote reflected prevailing realities: in 1936 a federal grand jury in Arkansas indicted a deputy sheriff for violating the Thirteenth Amendment when he falsely arrested several black men and forced them to labor on his plantation. The shadow of slavery seemed to hang most heavily on the black men and women forced to work on chain gangs. Southern highway construction, claimed the *Defender*, relied first and foremost on "slave workers" in which laborers could be arbitrarily beaten while the state became the beneficiary of (mostly) black men's uncompensated labor. Most of all, the language of black enslavement was used to describe limited and impoverishing economic circumstances, urban as well as rural, industrial as well as agricultural, and to suggest a level of exploitation that was shaped by a long historical legacy of racial injustice and so surpassed what whites experienced. Thus, it captured how much the Depression now imposed conditions—imprisonment, un- and underemployment, agricultural peonage—that disproportionately affected African Americans, building as it did on long-standing exploitation. In 1935, two NAACP writers, Ella Baker and Marvel Cooke, described the desperately degrading circumstances of black New York women competing for underpaid domestic work in an unregulated labor market, as the "Bronx Slave Market." Unable to secure the kind of domestic and industrial work they had done prior to the Depression, these black women now congregated in the new slave "markets" waiting "for Bronx housewives to buy their strength and energy." Few received a decent wage, and many were subjected to brutal work conditions, freely imposed on them by the new "Mrs. Simon Legree."[8]

By and large, African American activists expressed considerable skepticism about the power of government to end this persisting pattern of enslavement. Certainly many agreed that government, Lincoln especially, had done its part in initiating an important phase in the freedom struggle. But historical circumstances also revealed the state's limited powers, as well as waning interest, when it came to racial oppression. For years many wondered what had become of broken promises like the "forty acres and a mule" once held out to the recently freed. Doubts about government intentions may have even intensified during the 1930s, a time when the potential for change—as promised by New Deal officials—went largely unfulfilled. "Slavery has been re-introduced," proclaimed NAACP leaders in 1934 in response to the forced work policies that accompanied relief efforts in many southern rural areas. Others protested the newly proposed public works projects for instituting a "slave wage scale." Roosevelt's agricultural program, claimed a *Chicago Defender* headline in 1936, "Re-Enslaves Farm Workers in the South." Most of all there was a kind of weariness about having to express loyalty to a government that had ultimately done so little to further the cause of emancipation. "The Race," wrote *Defender* editor Enoch Waters, "feels that it has long since settled its debt to the government, which brought about its emancipation. The time has arrived when that government can expect no more in the way of loyalty than it is willing to give that group by upholding the constitutional amendments."[9]

Although they lacked a personal history with chattel slavery, white working-class people also spoke the language of bondage during the Depression years. Their slavery talk was meant to convey very different circumstances than those experienced by African Americans, not to mention different expectations. By and large, white working people reached for the metaphor of slavery to convey outrage with what seemed to be *new* indignities and insecurities brought on by the economic crisis. They did not necessarily use this language to talk about race, although their words pointed to the potential for recognizing shared hardships across the racial divide. Mostly, they seemed particularly mindful of class, and especially of the ever-widening chasm between those men and women (although mainly men) dependent on meager factory wages and those who helped maintain the dominance of capitalists and employers.[10]

A worker in Muskegon, Michigan, was disgusted at the brutality, even physical violence, foremen used on their workers. "If this is fair justice," he wrote in a 1935 letter to a New Deal official, "we certainly are drifting back to slave day's [*sic*]." A textile worker wrote that same year to describe his place of work, "a place which is laughingly called a factory," as a site of disease, overwork, and misery. He and his coworkers, he explained, had become "slaves—slaves of the depression!" The working people who composed these phrases drew on a language with deep historical roots. Since the eighteenth century, social commentators and workers had decried the way the modern factory system stripped laborers of their skills and independence, reducing them to a condition of "wage slavery," forcing men, women, and children to earn "slave wages." "Workers of the world, unite!" proclaimed Marx and Engels in their ringing conclusion to *The Communist Manifesto*: "You have nothing to lose but your chains." In the early nineteenth-century United States, where slavery was an ever-present reality, both southern slaveholders and laborers held up "wage slavery" as a symbol of capitalist cruelties. Northern workers, too, often complained about the particular injustice of "white slavery," suggesting that while chattel slavery for blacks might be necessary, restraints for white working people had no place in a free society. In the late nineteenth century, with racial slavery officially abolished, the righteousness of the emancipation cause continued to inform working people's characterizations of their oppressive work conditions. As factory work became even more subdivided and routine, as workers became ever more alienated from the work process and the final product of their labor, working people and labor reformers specifically targeted the injustice of the wage contract, which forced a worker to sell his time to an employer who could do as he pleased with the ten or twelve or even fourteen hours of a laborer's day. Mechanization further enhanced the sense that workers had lost control of the laboring process. An Australian writer observed the workers in Henry Ford's factory in the 1920s and explained, with a nod to Marx and Engels, how the man on the assembly line was "part of the chain, the feeder and the slave of it."[11]

Thus, when workers in the 1930s compared their workplaces to "slave driven shops," they tapped into a well-established labor tradition. Yet the cataclysm of the Depression also called for a break with tradition, prompting American workers to wonder, in fact, if the economic system was spiraling toward collapse. The language of slavery gave workers a way to address the extremity of the current crisis and a way to lash out at a system that seemed to be rapidly regressing back toward something obsolete and archaic, something that defied capitalism's promise of social mobility. If employers and employees stood as far apart as masters and slaves, then surely the chasm between classes was nearly unbridgeable. Slavery, in this way, defiantly challenged notions of American progress or prosperity, rebuking any celebration of the United States as the kingpin of the modern industrial order. In short, nothing screamed economic backwardness quite as loudly as slavery. "The stretch out system," a South Carolina mill hand explained, "is worse than Roman slavery." The widening chasm between classes, moreover, seemed to suggest something downright un-American, not only in terms of workers' treatment but also for the kind of response it might provoke. Work in the sugarcane fields, one Louisiana letter writer explained in 1937, was not only like slavery but also worse than conditions in "China or

Mexico or Africa." This, he believed, would surely push people down the path of communism.[12]

Particularly prominent among those speaking the language of slavery were labor leaders and trade union activists who helped shape the new culture of labor protest in these years. Following World War I, labor leaders helped revive trade union activity in a number of central US industries, including steel manufacturing and southern textiles. Immediately following the 1929 collapse, trade union membership declined because of extensive unemployment, but it rebounded mid-decade, thanks especially to the efforts of the Committee for Industrial Organization (founded in 1935) and its successor, the Congress of Industrial Organization (founded in 1938). The CIO was committed to organizing workers not in the traditional craft unions of the American Federation of Labor, but in a way that spoke to the new scale and skill levels of the 1930s workplace and that would allow for a more effective response to modern industrial capitalism. In these years US communists, too, played a prominent role in union organizing, creating ties that would become one important thread of an emerging Popular Front. Finally, labor leaders found support for their organizing efforts in New Deal principles. Not only had Roosevelt expressed sympathy for the "forgotten man," but his policies also seemed to give official sanction to working people's rights. The National Industrial Recovery Act, passed in 1933 at the end of FDR's first hundred days, included a provision—Title I, Section 7(a)—which recognized employees' right to organize and bargain collectively with their employers. Indeed, initiatives like this one helped generate the new conversation about slavery in the 1930s by prompting thousands of workers to write to New Deal administrators, a group assumed to be concerned with the "slave-like" conditions of industrial America.[13]

Union organizers used the language of slavery to protest the oppressive and arbitrary measures that stripped working people of their dignity and humanity. Among the most demeaning forms of treatment was the "stretch-out" system, a practice particularly prevalent in southern textile mills, in which bosses compelled workers to produce more, and at a faster pace, under the guise of promoting labor "efficiency." In one North Carolina mill, when employers got the idea that looms would run faster if workrooms were kept at an "awful high temperature," workers fought back. James Edmonds, who organized the protest, laid out the grievances to the manager and explained that workers would do whatever they could to defend their jobs. "We hate violence," Edmonds explained, "but we hate slavery worse." Gradually, and especially as union activists believed they had the support of the Roosevelt administration, they directed their arguments about slavery—as well as their hopes for challenging slavery—to government officials. When the workers in the hotel industry were not told what their hours would be, or were promised bonuses that failed to materialize, they were forced, explained a New Yorker writing in 1937 to Labor Secretary Frances Perkins, to live like "suffering modern slaves" caught in "the clutches of our modern Simon Legrees." When female textile workers in the Appalachian Cotton Mills remained ignorant of their earnings until they saw their pay envelopes, their situation, said one of their colleagues in Knoxville, Tennessee, was "no less than slavery." To address this slavery crisis, many contended, workers would have to "take matters into their own hands." This meant unions and other collective bodies that could offset the seemingly arbitrary power of foremen and bosses. It also meant marshaling government power on behalf of working people. Thus JMG wrote to FDR from Pittsburgh, in February 1938, to denounce "slavery in many of the mills mines factories in the United States of America" and the practice of giving bonuses to "Slave drivers" who worked the "people to death." Above all, JMG contended, people working under such conditions needed a congressionally mandated "Safety Council" to ensure that they "are not made Slaves of by being over burdensome with hard work." A New York City transport worker maintained that a union would allow the workers to "go to our bosses and talk to them like men, instead of . . . like slaves." With frequent reference to workers' committees, collective action, and union organizing, working people sought to resolve the crisis of slavery through worker-led initiatives, backed up by concrete actions and support from government officials.[14]

Labor leaders, and sometimes regular working folk as well, also portrayed slavery as a condition shared by blacks and whites. This argument challenged the dominant historical narrative of benign chattel slavery by recognizing the bitter reality of nineteenth-century racial bondage. Implied here, too, was a sense, albeit not always fully articulated, of empathy: that white workers understood at least some of the pain endured by black slaves. A textile labor leader, writing in a union newspaper, identified certain employers' tactics as nothing "less than slavery, for the abolition of which a war was fought more than sixty years ago." JMG, the Pittsburgh laborer demanding a workers' Safety Council, connected the current situation to the struggle of an earlier generation who "gave up their lives to banish Slavery and to make this a happy Christian country to live in." Black activists, too, sometimes referred to the bonds of white and black enslavement, including civil rights lawyer Hubert Delany, who struck this theme in an Emancipation Day speech in Harlem in 1938. "We in this country who are poor and at the bottom of the economic ladder," Delany insisted, "whether we be black or white, are still in slavery" and will be as long as we feel "economic insecurity." A Harlem resident likewise faulted a different Emancipation Day speaker, in 1934, for failing to recognize that "we negroes are merely the victims of the same social system that enslaves the whites."[15]

Here in these words about the abolition struggle and "black-snake-whip slavery" we can hear some of the dominant notes of a left-wing Popular Front culture: an insistence on the shared travails of oppressed people across racial lines and so an imperative to organize "black and white together" in a new type of "antislavery" struggle. This sentiment was inscribed in what was basically the Popular Front's anthem, "Ballad for Americans," composed in 1939 by communist and lyricist Earl Robinson: "A man in white skin can never be free while his black brother is in slavery." More than just catchy phrases, the 1930s Popular Front reflected a complicated blend of Communist Party ideas, emanating from both the Soviet Union and US party leaders, as well as ideas expressed, in more popular form, by left-leaning writers, artists, and activists. After 1935, the Communist Party in both the Soviet Union and the United States put the idea of a broad, popular front against worldwide fascism at the center of its political strategy. Although they followed the Soviet party's initiative, US communists never imposed a single, unified ideological perspective on this movement. Rather, at least in its US manifestation, the Popular Front consisted of a loose umbrella of left-leaning groups and individuals, including communists, socialists, and liberals associated with the New Deal who were committed to the fight against fascism abroad and at home and to the struggle to extend democracy to working people and ethnic minorities. Popular Front culture ran the gamut from labor union pamphlets to plays written by "card-carrying" communists but produced by New Deal appointees to Hollywood films in which left-wing writers blended their messages with those of more mainstream artists. The scholar Michael Denning identifies a kind of indigenous Popular Front culture, one that functioned independently from communist influence and gave voice to themes of labor justice, civil rights, and antifascism. Other scholars give US communists a more central role yet also suggest that in the labor movement, as well as in various artistic movements, they seldom advanced an explicitly communist agenda. Michael Kazin contends that the correlation of the Popular Front with the expansion of American mass culture meant that US culture gradually became more hospitable to a range of perspectives—including those sympathetic to certain communist ideals—but the cacophony of voices could also dilute any hardline ideological tendencies. Glenda Gilmore locates US communists at the forefront of labor and civil rights organizing in the South but finds that certain core ideological beliefs did not generally set the agenda, especially after 1935, when they turned their attention to building a "Southern Popular Front" in which socialists, labor organizers, black organizations, and liberal white southerners advocated greater interracial dialogue.[16]

Indeed, organizing in the South provided communists with deep and lasting lessons in the history of racial slavery that became core components of their thinking and their strategy. Angelo Herndon, grandson of slaves and son of an Ohio coal miner, joined the communist movement after moving South in the 1920s. He recalled chilling stories he'd heard about the tortures and beatings his ancestors had endured, explaining that he remembered "these stories, not because they were so different from life in my own day" but because "they were exactly like some of the things that happened to me when I went South." Herndon knew precisely how much the legacy of past racial oppression lived on. In 1933 he was convicted under a Georgia state law, passed in the Reconstruction period and designed to combat insurrectionary actions against the state. Yet Herndon also thought the past might have a message of hope. Recalling the secret organizing work he did for communists in the South, he likened it to the work done by "the Abolitionists in the South during the Civil War, behind shades and locked doors." The southern black communist Hosea Hudson likewise saw the struggles of the 1930s as integrally connected with those of the past. "When I was a small kid," recalled the Georgia-born Hudson, "that wasn't long after slavery . . . [when] the old slave people used to talk about the Yankees whupping the South. . . . I heard that talk so much until I always looked for the Yankees to come back one day and finish the job of freeing the Negroes." Black and white communists built on these associations and portrayed left-wing agitation in the Depression-era South as a continuation of the intersectional freedom struggles of the Civil War and Reconstruction periods. Several, in fact, consciously revisited the historical record in order to establish the precedent behind the present-day imperative to build an interracial alliance. Communist writer and one-time southern organizer James Allen, who was white, wrote a history of the Reconstruction period not only to address mischaracterizations of the Radical Republicans of the 1860s but also to show how "the Negro people can complete the unfinished tasks of revolutionary Reconstruction," aided by support from "the working class and other progressive elements."[17]

Perhaps no left-winger was more insistent on the links between the "antislavery" struggles of the 1860s and 1930s than Mike Gold. Born Itzok Granich to Jewish Romanian parents on New York's Lower East Side, Gold changed

his name in honor of a Jewish Civil War veteran who fought, he said, to "free
the slaves." The Jewish-black alliance formed a critical touchstone in Gold's
thinking. During the 1920s, Gold worked on his novel, *Jews without Money*, a
largely autobiographical account of the brutal conditions endured by Jewish
immigrants in early twentieth-century New York. Central to Gold's story is the
gang of Jewish street urchins led by a rebellious ruffian named "Nigger." After
the book's celebrated appearance in 1930, Gold became a regular columnist for
the Communist Party's national newspaper, the *Daily Worker*, where he often
reflected on the radical tradition in America history. Although he was mindful
of Jewish influences, the former and deeply secular Itzok Granich may have
found it particularly important to demonstrate just how *American* left-wing
radicalism was, especially given the anti-Bolshevist and anti-immigrant mood
of the times. "America," Gold wrote in one of his columns, "is better than the
Ku Klux Klan. America is also the land of Thomas Jefferson, and Walt Whitman, and the abolitionists who fought a civil war to free this land from black
slavery." If anything, Gold implied, it was right-wingers who drew inspiration
from abroad, including white southern novelists like Stark Young, who glorified
plantation slavery while casting admiring glances at Italy's Mussolini. When
Angelo Herndon was sent to a Georgia chain gang in 1933, Gold likened Herndon to John Brown, whose months in prison "roused millions of northerners
to his defense, and made them partisans against slavery." Gold hoped to see a
similar movement rally around Herndon.[18]

Remembering John Brown became one of Gold's most important artistic
objectives during the 1930s. To Gold, Brown embodied the deeply American
freedom struggle that first took shape in the fight to end chattel slavery but
continued in twentieth-century actions on behalf of overworked and underpaid "wage slaves." In 1936 Gold collaborated with a fellow left-winger, Michael
Blankfort, on a Federal Theatre play, *Battle Hymn*, which recounted the story
of John Brown's decision to fight against slavery in Kansas and Harpers Ferry.
Staged at the WPA Experimental Theater in New York in the summer of 1936
and then in San Francisco, *Battle Hymn* earned considerable, even mainstream,
acclaim. The play's subject also provided an ideal setting for advancing a central tenet of the Popular Front: "Labor, even in a white skin," says one abolitionist agitator paraphrasing Marx's *Kapital*, "can never be free as long as labor
with a black skin is enslaved." This same man seeks to educate John Brown
on the links between black and white bondage: "Today there are women and
children up North," an abolitionist agitator tells John Brown, "sweating their
lives away in textile mills. And before us there were Irish immigrants who died

in thousands building our railroads because slaves were too valuable to be so misused. And they were white men, supposedly free men like ourselves." The history lesson referred to the 1850s, but surely Gold and Blankfort had the 1930s very much on their mind when they had John Brown respond: "Preserve us from such freedom."[19]

The theme of "black and white in slavery" informed numerous artistic and journalistic works composed by communists as well as others in the Popular Front orbit, especially in the later years of the New Deal, from theater to fiction to dance. When photographer Margaret Bourke-White collaborated with her husband, the Georgia-born novelist Erskine Caldwell, in 1937, to produce a book on the rural South, they cast a particularly poignant spotlight on downtrodden farm laborers, white and black, both feeling the effects of "slavery." White southerners, Bourke-White and Caldwell explained, were forced to endure "the limitations of life imposed upon those unfortunate enough to be made slaves of sharecropping." At the same time, "the Negro tenant farmer" was not only "the descendant of the slave" but was "on a plantation . . . still a slave." The following year, choreographer Martha Graham also considered slavery in her 1938 dance piece, *American Document*. Presented under the auspices of the left-wing *New Masses* magazine, Graham's dance depicted several episodes from US history, including a sequence on slavery and emancipation. In that segment, a group of white women took up the emancipation dance, based on "an American Minstrel Show" but done in a manner that was "solemn rather than entertaining." So while the dancers were all white—and interracial performances were exceedingly rare in the 1930s—Graham's insistence that white women dance in a solemn reflection of black minstrelsy seems designed to suggest a feeling of interracial empathy. As one reviewer saw it, this part of Graham's work brought together "the emancipation of the Negro and the present economic situation."[20]

Artists like Gold, Graham, Caldwell, and Bourke-White sought, in their own ways, to surmount the rigid obstacles of Jim Crow segregation and to think about slavery as a condition that drew black and white together. Yet as they pressed intently on the metaphor, artists and writers also lost sight of the historically specific conditions that defined black enslavement, gave more attention to the plight of modern-day white "slaves," and minimized the present-day exploitation of blacks. African Americans occupied a distant and remote place in the past, a past that included their liberation, while white people emerged more and more as "the slaves" of the moment, the ones demanding the immediate attention of a public anxious to address the injustices and exploitation of the Depression era. Even Gold, with his acute awareness of nineteenth-century racial slavery, believed that antebellum black "slaves were too valuable to be so misused" in building railroads and so perhaps suffered less than poor and immigrant wage slaves. Graham's dance, too, reminded audiences of Negro emancipation while showcasing suffering in the movements of white female dancers. In *You Have Seen Their Faces*, Caldwell wrote captions for the photographs of black southerners that made black enslavement seem almost tolerable. "Just sitting in the sun watching the Mississippi go by," reads one description that accompanied an image of black men seated by the river. Perhaps this was always the way black folk had experienced their long history of bondage.[21]

The limitations of the "black and white in slavery" idea emerged with particular clarity in the 1937 Federal Theatre production of *The Lonely Man*, a play written by Howard Koch, a young lawyer-turned-writer who would go on to work with Orson Welles's Mercury Theater, collaborate with Julius and Philip Epstein on the screenplay for *Casablanca*, and prepare the screenplay for the pro-Soviet World War II documentary *Mission to Moscow*. Like many Popular Fronters, Koch was no communist ideologue, although he was prosecuted in the anticommunist hysteria of the 1940s and eventually blacklisted by Hollywood. *The Lonely Man* epitomizes many Popular Front themes of the Depression era. Set in the strike-torn Kentucky coal region of the Depression years, the play focuses on a small Kentucky college, Lincoln University, where students and administrators are divided by the surrounding labor tumult. In this, Koch's play addressed one of the central labor battles of the period, the bloody and violent struggle to organize mine workers in Harlan County, Kentucky. The chancellor of Lincoln University, a man who has sympathy for the mine workers yet is also beholden to the university's wealthy, mine-owning trustees, is preoccupied with the problem of "slavery." Reflecting on Lincoln's legacy, he observes: "He freed those who were called slaves; it is for us to free those who are called free." Clearing up any mystery as to who that might be, a group of men, presumably miners, march past his office carrying banners that read "Free the Whites." Later, when a new faculty member who bears an uncanny resemblance to Abraham Lincoln prepares to defend one of the white campus workers who has been arrested for syndicalism, he draws on a legal brief that describes the Thirteenth Amendment as "a charter of universal civil freedom for all persons of whatsoever color, race, or estate." Without question, Koch took aim at one of the most incendiary problems of the 1930s, exposing not only the greed of Kentucky mine owners but also the vacillating liberal views of some political leaders. And like thousands of workers, African Americans, and left-wing writers and artists, Koch gravitated toward the language of slavery in order to consider the degraded circumstances of the Depression and the brutal divide pitting workers against bosses. But his play also suggests how the Popular Front language of slavery could end up ignoring racial injustice, insisting on a color-blind approach in battling economic oppression, yet with a slant that ultimately put the problem of white enslavement at the forefront.[22]

WHILE WHITE "ENSLAVEMENT" emerged as a problem with immediacy, black enslavement, even in New Deal and Popular Front circles, was forced to occupy the kind of spaces allotted to the documentary folk culture of the Depression era. The 1930s, scholars have observed, drove numerous writers, musicians, and artists to focus their sights on marginalized groups, people outside the American mainstream who had supposedly been overlooked by the forces of modern industrial "progress." Disgust with the greed and corruption of American business encouraged this band of creative workers to take new interest in people on the fringes, as well as those whose culture provided a window to a "mythical time in the past when Americans were more vigorous, more honorable, and more self-sufficient." Such outcast groups—many of whom resided in the South—had historical experiences of marginalization that made them vibrant representatives (or so folk enthusiasts claimed) of a true "folk" aesthetic. Awareness of "the folk" thus spawned new interest in southern black culture, encouraging efforts to unearth distinct musical styles and to record vibrant stories from the past. This included the work undertaken by writers, editors, and interviewers associated with the WPA's Federal Writers' Project, particularly the massive undertaking to interview thousands of elderly black men and women, most still residing in parts of the South, about their memories of antebellum slavery. Initially a project devised by black scholars in the 1920s to counter the romanticized view of slavery that predominated in historical thinking and popular culture, the slave interview program became, in the 1930s, one of several New Deal ventures designed to give unemployed writers and artists and musicians a source of income while also bringing the stories of ordinary Americans into the public spotlight. Indeed, another reason talk about slavery, as well as the Civil War more generally, gained traction in these years was because the federal government put resources into collecting memories of ordinary, and often aging, Americans, including black men and women who had experiences with the chattel system.[23]

Although modern-day historians cast an understandably skeptical eye on the WPA slave narratives, careful reading might yield some insights, if not necessarily about slavery, then perhaps about things that older African Americans living in the 1930s chose to remember about their past, and what they preferred to forget. We might learn something, too, about how federal agents in these years approached the subject of slavery in the first place and what significance they attached to this critical chapter of American history. Because the ex-slave narratives had limited circulation and only a few collections were ever published, their influence on a broader public would have been limited. But the approach taken by project directors and interviewers certainly tells us something about prevailing sensibilities regarding the slave past. In one respect, that approach appears mixed, running the gamut from stereotyped depictions of loyal "aunts" and "uncles" to more disturbing portraits of slave markets and brutal plantation conditions, often depending on the point of view of the individual interviewer or how the head of each state's Writers' Program handled the project. The approach also shifted depending on input from editors at the federal level, including Sterling Brown, national Negro Affairs editor, and John Lomax, national adviser on folklore and folkways.[24]

Ultimately, it was Lomax, with his particular interest in "quaint and eccentric" customs among the former slaves, who shaped the script that most interviewers would rely on in their interrogations. As a project resting on the liberal edge of the Popular Front spectrum, Lomax's program drew very much on the 1930s fascination with discovering and documenting the American folk tradition. Working with his son Alan, John Lomax helped bring black performers like Lead Belly into the limelight and gave new attention to the music and culture of American slaves. When John Lomax became actively involved in the WPA slave interview project in 1936, he made the search for folk traditions a principal point of focus. This approach not only satisfied Lomax's intellectual curiosity; it also fit well with many of the narrow-minded assumptions of southern white interviewers who were more comfortable talking about courtship practices than about white slaveholders' brutality. Even John Lomax's son, Alan, regretted the missed opportunity to talk more about the economic exploitation of slavery and its impact on the postemancipation era. The interviews, remarked Alan and his wife Elizabeth, failed to grapple with such crucial issues as whether "any of the plantations [were] actually divided up" and whether any masters gave their slaves "money to make a new start." Any book that might emerge from these interviews, Alan and Elizabeth Lomax believed, should stress that "exploitation," not just slavery, "is a nasty thing."[25]

Indeed, ex-slaves had much to say about the nasty side of slavery, although their recollections about brutality are hidden in the folksy frame adopted by the interviewers. Countless interviews show an uncomfortable tug-of-war between the interviewers' orientation to folkways and the interviewees' focus on whippings, mistreatment, and stifled opportunities. One Georgia woman, for example, likely having been asked whether she believed in ghosts, told her interviewer: "I used to think I seed haunts at night, but it always turned out to be somebody that was tryin' to scare me." A South Carolina interview that recounted the story of an ex-slave killed by the Klan right after the war was titled—presumably by the white interviewer, Caldwell Sims—as "Folk Lore: Folk Tales (negro)."[26]

The WPA's predominantly white interviewers seemed mainly interested in turning slavery into a historical experience defined by its disappearing customs and cultural practices. Interviewers defined their subjects as "interesting specimen[s] of a rapidly vanishing type" and asked questions about what slaves ate, what games slave children played, and what folk sayings the old folks remembered. As the white interviewer saw it, the interview was a mission of recovery, designed to get old people to speak about an experience that, with its odd expressions and unscientific beliefs, clearly belonged to a bygone age. Minnie Ross, who interviewed the Georgia ex-slave Hannah Austin, apparently kept her interview short in part because Austin's family had been "classed as 'town slaves' . . . because of their superior intelligence." Presumably, as Ross saw it, Austin did not fit the profile of the country slave whose knowledge of precious and antiquated folk practices stood waiting to be unlocked by the probing interviewer.[27]

Black interviewers, writers, actors, and historians made attempts to counter the demeaning portraits of slavery that made their way into the WPA narratives, as well as other federal arts initiatives. Most notably, Sterling Brown, as editor of the Negro Affairs division of the Federal Writers' Project, managed to override some of the decisions being made by southern white writers and editors, even demanding revisions of particularly offensive formulations in the *American Guide* series. But Brown's overall influence was limited, especially in the face of what one writer called "the Old South disease," which became so pernicious toward the end of the 1930s. The difficulty of pushing back against white stereotypes about slavery was compounded by the reluctance on the part of many ordinary black folks, especially those in the South, to say much about the slave past. While some black activists saw political benefits in emphasizing the continuity from antebellum slavery to ongoing exploitation, others saw little to gain from an approach that would only accentuate a picture of black degradation and perhaps confirm how much African Americans of the 1930s had failed to lift themselves from the shadows of the past. When a white northern sociologist visited a Mississippi town to learn about racial attitudes and practices, he

"Mr. Tony Thompson, an ex-slave who studied at Atlanta University forty years ago. Off the Edenton Road, Greene County, Georgia." Farm Security Administration photographer Jack Delano took this picture in May 1941 as part of a broader government effort to document the experiences of ex-slaves in the New Deal era. Jack Delano, Farm Security Administration/Office of War Information Photograph Collection, Prints & Photographs Division, Library of Congress, LC-USF34–044281-D.

found black Americans exceedingly reluctant to discuss their ancestry, as "it tends to remind Negroes of slavery days; a remembrance which is bound to be painful while the pattern of Negro subordination persists as it does today." Leon Lewis, a writer for the Associated Negro Press, expressed a similar apprehension. Celebrations of emancipation, Lewis wrote, "tend to keep the Negro's mind clouded with inferiority complexes" and "clearly show that the modern day Negro does not relish the fact that his foreparents were slaves." Indeed, many African Americans may have regarded the Depression era's documentary impulse, and the emphasis on the folkways of the past, as an unwelcome development, since it seemed to trade in unflattering and stereotyped depictions of black folk. At a 1939 celebration in St. Paul, Minnesota, for example, meant to showcase American ethnic groups and their historic traditions, black participants voiced opposition to wearing the symbols that marked them as slaves. Indeed, the New Deal's turn toward cultural pluralism, designed to celebrate ethnic traditions that had been shaped in an imagined past, seemed to encourage an overemphasis on "the slave period" that many African Americans found offensive.[28]

THUS VARIOUS FACTORS conspired to make the African American slave past seem either quaint, inconsequential, or a subject best left unexplored. At the same time, New Deal politicians increasingly turned their attention to the problem of "slavery" only to discover a condition that primarily described white men's economic exploitation. Perhaps responding to the thousands of impassioned letters working people had written to the new administration, New Deal politicians, including Roosevelt himself, took up the theme of Depression-era slavery. Yet even more than Popular Fronters, New Dealers pointedly disentangled slavery and race and, in their language as well as their policies, made white workers, especially men, the principal focus of their concerns. Reluctant to challenge entrenched white Democrats in the South, Roosevelt generally acquiesced to discriminatory practices in the implementation of New Deal programs like the National Industrial Recovery Act and the Agricultural Adjustment Act. Black observers often noted, and historians have since confirmed, that New Deal policies generally gave a free hand to southern white administrators who pointedly excluded southern blacks from many New Deal relief efforts. Moreover, in his desire to showcase the federal government's emancipatory powers for a broad set of people, Roosevelt and his supporters took pains to emphasize a less racially oriented set of objectives, thereby elevating white suffering over black. When FDR castigated economic royalists for subjecting

Americans to a form of "economic slavery," he implied that the new slavery lacked a racial component. When he spoke about Lincoln, he portrayed him as an "emancipator—not of slaves alone but of those of heavy heart everywhere." By taking race out of the picture, Roosevelt allowed white people to occupy the central spot on the slavery landscape.[29]

Roosevelt's supporters echoed these themes. They emphasized a "new" kind of slavery that bore down with particular ferocity on the industrial sphere, a labor domain most knew to be overwhelmingly white. They also understood Lincoln's legacy, of ending chattel slavery, as an objective that had been successfully accomplished, but that some new and pernicious system of bondage now infected American industry. Frank Dorsey, a Democratic representative from Pennsylvania, for example, believed Lincoln would have recognized, in "some of our industrial ramifications, a new slavery just as deadly as the kind he obliterated." William Connery, a Massachusetts Democrat, cast aspersions on the Supreme Court for holding back the New Deal's promise of liberation. "Today," he intoned in a 1935 Memorial Day speech, "despite the fact that all our people are free in that they have the right to work and live where they please and are upon a basis of equality in electing public officials, there are many who contend that our toilers live in virtual economic slavery in that they are denied an income which will provide a decent standard of living for themselves and their families and too often they are denied the right of collective bargaining." Surely in assuming that all people had a "right to work and live where they please and are upon a basis of equality in electing public officials"—rights that were uniformly denied to African Americans—Connery made it clear that white people occupied his thinking.[30]

Connery's language also implicitly spotlighted men as the ones who bore the brunt of white enslavement, especially in speaking of those anxious for "a decent standard of living for themselves and their families." In this, Connery echoed predominant New Deal thinking that typically regarded "workers," and so those mostly likely to experience the "virtual economic slavery" of these years, as both white and male. There were some on the left—notably women artists and writers like Martha Graham and Ella Baker—who did occasionally imagine the particular problem of female enslavement, even black female enslavement. But just as Roosevelt had worried first and foremost about "the forgotten man," so New Deal legislators tended to construct their tropes and their policies by focusing primarily on those assumed to be most entitled to, and most likely to occupy, stable and consistent forms of employment and those who worked to support not only themselves but also "their families." Hence, Social Security legislation privileged steadily employed industrial workers over the largely black and female domestic and agricultural workforce when it came to funding old-age pensions. Throughout the Depression, too, relief measures generally overlooked women's poverty and unemployment, since so many assumed that jobs rightfully belonged to men and women rightfully belonged at home, certainly not in the labor market, where they might deprive men of work. The language of slavery, then, as it emerged in the 1930s, reflected not just racial assumptions about what constituted legitimate forms of white and black suffering but also gender conventions that imagined white men, more than women, as the ones most in need of emancipation.[31]

In New Deal speeches and in Popular Front literature and drama, the distinct historical circumstances that shaped African American slavery, along with the distinct experiences women faced in the job market and the domestic sphere, took a back seat to the economic crisis that shackled white men into a new form of bondage. Perhaps no one recognized the slipperiness of this language, especially in its racial dimension, as keenly as W. E. B. Du Bois. Du Bois understood North American slavery as a phase in a long-term struggle against capital and so called his chapters on antebellum slaves and the Civil War, respectively, "The Black Worker" and "The General Strike." But he also recognized the particular conditions that differentiated those black workers from white ones. "We may think of the ordinary worker," Du Bois wrote in Black Reconstruction, "slaving ten, twelve or fourteen hours a day with not enough to eat . . . and we say here too is a slave called a 'free worker' and slavery is merely a matter of name." However, Du Bois argued, the slavery of the nineteenth century, as it affected nonwhite peoples, "was without doubt worse in these vital respects than that which exists today in Europe or America." If there was a "new enslavement of labor," Du Bois suggested, it was not in America—where "home labor" had been bribed by high wages and political office—but among black, brown, and other nonwhite workers in places like China or India or Africa. Du Bois, far more than many of his contemporaries, recognized the international power of capitalism to create an "analogue" to slavery in other parts of the globe. Du Bois, too, recognized the problem in using the "slavery" label indiscriminately, without considering the difference between those who had gained certain privileges from capital and those who had not—whether in the present or the past.[32]

When writers and artists, liberals and leftists, failed to make these distinctions, they could make black enslavement seem long-standing and almost natural, while white enslavement became the problem that symbolized the specific crisis at hand. Margaret Bourke-White and Erskine Caldwell might call black southerners of the Depression years "slaves," but they portrayed them as a people living with the unbroken, and perhaps never-to-be-broken, chains of slavery. When white people appeared as slaves, however, it assumed an urgency that spoke to "the present economic situation." Black slavery, in contrast, was a condition that was more deeply rooted in a culture that seemed almost impossible to disrupt, a culture that had "folk" ways that linked 1930s African Americans with their ancestors of long ago. The southern white historian Avery Craven gave academic cover to this idea that black slavery was a product more of cultural than of economic developments. The Negro slave, Craven wrote in 1938, "was far more important as a Negro in shaping life and giving peculiar quality to the South than he was as a slave. His status as a slave was, in fact, but a passing incident." Even liberal writers and artists who brought some concern about racial oppression into their films or their books or other artistic creations similarly took a less insistent tone about black suffering under slavery. At the edges of Popular Front culture, where artistic sensibilities edged away from radical politics and more into the liberal mainstream of the New Deal and then even further into the "mass" culture of Hollywood, white "enslavement" tended to efface, even more thoroughly, the historical problem and persistent legacy of black bondage.[33]

Consider, for example, how Americans in the 1930s saw the chain gang problem, a system that many writers and observers understood as a modern-day manifestation of antebellum slavery. In 1932, socialist author John Spivak published a fictionalized account of his investigations into the Georgia penal system. Spivak's book, *Georgia Nigger*, told the story of a black sharecropper's son, David Jackson, trapped between different versions of enslavement: the peonage system of southern planters and the state's chain gang scheme. As Spivak saw it, the twentieth-century arrangements represented a direct continuation of the nineteenth century's, with an earlier system of racial slavery evolving into a modern-day problem that allowed whites "to maintain an economy based on slave labor which had been set free."[34]

Georgia Nigger received considerable praise from mainstream journals, but the ink was hardly dry on Spivak's book when his story, essentially one about the barely perceptible change from one system of black enslavement to another, was eclipsed by another chain gang book: Robert Eliot Burns's *I Am a Fugitive from a Georgia Chain Gang*. Burns, a white Brooklyn native and World War I veteran, wrote, more or less, of his own experiences of hardship following his

"Ex-slave and wife who live in a decaying plantation house. Greene County, Georgia."
Taken in July 1937 by Dorothea Lange, the photograph and its caption underscored what
many white Americans saw as a kind of timeless quality in the African American slave
experience. Dorothea Lange, Farm Security Administration/Office of War Information Photograph Collection, Prints & Photographs Division, Library of Congress,
LC-USF34–017944-C.

arrest in Atlanta in 1922 for petty theft. Sentenced to a Georgia chain gang,
Burns documented the brutalities and cruelties of the system, including specific
abuses meted out to black prisoners; he recounted his own flight to freedom and
his reincarceration after being tracked down by Georgia state officials, followed
by a second successful escape. Capitalizing on the sensationalism of the book,
notably Georgia officials' continued pursuit of Burns, Warner Brothers bought
the rights, hired Mervyn LeRoy to direct and Paul Muni to play the protagonist,
and quickly released the film, *I Am a Fugitive from a Chain Gang*, to immense
critical acclaim. Known for its "social problem" films of the 1930s, Warner Brothers employed a larger than usual share of writers and actors with Popular Front
inclinations. Indeed, the original scriptwriters for LeRoy's movie, two authors
with left-wing sympathies, and likely familiar with Spivak's book, demonstrated

a keen awareness of the chain gang's racist structure and spotlighted numerous black characters in their story line.[35]

In the end, though, audiences saw a movie that drew on historical tropes about slavery, and offered some acknowledgment of black suffering, but gave the bulk of its attention to the way one of the central institutions of modern-day slavery, the southern chain gang system, made white men its principal victims. In effect, the film married the 1930s concern with "the forgotten man" to the story of chain gang slavery and in the process largely erased black people. In LeRoy's movie, Paul Muni plays James Allen, celebrated on his return home from the Great War but quickly trapped by an economic system that crushes his aspirations to "build things." Unwilling to do monotonous and emasculating labor in the shoe factory, Allen becomes a hobo, traversing the country in search of work, spending most of his time in flophouses. The scenes of his drifter life may not have been historically accurate for the early 1920s, but they certainly resonated with audiences in the early Depression. After being coerced into help-ing in a botched robbery, he is sent to the chain gang somewhere in the South. Everything about life on the chain gang screams slavery: not only the southern locale, but also the shackles firmly fixed to workers' ankles; the foremen who whip recalcitrant laborers at day's end; the bloodhounds used to track down "fugitives." And when, several years after Allen's escape, Georgia officials find him living comfortably in Chicago, they mount a "states' rights" campaign to seek his extradition. Allen, in effect, is the fugitive slave who Georgia slavehold-ers insist is their property, the tragic victim in a story not unlike the abolitionist tale told by Harriet Beecher Stowe eighty years before.[36]

During both of Allen's terms of imprisonment, black prisoners do figure prominently, but less as individual characters and more as a mass who, by their collective presence, convey an atmosphere of slavery. The black parts from the original script have been erased, apparently due to the pressures of Hollywood's Motion Picture Production Code and concerns that depictions of numerous black prisoners would provoke "resentment in the South." Black characters who do stand out in the film offer cautionary tales of just how bad slavery could be, so bad no white man would be able to endure it. When one of the white pris-oners observes a hard-working black chain gang member, he suggests that the warden likes the black man's work so much he intends to keep him there for the rest of his life, thus turning a prisoner who was implicitly a slave into an actual one. Allen ultimately turns to this same black prisoner to hammer apart his leg shackles so that he can run away. The black man willingly complies, hoping Allen will truly get away from the "misery" of the chain gang.[37]

Ultimately, *I Am a Fugitive* drew its main power from the nightmare of a middle-class white man repeatedly trapped in a coercive system: from the factory system to Depression-era poverty and then the chain gang itself. The real "horror of imprisonment on the chain gang," one scholar has noted, "is that it disrupts the racial boundaries that had previously secured for [James] a more privileged form of citizenship." The real problem, in other words, is being enslaved while white. This notion is reinforced when a prison official at one point makes a count of the inmates and tallies ninety-four white men and sixty-nine "negroes," a number clearly at odds with the reality of a black-majority prison population. Given the sympathies of some of its creators, it's not surprising to find snippets of a Popular Front sensibility in LeRoy's film: the few glances given to downtrodden black prisoners, for example, and the aid given by one black prisoner to the white protagonist. Yet in the end the film spotlighted the miseries of white men while black men provide the atmosphere—through their singing and their sledgehammering and just their presence—that tells us this is "slavery," a bad condition that white men should resist.[38]

I Am a Fugitive ends on a note of desperation and, like many early Depression films, sympathizes with figures who defy the American success story. Asked how he will live, Paul Muni's character famously replies, "I steal!" After Roosevelt took office, Hollywood reflected the nation's changing cultural sentiments, especially with films that took a more optimistic approach to weathering the crisis and that increasingly looked to the American past to find values and character traits worthy of emulation in the present. As a result, after 1934 Hollywood's vision of enslavement focused less on immediate conditions of degradation and more on historical accounts, particularly ones dealing with the South and the Civil War. These films continued to show a fascination with white suffering and devastation, sometimes even with all the symbols and trappings of slavery, thus evoking the sympathies of a largely white Depression-era audience, mindful of the new ways white people had experienced the economic crisis. Even more, with films set in the Old South or during the Civil War era, the tendency to show white people's misery echoed a kind of neo-Confederate tendency to cast the central spotlight not on black slavery, assumed by many to be benign and relatively humane, but on the "slave-like" oppression white people suffered at the hands of Yankee invaders and carpetbagging meddlers. Showcasing any of the actual cruelties of black enslavement would not only have challenged the predominant historical view of the South's "peculiar institution"; it also would have made white southerners seem less like victims and more like perpetrators. This choice, of course, fit squarely with filmmakers' stated intention to make movies that would be more appealing and "salable" to white southern audiences. It also conformed to production codes that showed little tolerance for scenes of racial conflict or unrest.[39]

In depicting African American slavery as a bygone and even quaint relic of the distant past, Hollywood movies in the 1930s revealed their debt to the long-standing, and white supremacist, historical narrative, but also to the kind of "folk" sensibility showcased by the WPA. When slaves appeared, they were repeatedly portrayed as the happy beneficiaries of a relatively benign institution as well as a people with appealing cultural traditions rooted in music and religion. By contrast, those who suffered and endured oppression, perhaps as the result of small-minded thinking or a miscarriage of justice, were southern whites. After Roosevelt took office, cinematic depictions of white enslavement also opened up a window for white emancipation, inserting a message of hope in contrast to the despairing tones of films like *I Am a Fugitive*. Liberation sometimes came from a personal act of courage, but more often by an act of political enlightenment. These films thus suggested the emancipatory power of government to direct its humanitarian impulse toward white people who, in their state of oppression, always bore the marks of "enslavement." In the 1935 film *The Littlest Rebel* Shirley Temple stars as "Miss Virgie," the daughter of a dashing Confederate officer who must leave his family and plantation when duty calls. The war then forces suffering and indignities on the plantation, quickly ending the happy days of children's birthday parties and tap dancing. When Miss Virgie and "Uncle Billy" (Bill Robinson) discuss the war and the plan to "free the slaves," they are both stumped by what that phrase even means. The one who suffers most from wartime indignities is Miss Virgie, who at one point puts on blackface to pass as a slave during the Union invasion. Then, when Virgie's mother dies, she is swept up in the mourning of the plantation's black inhabitants, who sing of the young white girl's misery: "Sometimes, I Feel Like a Motherless Child." In the end, she travels to Washington to see the man who planned to "free the slaves" and asks him to do his work of emancipation. In this case, though, it is freedom not for herself, or for her slave companions, but for her father and a friendly (white) Union soldier who have been imprisoned for suspected espionage. Baffling as it might be to understand why Lincoln might "free the slaves," it is clear how important it is for Honest Abe to free these two white men.[40]

The Littlest Rebel conforms to what one film scholar has identified as a long tradition of racial melodrama in US popular culture. Beginning with *Uncle Tom's Cabin,* and extending through films like *Showboat* and *Birth of a Nation,*

audiences learned to sympathize with both white and black characters by seeing them linked to particular "forms of racial victimization." White settlers, for
example, suffering at the hands of savage Indians in Wild West shows, achieved
a kind of moral legitimacy designed to counter any notion that they may have
been land-grabbing conquerors. And with the advent of sound and music in
1920s films, white characters in movies such as *The Jazz Singer* and *Showboat*
likewise earned audience sympathy "by musically expressing a suffering that
is recognizable as 'black'": they sang the "blues" or put on blackface to sing
about "Mammy." This tradition of racial melodrama remained a powerful force
in films of the 1930s. The knowledge that Miss Virgie was, in her own way, a
slaveowner was readily displaced when she made herself look like a slave and
got a sharp kick from a Union soldier who believed her disguise. Indeed, the
circumstances of the Great Depression and New Deal gave particular shape
and urgency to this aesthetic form of racial melodrama, precisely because white
suffering had captured the gaze of white America and because white Americans
had found in the language of black enslavement a powerful vehicle for conveying their own immiseration.[41]

Yet while some of the earlier films and novels, like *Uncle Tom's Cabin* or *I Am
a Fugitive*, retained references to black oppression and enslavement, later in the
New Deal era there was a pronounced tendency to banish black suffering more
thoroughly from the picture and make whites more completely the victims of
slave-like suffering. In *The Littlest Rebel*, the very idea of freeing black slaves is
preposterous. In similar fashion, John Ford's films of the 1930s cast a spotlight
on white victimhood and eventual liberation. Born in 1894 to Irish-born parents, Ford became one of Hollywood's leading filmmakers during the 1930s and
one of the principal creators of a new type of Civil War story, one that would
replace the old—more blatantly racist—tale of reunion over race. Ford, though,
knew the old story well, having started his movie career as an extra playing a
Klansman in D. W. Griffith's *Birth of a Nation*. After directing numerous shorts
and feature films in the silent era, Ford emerged as one of the Fox studio's most
popular talkie directors. Perhaps his early work in the Griffith era instilled in
Ford a fascination for the Civil War; certainly it remained a persistent theme
in his work. And while Ford seemed to replicate long-standing tropes of white
reunion, southern romanticism, and loyal slaves, he also adjusted that story line.
Ford drew on the Depression era's concern for "the forgotten man," portraying
him as a figure—a humble doctor, an industrious blacksmith, even Abraham
Lincoln—scorned by the powers that be. And while white men's emancipation
was paramount in Ford's accounts, he did show an occasional sensitivity to race.

Like other white directors in this period, Ford preferred a paternalistic view of "racial intimacy" to the vicious racist brutality of Griffith.[42]

John Ford's *Judge Priest*, a top-grossing film for 1934, drew from a popular short story collection by Kentucky writer Irvin Cobb. Set neither in the Civil War past, like *The Littlest Rebel*, nor in the present, like *I Am a Fugitive*, *Judge Priest* takes place in 1890s Kentucky at a time when Confederate commemoration was at its height. Ford's film, however, is no weepy tribute to the traditional female keepers of the memorial flame. Instead it displays its class consciousness, not to mention misogyny, by honoring the hard-working veterans deemed too uncouth by elitist daughters. The film gives particular attention to the hard-working blacksmith, Gillis, who had long been considered an outcast in his Kentucky community but had, in fact, performed numerous acts of bravery for the Confederate cause. When Gillis is accused of attacking another man who made insulting remarks to young Ellie May, Gillis's case comes to trial in Judge Priest's court. Surprising testimony reveals Gillis's secrets: not only was he Ellie May's father, but he had also, during the Civil War, been a chain gang prisoner; he had been freed from the gang, along with the other imprisoned white men, because the Confederacy needed more soldiers. In an apparent homage to Griffith, Henry Walthall, the actor who played "the Little Colonel" in *Birth of a Nation*, makes a cameo appearance to recount Gillis's past. Yet Ford's film is a far cry from Griffith's: *Judge Priest*'s blacks, although stereotyped, play crucial roles in alleviating white suffering and unifying the white community. There is even a reference to Judge Priest helping save a black character from a threatened lynching, although the scene was cut, perhaps because of Hollywood fears about its reception in the South.[43]

Echoing *I Am a Fugitive*, *Judge Priest* also presents a disrespected white veteran, forced to endure an oppressive imprisonment akin to slavery. But in *Judge Priest*, the chain gang is clearly an all-white affair—so white, in fact, that it is a pool for potential Confederate reinforcements. Even more, Gillis is twice liberated by benevolent political officials: first by the Confederate governor of Virginia, who agrees to have the chain gang men turned loose, and then by Judge Priest, who allows the truth about Gillis's past to emerge in his court so that the jury will find him innocent. Indeed, there may have been no better emblem of government beneficence than the actor portraying Judge Priest—Will Rogers, who used his early 1930s radio program to support New Deal initiatives and was known as the "Number One New Dealer." Ford, then, makes a few gestures toward racial empathy—much like the New Deal itself—but firmly keeps the focus on political benevolence directed toward white emancipation.[44]

Similar themes of white liberation are woven into John Ford's 1936 depiction of the trial and imprisonment of Dr. Samuel Mudd, the Maryland man accused of assisting John Wilkes Booth after the assassination at Ford's Theater. In *The Prisoner of Shark Island* Ford presents a telling example of how a historical event involving black enslavement could be imaginatively transformed into a portrait of white bondage and—eventually—liberation. The film depicts Samuel Mudd at the very end of the war: a kind and well-intentioned slaveholder, always attentive to the physical needs of his workforce. In turn, the black folk on Mudd's plantation treat him with respect. Properly implemented, then, chattel slavery was not a source of black oppression but, potentially, a moment of interracial harmony. Republican hysteria in the aftermath of Lincoln's assassination—part of the doctrinaire policies of the carpetbagger government that "enslaved" the South—leads to Mudd's arrest and, essentially, his "bondage": heavily shackled after a spurious trial and conviction; joining the ranks of other shackled (white) prisoners in what could be a chain gang or slave coffle; shipped off to the heavily guarded prison on Shark Island. In the publicity for the film, audiences were enticed with the slogan "The chains that cut his flesh to shreds will rip your heart apart." At one point—when Mudd takes on his former slave Buck as a companion in suffering—Ford hovers, ever so subtly, around the possibility of interracialism. But it is Mudd, of course, who is the focus of our concern and whose own suffering is most like slavery, especially since we know that Buck is only suffering because he has chosen to render assistance to his former master. Like *Judge Priest* and *The Littlest Rebel*, *The Prisoner of Shark Island* also ends with freedom for white men, with liberation again being dispensed by kindly political officials: after Mudd renders crucial assistance during a yellow fever outbreak, the president of the United States issues a pardon.[45]

More rarely, Hollywood applied the tropes of white enslavement to female characters, although white women seldom elicited the same kind of sympathy and concern as white men forced into bondage. In William Wyler's 1938 film, *Jezebel*, Bette Davis plays the spoiled and tempestuous Miss Julie, a southern belle who shows little interest in conforming to expected norms of ladylike behavior. Her most glaring act of rebellion comes when she wears a red dress instead of the usual, and far more demure, white gown, to the big New Orleans ball. This behavior is considered so outrageous that it nearly prompts her fiancé to beat her physically, with a cane. The trailer for *Jezebel* even heralded this as a film about a woman who, instead of being loved, "should have been whipped." Later Miss Julie solidifies her slave-like status when, distraught at having lost her fiancé, she sits with her slaves and adds her voice to their tuneful

Scene from the 1936 Twentieth Century Fox Film *The Prisoner of Shark Island*. As in many other 1930s films, white men figured prominently as the victims of enslavement. Here Warner Baxter, playing Dr. Samuel Mudd, wears the shackles of his imprisonment while a black guard looks on. Photofest.

lamentations. But if Julie wears some of the symbols of enslavement, she is not the same type of "slave" as Samuel Mudd or the blacksmith Gillis. Rather, as a woman defying traditional gender expectations, Julie seems more like a job-seeking or power-craving woman of the 1930s, a woman intent on disrupting patriarchal order at a moment when such order required reinforcement. Julie, in other words, is the white female slave who, until she learns to modify her unruly behavior, deserves her enslavement.[46]

More typical were the films that demanded sympathy and concern for white men whose enslavement signified the injustices and indignities they had been forced to endure. These films, like others produced throughout the Depression decade, drew on slavery-based language and imagery that had become nearly ubiquitous in this time of economic devastation. Of course, the enslavement of black characters in these films bore little resemblance to the brutal whippings and forced separations depicted in Carter Woodson's *Journal of Negro History*, or even the struggles imagined by Mike Gold or Martha Graham. So far removed were these movie characters from the historical realities of the nineteenth-century South that they were even confused, like Bill Robinson's character in *The Littlest Rebel*, by the very concept of "freeing the slaves." Instead, those who bore all the marks of enslavement were white people—Paul Muni's James Allen, the white blacksmith in *Judge Priest*, the falsely accused Samuel Mudd. These were the "forgotten men" whom Franklin Roosevelt had in his sights: the white folks, usually men, who suffered, often without complaint, and who had received scant acknowledgment from political leaders. Hollywood did not let these white victims persist in their suffering but offered them, at least after 1933, a timely and beneficent intercession by political leaders so they might break their shackles for good. And no political leader, symbolically, was more important in this act of liberation than Abraham Lincoln, the object of one of the most powerful cults of the New Deal era.

[4]

A PASSIONATE ADDICTION
TO LINCOLN

"OH FOR BUT ONE STATESMAN as fearless as Abraham Lincoln, the amancipator [*sic*] who died for us." This poignant plea, written in December 1930 to the head of the president's Committee on Employment, seemed targeted for Herbert Hoover and his uninspiring response to the Depression. It was also something more specific: the supplication from the wife of a World War veteran desperate for support from a nation so many soldiers had given their lives to defend. As the economic collapse began to push Americans—miners, sharecroppers, factory workers, and veterans—to think about their conditions of "slavery," it also encouraged hopes and longings for a figure of salvation, an Abraham Lincoln who might free people from their dismal circumstances. Herbert Hoover would never play that role, but many Americans pinned their hopes on his successor. Carolyn Harrow of New York City felt a surge of optimism after listening to Franklin Roosevelt's first fireside chat, in March 1933, and believed that "at the end of four years," FDR's name would be mentioned "in the same breath with the name of Abraham Lincoln." A few months later, Rocco Verri of Dania, Florida, did just that: "Abraham Lincoln freed the chattel slaves and now Mr. President you are about to free the child and wage slaves."[1]

In the 1930s and '40s, the signs were everywhere of American people hoping for, longing for, and reimagining the sixteenth president of the United States. Long figured as a predictable staple in Republican Party propaganda, Lincoln now became an object of intense political contention, fought over by New Deal Democrats, Republican stalwarts, black civil rights workers, and left-wing activists. Once relegated to vague political pronouncements, Lincoln now took center stage in volatile discussions about economic collapse, race and civil rights, and global conflict. Those interested in Lincoln's symbolic power seldom agreed on which aspects of Lincoln's legacy to emphasize. What, for example, did it mean that Lincoln stood for "emancipation"? Was he a president offering solace just to white Americans, or to African Americans as well? If Lincoln represented the deployment of federal power, whose interests and goals would that federal power serve? The political battles over Lincoln became even more fraught because of the cultural resonance Lincoln achieved in these years, as Americans became well versed in the stories of his childhood hardships and youthful ambitions, especially when those stories came from the pen of Carl Sandburg or took shape on movie screens across the country. Indeed, not since Reconstruction had Lincoln's legacy been so sharply contested or had Lincoln assumed such a prominent place on the public stage. Out of these contests, starting in the early 1930s and extending through the years of the Second World War, the sixteenth president underwent a series of remarkable transformations: no longer a bland symbol of reconciliation, he emerged as a figure more firmly associated with federal power and racial justice, although the racial message was often tempered by an appreciation of Lincoln's racially neutral "humanitarianism." By the end of the 1930s, the Lincoln image changed again, with Honest Abe transformed into a singular representative of Americans' rebuke to global dictatorship. In this regard, Lincoln did not simply mirror cultural and political trends. Rather, he occupied a fiercely contested space and, for some Americans, offered an imaginative repository—a kind of cultural testing ground—allowing them to explore more hopeful responses to the social and economic crises of the 1930s.[2]

"GETTING RIGHT WITH LINCOLN" was already a well-established political tradition, as historian David Donald has suggested. By the 1930s all political persuasions had to demonstrate their firm adherence to all things Lincoln. While this included mainstream parties and political movements, in the Depression era there were signs that some politicians and activists now wanted to get left with Lincoln, too. Democrats increasingly challenged Republican claims to the sixteenth president as they worked to associate Lincoln with New Deal efforts. Indeed, for every Republican who summoned Lincoln as the "great defender of freedom," there was at least one Democrat honoring him as the New Dealer of the 1850s and '60s. Lincoln likewise took a starring role in several New Deal plays, including Howard Koch's *Lonely Man*, which placed him at the forefront of contemporary workers' struggles, imagining him as a reincarnated college professor who visits a Kentucky campus and expresses sympathy for striking coal miners. Moving further left, US communists made Lincoln an object of veneration, inviting Americans who wanted to fight fascists in Spain to join the Abraham Lincoln Brigade. The left-wing Mexican muralist Diego Rivera even proposed pairing Lincoln with Lenin in his short-lived fresco at Rockefeller Center.[3]

Scene from the 1935 Twentieth Century Fox Film *The Littlest Rebel*. Two of the biggest stars of the 1930s, Shirley Temple and Abraham Lincoln (played here by Frank McGlynn), teamed up in this Civil War film, in which Temple played the part of a youthful Confederate who pleads with Lincoln to save her father's life. Photofest.

Yet Lincoln's popularity in these years went far beyond leftist political boundaries. In 1939 the *Los Angeles Times* called Lincoln "one of the greatest peacemakers of all time," while the *Boston Globe* celebrated him, perhaps only slightly more modestly, as "the greatest American humorist." Lincoln also acquired a new standing in American popular culture, appearing as the star attraction in novels and radio programs and theater performances. Perhaps the capstone to Lincoln's new celebrity status came with his emergence as a Hollywood icon. In 1930 he took top billing in an early biopic by legendary filmmaker D. W. Griffith and starred in the two better-known films from the end of the decade: John Ford's *Young Mr. Lincoln* and John Cromwell's *Abe Lincoln in Illinois*. In the 1935 film *The Littlest Rebel*, Lincoln teamed with the most financially successful movie star of the 1930s, Shirley Temple. The two shared an apple and then Lincoln freed Shirley's father, falsely accused as a Confederate spy, from prison.[4]

The pairing of Shirley and Abe did not simply make for good box office returns; it spoke, too, to the powerful emotional weight each one had assumed in 1930s America. If, as John Kasson has suggested, Shirley Temple and Franklin

Delano Roosevelt radiated a kind of resolve and resiliency in the face of un-precedented challenges, so too did Lincoln inspire Americans in the way he confronted the anguishing conflict of his own time. While he may not have projected Shirley Temple's engaging smile, Lincoln, at least as he was imagined in these years, held appeal through his sense of empathy and his commonsense thinking. As with FDR—and unlike with his predecessor, Herbert Hoover—Americans saw Lincoln as a leader who tackled problems without dispensing platitudes. As an apparent outsider and "common man," Lincoln also struck an emotional chord for those who felt alienated from corporate power and the established elite. The emotional stock many placed in Lincoln may have even helped him transcend politics, allowing people to see him as far more than the representative of one or another political ideology. The composer Aaron Copland, who honored the Civil War president in his 1942 *Lincoln Portrait*, was drawn, like many, not to Lincoln's political pronouncements but to his "gentle-ness and simplicity of spirit." Observing the kinds of emotional responses Lin-coln seemed to elicit, the writer and literary critic Alfred Kazin remarked in 1939 that Depression-era Americans had developed "a passionate addiction" to Lincoln. After having written two Lincoln poems and completed three portraits of the sixteenth president, the painter Marsden Hartley used even stronger lan-guage when he said: "I am simply dead in love with that man."[5]

A good deal of this attraction to Lincoln, as a living and breathing human being, could be traced to the work of Carl Sandburg. Published in 1926, Sand-burg's *The Prairie Years* chronicled the life of Lincoln up to his 1860 presidential victory. Sandburg, though, was hardly the first to humanize the Lincoln legend. Some writers and artists during the Progressive Era had already begun to make Lincoln more accessible and more attuned to the concerns of "ordinary" Ameri-cans. Sociologist Barry Schwartz has argued that in these years Lincoln suited the culture of progressivism, especially the desire to close the divide between "the genteel and the common people," leading many biographers to highlight Lincoln's emotional complexity and his affinity for the challenges and obsta-cles facing regular folk. Ida Tarbell, prior to Sandburg the foremost delineator of Lincoln's life, offered one of the most popular versions of this humanized Lincoln. In Tarbell's telling, Lincoln's greatness came precisely from his close proximity to the trials and hardships of frontier life, a narrative strategy that, Schwartz explains, allowed Tarbell to bridge the gap between Lincoln's rustic beginnings and his powerful presidency.[6]

Sandburg, an Illinois-born folklorist and poet of Swedish descent, imbibed this "common man" portrayal of Lincoln and seemed even more enthralled

than others with Honest Abe's "commonness." "Lincoln," he wrote in a 1911 article for the *Milwaukee Social Democratic Herald*, "was a shabby, homely man
who came from among those who live shabby and homely lives." In poems and
essays, as well as full-length biographical accounts, Sandburg did not just show
how a rude frontier culture could inspire political greatness but also explored
the full range of difficulties that informed the life of young Abe and his fellow
Americans. Sandburg's Lincoln remained, in other words, always in the cross-
hairs of democracy, never far removed from the trials and occasional joys of regular folk, whether that meant grueling factory labor, backbreaking farm work,
or crude and earthy humor. Despite appearing several years before the onset
of the economic crisis, *The Prairie Years* clearly resonated for Depression-era
Americans, especially with its celebration of the American "folk"—native-born
white people in particular—and their indigenous political wisdom. Sandburg's
work was, in this way, very much in keeping with the documentary folk culture of the New Deal years and the impulse to unearth the decent and morally
upstanding traits embodied in past generations of everyday Americans. Lincoln, Sandburg maintained, was inextricably linked to the honest and resilient
culture of the ordinary folk: one of those people who "in the short and simple
annals of the poor . . . breathe with the earth and take into their lungs and blood
some of the hard and dark strength of its mystery." Writing to his editor as he
gathered the material for his next set of Lincoln books, Sandburg believed that
amid "the garland of short stories and a gallery of interacting characters," the
reader would find "enough political wisdom to guide this country thru several
crises and depressions."[7]

During the 1930s Sandburg became one of the most recognized proponents
of the Lincoln tradition, frequently expounding in interviews and articles on
Lincoln's relevance to contemporary problems. He often wrote and spoke about
parallels between Lincoln's challenges and those faced by the present White
House occupant. He also probed deeply into Lincoln's character and person-
ality. In 1932 he profiled Mary Todd Lincoln, confirming a familiar picture of
an anxious, high-strung, and socially ambitious woman. Rather than detract-
ing from the image of the humble and common Lincoln, such a portrait only
made it stronger: the marriage to Mary allowed her husband's "patience and
gentleness" to grow and develop a "more tender and moving sympathy for the
common people of a suffering nation." In *The People, Yes*, a book-length poem
published in 1936, Sandburg took a wider lens on "the people" who helped give
substance to leaders like Lincoln. All of this work, in addition to the success
of *The Prairie Years*, made Sandburg well situated to influence the expanding

commercial culture of this decade as countless filmmakers, radio producers, and playwrights looked to his work as a source of inspiration. More than a few thought of Sandburg as a kind of stand-in for the Civil War president—"the most Lincolnian of our poets," one reviewer put it. When Sandburg finally, in 1939, published *The War Years*, his second set of volumes on Lincoln's life, he produced a work that spoke even more directly to the economic chaos, social turmoil, and global conflict that engulfed Americans in the New Deal period.[8]

Despite the previous era's humanizing biographies, when the 1930s began Lincoln lacked the kind of political vibrancy he would acquire later in the Depression decade. In pronouncements on his presidential leadership, he appeared primarily as a bland and unifying symbol, committed above all to moderation and reconciliation. To Republicans, he remained an upstanding party man who, as one representative proclaimed, "knew no such word as insurgent." In the image enshrined in the 1922 memorial, Lincoln stood, as former president William Howard Taft put it, for the "brotherly love" between North and South. In 1930, with economic collapse looming, President Hoover hailed Lincoln not as a Great Emancipator, but as a Great Moderator. His words "poured their blessings of restraint" on each subsequent generation. That same year, D. W. Griffith made his first talking film, taking Lincoln as its chief subject. Inspired by his reading of *The Prairie Years*, Griffith tried to persuade Sandburg to be a paid consultant for the film, but he found the poet too expensive for his budget. Ultimately, though, even Sandburg probably could not have saved Honest Abe from the maudlin sentiment of Griffith's cinema. Under Griffith's direction, Lincoln emerged as the standard-issue reconciler who, as one reviewer explained, made a "notable attempt to be fair to the two halves of our nation." In addition, Griffith apparently found it difficult to pivot from Lincoln's backwoods upbringing to his rise to national leadership: in a scene that does little to incite admiration for Lincoln's gravitas, the president, soon after arriving in Washington, flops down on the White House floor to take a nap.[9]

This bland, neutral, and apparently fatigued Lincoln reflected a reluctance on the part of many white Americans to invest the sixteenth president with real and substantial power, precisely because Lincoln in these years had to be safe and moderate, someone who could reach out and heal the wounds of sectional division. This Lincoln was, in other words, one suited to the reconciliation narrative that had captivated American culture and thinking at least since the end of the nineteenth century, the kind of narrative that still, in the 1930s, informed many fictionalized accounts of the sectional conflict and interpretations at Civil War battlefields. That narrative had given pride of place to a kind of brotherly

reunification, most vividly imagined in the form of white soldiers from opposing sides shaking hands across the bloody chasm. The appealing fiction in the
idea of reconciliation was that men and sometimes women from across the sectional divide willingly came together in a mutual embrace. Lincoln, though,
could be a potentially troubling symbol in this narrative, since he was not just a
man of "the North" but was really a figure of federal authority. To keep things
balanced, the pre–New Deal Lincoln generally took a backseat to the emotional
bonding of white northerners and southerners.[10]

This kind of Lincoln even found favor with southern whites. With so much
emphasis placed on his personal struggles, many could view him as a classic
symbol of American achievement: someone who rose from poverty to success
by working and studying hard. Jimmy Douglas, a southern mill worker, seemed
to have this Lincoln in mind when he set out to prepare himself for college
and a life better than what his parents had known. "I'd think of what I'd read
about Lincoln and all those others and it seemed to me I could do it, too," he
explained. A 1929 survey of white school-age boys in Alabama, who were asked
to name their top choice among national leaders, yielded a strong third-place
showing for Lincoln, behind Washington and Charles Lindbergh and ahead
of Robert E. Lee. Whatever their rankings, white southerners apparently felt
relatively little conflict about honoring Lincoln while also celebrating the Confederacy. To South Carolina journalist Ben Robertson, "Lee and Jackson were
our generals and Lincoln was President of our United States." Only Sherman,
he thought, was "not of America at all." North Carolinian Dorothy Hankins told
Carl Sandburg that while both her grandfathers had fought for the Confederacy,
"as far back as I can remember [Lincoln] and Robert E. Lee were my greatest
heroes." The historian Louis Rubin likewise recalled learning to revere both
the Confederacy and Abraham Lincoln during his youth in the South. Lincoln,
Rubin recalled, was known for his fair-mindedness and his insistence on bringing, and keeping, the union together. Hence, "it was well known that had that
great and good man not been assassinated by the dastardly John Wilkes Booth,
he would have eased the burden of the defeated southern states" and helped
avoid the horrors of Reconstruction.[11]

This was the Lincoln portrayed in D. W. Griffith's wildly popular 1915 film,
Birth of a Nation. Referred to as "the Great Heart," Griffith's Lincoln is revered
by southern whites for his forgiving nature. But this kind and merciful man,
so bent on bringing his feuding children together, is also oddly androgynous:
weepy, wearing a shawl, serving, as film historian Melvyn Stokes says, as both
father and mother figure to the American people, although the mothering

seems more prominent than the fathering. Still, in the end, Lincoln is not even an effective mother: it is not the president, in Griffith's film, who gives birth to the nation; it is the consolidated power of white men, North and South, and especially the Ku Klux Klan. This image of a relatively weak Lincoln presidency may also be one reason, too, that the story of Lincoln's youth—his frontier up-bringing, his awkward but heartfelt romantic encounters, his less-than-stellar performance as the New Salem postal clerk—became so captivating in the early twentieth century. Here was territory that one could mine for engaging human material without having to venture into the decidedly more messy business of Lincoln as a figure of power who actually enacted measures, emancipation for example, that did not meet with universal acclaim.[12]

Over the course of the 1930s, Lincoln started to look different. For one, he became less feminine. In his 1938 drama, *Abe Lincoln in Illinois*, Robert Sherwood shows Lincoln's masculine force emerging slowly, but inexorably, during his pre-presidential career. Sherwood initially posits the possibility of a political cabal who promote Lincoln's candidacy with the goal of making him their pawn. This notion, however, is quickly dispelled when, in a crucial moment in the play, the newly elected president angrily confronts his wife for her whining and reckless display of emotion on election night. The confrontation makes it clear, notably in this pivotal rebuke to Mary and not to the cabal, that Lincoln will be a forceful leader who has no intention of being ruled by others. The 1939 film *Young Mr. Lincoln* also spotlights Honest Abe's masculine strength, portraying him as the lawyer who defends helpless—and fatherless—brothers who have been falsely accused of murder. Not only does Lincoln here assume the part of paternal stand-in for the innocent Clay brothers' missing patriarch; he even manages to reduce his adversary, and the real murderer, to simpering tears during a withering cross-examination.[13]

Lincoln's enhanced masculine strength also allowed him to emerge, more decisively, as a figure of relevance in a modern, twentieth-century world. He was a figure not held back by old-time sentiments but ready to engage with contemporary problems. Although John Dos Passos had, in his *USA* trilogy (1930–36), mourned the passing of the old artisan-centered "Lincoln Republic," Sandburg countered that view with his insistence on Lincoln's timelessness, embodied in his energetic commitment to new ideas and a desire to break free of old fetters. With Lincoln's arrival in Washington, Sandburg wrote, the "very air of the city" suggested "a sense of change, of some new deal, of an impending program to be wrought out on historic anvils in smoke and mist and reckless slang, of old bonds and moorings broken beyond holding by old thongs and anchors." The

"new deal" reference was, of course, no accident: politicians and writers, Sandburg among them, had begun to cast Lincoln as a forerunner for the groundbreaking work Franklin Roosevelt had undertaken. Lincoln, then, was being
ushered into a new era, one that demanded more than just handshakes and healing and instead required a more vigorous assertion of state power.[14]

Lincoln, as the head of state, was well-positioned for encapsulating this new
concern about national power and could be more forcefully aligned with this
agenda than other figures associated with the Union cause. Although Ulysses
Grant had once ranked high in the pantheon of Civil War heroes, especially
at the time of his death in 1885, Lincoln's rise to prominence seemed to push
Grant, along with other Union figures, to the sidelines. One *New York Times*
reader expressed displeasure, in 1935, about the "current program of featuring
Lincoln and Lee as our only great men of the Civil War period." What, Stuart
Henry wondered, had happened to Grant, "the one man who saved our American nation"? As Henry perceptively noted, 1930s Americans recognized Lee, a
man representing the doomed but allegedly noble military effort of the South,
and Lincoln as their central heroes of the sectional conflict. And it was Lincoln,
a man associated more with government than with warfare, who was emerging
as the most important figure of all. Surely some of this was related to the current
celebration of the benevolent potential of the nation-state.[15]

A crucial manifestation of that state benevolence was slave emancipation.
In Howard Koch's 1937 play *The Lonely Man*, the first point made about Honest Abe is that "he freed those who were called slaves." True, academics and
popularizers had always paid some attention to Lincoln's efforts as a "great
emancipator," but that aspect of Lincoln's presidency came even more to the
forefront during the New Deal years as a way to underscore the parallels between the sixteenth president and Roosevelt and to emphasize the kind of har-
nessing of state power needed to achieve munificent results. As early as 1934,
Carl Sandburg compared FDR's National Recovery program and its assistance
for industrial workers with Lincoln's role in emancipation. Both presidents,
Sandburg insisted, used their executive position to proclaim a new status for
an oppressed people. The religious leader and writer Charles Sebold likewise
urged Roosevelt to "use the precedent set in the Emancipation Proclamation
for the complete fulfillment of his program," perhaps going so far as to confis-
cate private wealth in order to ameliorate the condition of "slavery" American
workers currently endured. FDR, too, argued that Lincoln's foremost political
contribution was not just about healing the sectional rift but about transcend-
ing sectionalism to bring "new meaning [to] the concepts of our constitutional

fathers and to assure a Government having for its broad purpose the promotion of the life, liberty, and happiness of all the people." FDR, in other words, aimed to make Lincoln part of a liberal tradition, one that would enlist the power of government to guarantee individual well-being. No longer just a healer and a reconciler, Lincoln now became aligned with the centralizing efforts of New Deal liberalism.[16]

Abolishing slavery was, of course, one critical way in which Lincoln used enhanced federal power to promote "life, liberty, and happiness." Yet the Lincoln who emerged in the 1930s might be described more accurately as a "Great Humanitarian" than a "Great Emancipator." Few nineteenth-century Americans would have described Honest Abe as a "humanitarian," but the term was, nonetheless, often employed to describe the sixteenth president in the 1930s and '40s. For many, in fact, it captured Lincoln's most essential quality. To one of Sandburg's readers, Lincoln's "great humanitarianism was the great thing that gained his place as President," a quality he equated with his intention to "strike hard" at the slavery problem. For some, humanitarianism pointed to a powerful character trait that made Lincoln deeply concerned with the human condition. The *New York Times'* theater reviewer, Brooks Atkinson, faulted a new Lincoln play for failing to show how Lincoln's "commonness ... later blossomed into humanitarianism." Lincoln, Atkinson believed, was more than just a friendly character: he was a strong and rugged individual who sought to improve humanity.[17]

Perhaps most importantly, the notion of Honest Abe's "humanitarianism" allowed people to see Lincoln's benevolence in broad and less racially specific ways. Roosevelt, asked to explain what Lincoln meant to him, called him "the greatest humanitarian," a notion that surely allowed FDR to take refuge in something big-hearted yet vague. Perhaps responding to Roosevelt's point, one of Sandburg's readers was prompted to wonder about the term's meaning. "Does the definition of humanitarianism today," asked Martha Prins of Brooklyn, "agree with the humanitarianism which Lincoln practiced?" Representative John Murdock of Arizona saw a difference between the two—a difference that hinged on race. "The present occupant of the White House," he argued "is as great a humanitarian as was Lincoln, with this difference: That Roosevelt's sympathies extend to all the underprivileged or the oppressed and are not centered or emphasized by race or color." Murdock, here, drew an unusual point of contrast: more often Lincoln, too, was assumed to be a humanitarian who also extended his sympathies without regard to "race or color." Representative Frank Dorsey of Pennsylvania thus argued that Lincoln's basic regard for humanity, his abhorrence of "precious human beings becoming mere chattel," meant he would easily recognize the "new slavery" that placed men in "economic peon-age." This, Dorsey argued, made Lincoln, essentially, a "new dealer of the late 1850s and the early 1860s."[18]

Portraying Lincoln as a broad-minded "humanitarian" made him an ideal symbol for projecting sympathy for "the common man," frequently figured in New Deal culture as a white man working for wages. As Lincoln himself was now presented in more masculine terms, he offered a more potent symbol for labor leaders, as well as ordinary working men, as they railed against the eco-nomic "slavery"—generally understood in terms of its specific effects on men—of the Depression era. Union organizers frequently referenced Lincoln's sym-pathies for working men and suggested that industrial workers would be the new recipients of Lincoln's emancipation efforts. "Our idea of a 'new birth of freedom,'" wrote the CIO official Len De Caux, "is an expansion of collective bargaining and industrial democracy." CIO leaders also liked to stress that CIO president John Lewis and Abraham Lincoln shared the same birthday. The play-wright Robert Sherwood, also interested in these connections between Lincoln, workers' rights, and New Deal labor relations, imagined Lincoln standing up for the laboring man when he debated Stephen Douglas. "Thank God," Sher-wood's Lincoln intones, "we live under a system by which men have the right to strike."[19]

Lincoln's life story, especially tales of his rise from obscurity and his persis-tent battles with detractors, also made him a sympathetic figure for American immigrants. "Even foreigners who have little grasp of the English language," wrote the reviewer of one Lincoln play, "love the story of the man Lincoln." Per-haps not surprisingly, the most successful Lincoln writer in these years was the son of Swedish immigrant parents; he likely interpreted the former president's saga through his own understanding of what American immigrants endured and experienced. Sandburg and other Lincoln delineators no doubt saw a par-allel between Lincoln and immigrants, both having to make their own way in new and sometimes hostile surroundings. The 250 Polish American residents of Brooklyn probably grasped those parallels when they planned celebrations, in February 1939, that would honor the birth of both Lincoln and the Polish hero of the American Revolution, Thaddeus Kosciuszko. And Roosevelt, too, seemed implicitly to understand Lincoln's appeal to twentieth-century immi-grants, precisely the kind of immigrants Roosevelt wanted in his own political organization. "Dig me up fifteen or twenty youthful Abraham Lincolns from Manhattan and the Bronx," FDR wrote to a New Deal associate in 1936, an ap-parent reference to socially conscious Jews whose sympathies would mesh with the New Deal program. In short, the social and political developments of the 1930s expanded Lincoln's reach, making him more available and accessible to a more diverse range of Americans than ever before.[20]

These ways of imagining Lincoln placed Honest Abe in the thick of the ethnic and cultural pluralism of the New Deal era. New Deal–sponsored pageants, parades, and dramatic programs put a spotlight on the proud folk customs of Irish, Italian, and Slavic immigrants, groups that were also, not coincidentally, being recognized by Roosevelt as critical players in an expanded "New Deal coalition"—the broad and diverse range of voters who would lend their support to the Democratic Party for decades to come. Black Americans were also, at least nominally, a part of that coalition, and also among those with a unique relationship to Lincoln; yet, compared to immigrant voters, they occupied a far more ambiguous place in the New Deal alliance. As a Democratic president who needed the support of powerful white southerners in his party, Roosevelt had little interest in making any explicit statements about changing the racial status quo in the Jim Crow South or endorsing a program with obvious racial implications. The New Deal, as the scholar Ira Katznelson has observed, frequently paid its debts to southern white demands, perhaps most notoriously when the president refused to lend his support to the federal antilynching law being urged by some members of Congress. And since most African Americans lived in the South and so had little recourse to the ballot, black political support counted for less in FDR's political calculations. As a result, he had little interest in turning Lincoln into a vibrant symbol of racial justice and so preferred a Lincoln who abhorred "slavery" and who practiced a broad-based "humanitarianism": one who freed not just black slaves but "those of heavy heart everywhere." In his own way, Robert Sherwood, later a key speechwriter for FDR, also tried to elevate Lincoln's concern for white immigrants over his regard for blacks. In *Abe Lincoln in Illinois*, Honest Abe emerges as a strong opponent of the anti-immigrant views of the 1850s Know Nothing Party, a party "dedicated to the proposition that only Protestants of pure Anglo-Saxon blood should rule America, that all Catholics, Jews and 'foreigners' in general (including Germans) should be reduced to the status of Negroes." Although not a wholly accurate rendering of the Know Nothing Party's platform, Sherwood's statement surely spoke to the New Deal's emphasis on ethnic plurality.[21]

Still, over the course of the Depression, numerous New Dealers felt the pressure to make Lincoln more responsive to black concerns. As African Americans were drawn into the political debates of the era, and northern black votes were able to make a difference at the polls, Roosevelt and his supporters engaged in a kind of symbolic politics that involved making gestures and sending signals that seemed to open some doors toward racial progress. Thus while Roosevelt and his supporters backed away from explicit challenges to many oppressive features of the Jim Crow system, they acceded to more incremental changes: appointing black men and women to a few New Deal posts, pushing the National Recovery Administration to reject the wage differentials in the South that permitted reduced pay for black workers, supporting a few public programs that gave greater visibility to civil rights issues. Similarly, they found ways to uphold Lincoln—supporting anniversary celebrations of the Emancipation Proclamation, helping stage Marian Anderson's Lincoln Memorial concert in 1939—that might hint at certain sympathies without compelling a definite shift in policy.[22]

Southern white liberals, a constituency FDR hoped to nurture, had even less interest in making Lincoln an active crusader for racial justice. White men like Howard Odum, the region's foremost sociologist, and Will Alexander, one-time head of the Commission on Interracial Cooperation, resisted any hasty abandonment of Jim Crow, preferring to make the system, in Glenda Gilmore's words, "work more smoothly." To these men, Lincoln was a comforting figure of racial moderation, committed to ending slavery but not to advancing racial equality. W. T. Couch, head of the University of North Carolina Press and a leading southern moderate, thus liked to reference the pre–Civil War Lincoln, who frequently disavowed any calls for civil or political rights for African Americans. Couch, like other liberal whites of this period, affirmed the notion of black inferiority, a condition which he saw as the product of generations of slavery and oppression but which he believed could, in time, be "overcome."[23]

Black activists and intellectuals fiercely resisted the kind of gradualist and paternalist approaches voiced by Couch and Odum, not to mention FDR, and tried to work out a different type of relationship with Lincoln. Since the Civil War, African Americans had both honored Lincoln's legacy and acknowledged the blind spots in Lincoln's commitment to racial justice. Recognizing the symbolic power of Lincoln, as well as the concrete policies enacted by Republicans both during and after the war, most blacks maintained steadfast support for "the party of Lincoln" into the first few decades of the twentieth century. A simultaneous tradition, however, could be traced back to Frederick Douglass, who recognized Lincoln as "preeminently the white man's President, entirely devoted to the welfare of white men." In the early and middle years of the Depression decade, many black Americans, no doubt frustrated with the continuing grind of Jim Crow, called attention to Lincoln's limitations. A prominent black newspaper editor contended that Republicans, including Lincoln, had no real love for Negroes or sincere hatred of slavery and disliked the institution for "purely economic reasons." The black historian Carter Woodson believed that Lincoln was "often overrated as the savior of the race" and took aim at the political damage that could be done by Lincoln idolatry. "Admiring others will hold the Negroes forever in bondage," Woodson explained in 1932. "Abraham Lincoln did not 'set my people free.' They are still in chains." And at a 1933 gathering in Brooklyn, black journalist Ted Poston, responding to historian Arthur Schomburg's more celebratory portrait of the sixteenth president, suggested that black Americans would still be slaves if Lincoln had had his way.[24]

These types of reckonings with Lincoln came increasingly to the forefront in the 1930s as blacks confronted the shifting political terrain of the Roosevelt years. How much, many wondered, should remembrance of Lincoln matter in light of the political choices that had to be made in the 1930s? Even more, how much could really be trusted about the memory of Lincoln that had been handed down, especially when it came from partisan manipulators in the Republican Party? Surely it was not hard to imagine that white Republicans had only burnished Lincoln's reputation in a crass attempt to win black votes. As early as 1932, the editor of the *Pittsburgh Courier*, Robert Vann, argued that it was time for black Americans to cut themselves loose from the Republican Party's callous misuse of the Lincoln image. "So long as the Republican party could use the photograph of Abraham Lincoln to entice Negroes to vote a Republican ticket," Vann argued, "they condescended to accord Negroes some degree of political recognition. But when the Republican party had built itself to the point of security, it no longer invited Negro support." By the time of FDR's second presidential campaign, in 1936, this had become a more pronounced line of argument in the black press and especially among northern blacks able to cast ballots. While Roosevelt had not tackled Jim Crow, he had offered some measure of relief and so, argued some black leaders, had at least provided something more tangible than an empty memory bandied about by Republican lawmakers. Earl Brown, a black political scientist, believed African Americans would cast their ballots for Roosevelt in November 1936 "because they are sick of the Abe Lincoln–Civil War claptrap and because they are still being fed by Roosevelt relief." Others agreed it was time to cut loose from old memories in light of present-day politics. "Would you have us be Republicans," asked Mrs. Redmond Garrett, a *Pittsburgh Courier* reader, simply "because our ancestors were"? A Baltimore newspaper, urging its black readers to vote for Roosevelt, put the point even more succinctly: "Abraham Lincoln," the editors wrote in 1936, "is not a candidate in the Present Campaign." Arthur Mitchell, a black Democrat from Chicago and the sole black representative in Congress, not only expressed irritation with Republicans for peddling Lincoln in the black community; he also questioned how much Lincoln deserved to be celebrated. "There is absolutely no truth," he declared in a congressional speech in April 1936, in the notion that Lincoln "was elected to free the Negro slaves."[25]

Still, cutting ties with Lincoln could prove politically risky for African Americans. For one, breaking with Lincoln would be difficult for ordinary folk in the black community, many of whom continued to see Lincoln in a hallowed light and prominently displayed his picture in their homes and schools. There was also a long-standing tradition of honoring Lincoln's birthday in the black press and attaching Lincoln's name to civil rights work. The National Equal Rights League opened a new campaign for a federal antilynching law in February 1931, "in the name of Lincoln and [Frederick] Douglass" and "through the medium of the Lincoln [birth]day and Douglass [birth]day observances." Additionally, black activists had often juxtaposed their own high regard for Lincoln with the way pro-Confederate southerners disparaged the sixteenth president. In condemning a UDC attack on Honest Abe, the *Chicago Defender* explained: "The same voices that raise the cry against the memory of Abraham Lincoln go about preaching the theory of white supremacy." Praise for Lincoln was thus an important strategy for establishing black loyalty and for undermining the patriotism of those who promoted racism.[26]

An exchange on the floor of the House of Representatives, in June 1936, between black Democratic representative Arthur Mitchell and white Republican representative John Robsion highlighted the political costs blacks might incur if they disregarded Lincoln. Mitchell had arrived in Congress from Chicago in 1935 after defeating Oscar DePriest, the black Republican representative from Illinois's First District. Mindful of this significant political shift, Mitchell no doubt was anxious to affirm his, and his black constituents', commitment to the Democrats' New Deal agenda and their disavowal of the GOP. "More Negro boys and girls," Mitchell explained, "are attending high schools than heretofore, and they will not fall for the old line that a vote for the Republican Party is a vote for Lincoln." Perhaps, Mitchell suggested, it was even time to question just how dedicated Lincoln had been to slave emancipation. Robsion, a representative from Kentucky, offered a long and impassioned tirade against Mitchell's charges. Observing that Mitchell was himself a descendant of slaves, Robsion questioned the Chicago representative's portrayal of the historical record and his denunciation of "the great services rendered by Abraham Lincoln and the Republican Party to his own father and mother and to millions of his own race." Noting how Mitchell and other black leaders had, until recently, celebrated Lincoln's memory and had discovered "only 4 or 5 years ago that Abraham Lincoln and the Republican Party did not free the Negroes," Robsion turned the charge of political manipulation back against Mitchell. And in no uncertain terms he questioned the black representative's patriotism. "Our colleague from Chicago," Robsion asserted, "belittled Abraham Lincoln and his service."[27]

Robsion, here, was playing a time-honored game: in highlighting Lincoln's act of lifting up a subordinated race, he underscored how much American blacks should feel themselves forever in Lincoln's debt. This notion, what the historian David Brion Davis refers to as "the Emancipation Moment," was a powerful one, frequently invoked in many of the conversations that black Americans had about Lincoln in these years. Even more, it made it clear how difficult it would be for African Americans to distance themselves from Honest Abe. Mitchell himself, responding to Robsion, thus felt forced to affirm: "I take second place to no person from Kentucky or any other State in admiring that great statesman." African Americans may have felt even more pressure to line up with Lincoln after 1936, when New Deal Democrats promoted a closer political alliance with Honest Abe and when African Americans developed a closer political alliance with New Deal Democrats. As various writers, artists, and politicians began to make firmer links between Roosevelt and Lincoln, they also implied that Democrats, more than Republicans, were the true inheritors of Lincoln's legacy. Consequently, black Americans would not be compelled to "forget Lincoln," and may have even felt the need to make more pointed tributes to Lincoln as part of affirming their support for Roosevelt. "Slaves Freed Twice as New Deal Blooms," shouted a headline from the *New York Amsterdam News* in October 1936. "Dixie Man Asserts Abe Lincoln Began It; FDR Next."[28]

This strategy, of embracing a newly "Lincolnized" Roosevelt, also carried political risks, especially a tendency to gloss over Roosevelt's weak record on civil rights. The *Amsterdam News* seemed willing to take the risk: by promoting FDR as the inheritor of Lincoln's emancipation policies, they argued that Roosevelt had greatly improved "the strained relations between the two major racial groups in this country." Other activists, however, took a different approach to the problem: they chose instead to reimagine Lincoln as a firm civil rights champion, implicitly sending a message that the struggle for racial justice had a long and illustrious history in the United States, one that should be embraced by anyone who honored Lincoln's legacy. While activists and political leaders frequently linked memory and politics, civil rights politics increasingly compelled black Americans toward a certain type of memory of the sixteenth president, one that imagined him as a more forceful champion for racial justice. Writing, in February 1937, in the pages of the *Chicago Defender*, the black biographer and attorney William Lilly discussed how much Lincoln was not simply an antislavery politician, but also one who opposed "race hatred" and even embraced the idea of black citizenship. With heated debates taking place in Congress regarding new federal antilynching legislation, Lilly likely understood that emphasizing Lincoln's antiracist past had important contemporary ramifications.[29]

NAACP leaders likewise recognized the benefits of enhancing Lincoln's status as a champion of racial justice, especially during the planning and publicizing of Marian Anderson's 1939 concert at the Lincoln Memorial. When the Daughters of the American Revolution barred Anderson, because she was black, from singing in their auditorium, NAACP activists played a critical role in finding an alternative place and were particularly attuned to the symbolism of organizing an outdoor concert at the Lincoln Memorial. "It would be far better . . . for Miss Anderson to sing out-of-doors," the NAACP board wrote as the concert was being planned, "for example, at the Lincoln Memorial, erected to commemorate the Memory of Abraham Lincoln, the Great Emancipator, or not to sing in Washington at all until democracy can surmount the color line in the nation's capital." The association with Lincoln allowed civil rights workers to connect their struggle with an American icon and an American tradition while at the same time portraying their DAR opponents—and the larger Jim Crow system—as callously un-American. And because using the Lincoln Memorial required the support of New Deal administrators, notably Harold Ickes's Department of the Interior, the event made Lincoln's racial justice agenda seem even more compatible with the New Deal program.[30]

Still, New Dealers continued to emphasize a moderate Lincoln, a "Great Emancipator" of the long-ago past, rather than the civil rights Lincoln favored by NAACP activists. In introducing Anderson, Secretary Ickes called attention to the appropriateness of Anderson singing at this shrine to "the Great Emancipator who struck the shackles of slavery from her people seventy-six years ago." Here, again, was Lincoln, the benevolent dispenser of liberation to an oppressed race of people. Yet despite these efforts to contain Lincoln, other progressives, especially in and around the Popular Front, continued to push hard to make Lincoln a champion not just of abolition but of racial justice more broadly. The magazine of the Southern Negro Youth Conference, a Popular Front organization

Marian Anderson at the Lincoln Memorial, 1939. Anderson's 1939 concert demonstrated the significance of Lincoln's image for the emerging civil rights struggle. Thomas D. McAvoy, The LIFE Picture Collection, Getty Images.

headquartered in Birmingham, Alabama, published a poem by its editor titled
"The People to Lincoln, Douglass" that imagined Lincoln as a partner in the
inter-racial struggle that was so central to the Popular Front agenda:

> Abe Lincoln clench your fists once
> more, straighten your back,
> and take the hand of Fred
> Douglass, the ex-slave,
> And turn to the people—
> We are ready, again, Abe Lincoln.
> We, the people will drive out the
> slavemaster. . . .[31]

Many black activists probably would have preferred to keep the spotlight
solely on Frederick Douglass, a far more adamant symbol of the black freedom
struggle. Black newspapers in these years were filled with tributes and notices of
public celebrations to Douglass, suggesting the power this militant abolitionist
had for the emerging civil rights agenda. But connecting Lincoln to the modern civil rights movement had its own obvious benefits because Lincoln was
such a crucial icon in America's pantheon of patriots. Even William Pickens, the
NAACP field secretary who expressed skepticism about Lincoln's friendship
with blacks, believed that Honest Abe would "oppose disfranchisement, caste
segregation and lynching."[32]

A little bit of this civil rights Lincoln even found its way into John Ford's 1939
film, *Young Mr. Lincoln*. Here Henry Fonda is cast as Honest Abe, working as a
young lawyer in Springfield when he is called on to defend two white brothers
accused of a murder. Prior to their trial, the two face the wrath of a lynch mob
that threatens to derail the judicial process. In a key dramatic moment, Lincoln
angrily rebukes the mob and prevents the lynching. "It gets so a man can't pass
a tree or look at a rope without feeling uneasy," Fonda's Lincoln intones. True,
Young Mr. Lincoln follows a pattern prevalent in other Ford films of the 1930s:
white men's suffering, in this case the ordeal of the imprisoned brothers, once
again wears the cloak of black oppression. Unlike *Judge Priest* and *The Prisoner
of Shark Island*, though, *Young Mr. Lincoln* imagined white men not as slaves but
as potential lynching victims. Surely, it is hard to imagine that a 1939 audience
would *not* have heard echoes of the contemporary lynching problem—and its
explicitly racial target—when Lincoln took his stand against the wild and fren-
zied mob in Springfield. By having Marian Anderson perform for the film's Memorial Day opening, in Springfield, Illinois—just a few weeks after her historic

Lincoln Memorial concert—the film's publicists made another connection between Lincoln and the modern civil rights struggle.[33]

NOT SURPRISINGLY, conservatives in this era had little interest in champion-
ing Lincoln as a figure of racial justice or even interracial compassion. Many
objected to connecting him to any kind of partisan agenda. Republicans were,
of course, appalled at the Democratic appropriation of their party's standard-
bearer and repeatedly made the case for Lincoln's commitment to laissez-faire
capitalism. "Are we obliged to accept the great founder of our [Republican]
party," wondered the Massachusetts politician Robert Bradford, "as nothing
but a groping New Deal Democrat born unhappily before his time?" Some conservative Democrats and Republicans made an even more forceful attempt to
reclaim Lincoln by using the newly organized House Un-American Activities
Committee (HUAC). Formed in 1938, one of HUAC's first targets was the Federal Theatre Project, the drama wing of the WPA, and one of the principal are-
nas where an intensely democratic Lincoln had been showcased. One play that
drew pointed ire from HUAC was the very popular Federal Theatre production
of E. P. Conkle's *Prologue to Glory*, another story of Lincoln's early life in Illinois
and the people and events that launched his political career. HUAC's attack
clearly reflected concern over how much Lincoln had been recruited for contemporary, and often progressive-oriented, political struggles. Widely praised
by mainstream reviewers, Conkle's play was dubbed, by HUAC, "a propaganda
play to prove that all politicians are crooked." One HUAC member, J. Parnell
Thomas, told Hallie Flanagan, the head of the Federal Theatre, that he particularly objected to a scene in which Lincoln tells a New Salem audience that
political debates ought to focus on "subjects for action, useful for living." That,
Thomas claimed, "is Communist talk." One wonders if Thomas, a Republican,
might have been using "Communist" as a euphemism for "Democrat."[34]

HUAC's campaign did manage to defund and effectively kill off the Federal
Theatre Project, although its specific case against Lincoln failed to gain much
traction. Critics and audiences generally liked Conkle's play, and the political
subtleties of the HUAC charge were likely lost on most of them. The influence
of Sandburg's biography, and the films and novels and other artistic offerings
that spotlighted Lincoln's sympathies with the people, probably made it hard
for most Americans to see anything communistic in Lincoln's democratic activism. The folk portrait of Lincoln, which was consistent with other celebrations
of indigenous Americana, made Lincoln seem like the antithesis of foreign-
born radicalism. As Hallie Flanagan put it, *Prologue to Glory* "could be called a

Poster for the Federal Theatre production of *Prologue to Glory*. Among the many other New Deal arts initiatives that celebrated Lincoln, *Prologue to Glory* was one of the Federal Theatre's most successful, yet still controversial, offerings. Harry Herzog, Federal Theatre Project Collection, Prints & Photographs Division, Library of Congress, cph 3f05319.

propaganda play in its intense emphasis on the distinct value of sturdy American qualities and simple living."[35]

Ultimately, though, it was precisely Lincoln's fierce association with "sturdy American qualities" that helped transform him, yet again, into a very different type of "propaganda" figure, one who could win admiration from both New Deal liberals and many conservatives. By the time of Marian Anderson's

Lincoln Memorial concert, there were already indications that a new iteration of Lincoln might overshadow the racial justice Lincoln of the NAACP, or the antilynching Lincoln of the Popular Front. Oscar Chapman, the assistant secretary of the interior who helped arrange the Anderson event, helped push the Civil War president in this new direction. After comparing Jewish singers being banned from the Nazi stage and Marian Anderson being shunned from a Washington, DC, concert hall, Chapman summed up the difference this way: "In Washington we have a shrine for Abraham Lincoln." Lincoln here symbolized a national tradition of racial and ethnic tolerance, not militancy. He also now became a figure of global importance, a figure whose work might transcend the domestic struggles of workers, immigrants, and African Americans and become part of the worldwide effort to rebuke the fascist agenda.[36]

Honest Abe, as we will see, did go on to play that role as US involvement in the new world war became more and more likely. But Lincoln could not wage war against global dictatorship if he was dragged down by his own authoritarian baggage. In a 1931 volume, the poet Edgar Lee Masters had made Lincoln look like a formidable strongman bent on an imperialistic crusade. Biographers more sympathetic than Masters had also noted Lincoln's tendency to amass more and more power over the course of his presidency. Even Sandburg wrote that in the aftermath of the Fort Sumter attack, the president "was taking to himself one by one the powers of a dictator" and that during his presidency he "had many of the powers of a dictator." But Sandburg also employed some clever strategies to counter such troubling speculation. For one, he often stressed—as have more recent historians—Lincoln's lack of firm policy, frequently quoting Lincoln's statement "My policy is to have no policy," a remark that, in a 1930s context, distanced Lincoln from those with dogmas and isms attached to their agendas. Even more effective was Sandburg's repeated invocations of the Lincoln "mystery" and "mystique": a tendency to describe Lincoln's power over the people as something unfathomable and enigmatic.[37]

Not one for deep political or historical analysis, Sandburg often employed this language to describe the Civil War president: he was "a mystery in smoke and flags saying . . . yes to the paradoxes of democracy"; he had a "mystic dream of a majestic Republic holding to human freedom and equal opportunity"; and he inspired "a feeling of mystic and heroic quality" among his nineteenth-century admirers. Critics who reviewed Sandburg's work and writers and artists who drew inspiration from Sandburg likewise gave Lincoln mystical qualities. "What is the power behind the mystic hold which Abraham Lincoln has upon the imagination of all people?" queried one reviewer of Robert Sherwood's Lincoln play, one of many works that paid homage to Sandburg. A student's guide to the film *Young Mr. Lincoln* began by calling Lincoln "our greatest American" and "our greatest mystery." "Mystery," "mysterious," "mystic": these words—used so often in Sandburg's descriptions and then echoed by Sandburg's reviewers and imitators—provided a literary and historical sleight of hand, a way to deflect analysis and avoid difficult assessments about power, freedom, and democracy. Americans in the 1930s and '40s were drawn to the "mystical" Lincoln because he resolved a central paradox about balancing democracy and authority. The "mystic" and "mysterious" Lincoln could thus be a single, powerful individual, yet not a totalitarian, because he somehow—mystically and mysteriously—was in sync with the will of the people. The mystery, in short, was how Lincoln could hold such awesome power yet also be one of the folk.[38]

For some Lincoln delineators, this sense of Lincoln's mystical power expressed itself in a self-conscious desire to mythologize the sixteenth president. Several writers made a point of departing from the more ordinary and human Lincoln in favor of someone who ultimately became a larger-than-life figure in the minds of those who loved and admired him. Embracing the Lincoln myth offered a way to celebrate the kind of exalted reverence with which Honest Abe was regarded and to simply concede that there was something, ultimately, that would remain mysterious, something that mere mortals might not fathom. The poet John Malcolm Brinnin, for example, described the twenty-eight poems that made up his *Lincoln Lyrics* as "an attempt at myth-making." New Deal politician Thomas Smith honored both "the Lincoln person and the Lincoln personage" but gave more weight to the personage. "Men," Smith believed, "hardly dare to disrespect the deities which their own creative imaginations have cooperated in calling from the vast deeps of chaos." Lincoln, in other words, was not actually a figure who had amassed a disturbing degree of power; he was only raised up to that height in people's imaginations. Although Sandburg intended his own work as a rebuttal to the Lincoln myths of the past, he nonetheless acknowledged the power of the Lincoln mythology, how "around the world and into the masses of people whose tongues and imaginings create folk tales out of slender fact, there ran this item of the Strong Man who arose in his might and delivered an edict, spoke a few words fitly chosen, and thereupon the shackles and chains fell from the arms and ankles of men, women, and children born to be chattels."[39]

In reviewing *The War Years*, the critic Max Lerner brought the lesson of Lincoln's democratic, if mystical, ethos into the present, arguing that in the current world of so-called war democracies, "we have reason to be proud of Lincoln. We have reason to be proud that with every opportunity for setting up a dictatorship, he did not succumb." Surely the underlying concern here was that FDR, too, not succumb, despite the charges often made about Roosevelt's own authoritarian ambitions. It helped, of course, that people had become accustomed to thinking of Roosevelt as another Lincoln and so saw in FDR someone similarly— and mystically—connected to the popular will. The poet Stephen Vincent Benét compared FDR to Lincoln in a 1940 Election Day poem. "You never were a Fuehrer and never will be," Benét said of Roosevelt, just "a man who knows the tides and ways of the people / As Abe Lincoln knew the wind on the prairies." Robert Sherwood, the Lincoln playwright who became one of FDR's advisers, likewise had Lincoln on his mind when he advised Roosevelt that "if people make you into a myth, you must live up to that myth, and be what they expect of you—yes, exploit to the fullest that confidence and faith." Sherwood, like many others, had learned from Lincoln how the power of myth-making might allow a historical figure to acquire great, even unprecedented power, but in a way that made that power seem rooted in the "mystical" power of the people. This sense of Lincoln's power would prove invaluable when the Civil War president more fully assumed his new and all-consuming role of leading Americans into a new foreign war to defeat, once again, the looming threat of "slavery."[40]

During the 1930s, Abraham Lincoln stood out as a kind of lightning rod for the constantly shifting and conflicting views about the New Deal. As a useful measuring stick for assessing the new political challenges and realities of FDR's administration, Lincoln emerged as a far more consequential and influential figure than he had been before. Many black Americans pushed aside misgivings about Honest Abe's emancipation record and made a renewed commitment to Lincoln, especially as he became a central New Deal icon. In doing so, however, they hoped to infuse the Civil War president with a strong and unwavering commitment to racial justice, a commitment they hoped Roosevelt himself would echo. Those at the center of the New Deal, however, hoped to separate Lincoln from a race-centered agenda and sought to make him a powerful national leader but a race-neutral humanitarian. At the same time, conservatives and anticommunists, mindful of Lincoln's enhanced stature, tried to reclaim the sixteenth president from any type of liberal agenda. All of this meant that by the end of the 1930s the Lincoln image was sharply contested, ever pliable, and awaiting further manipulation in the context of the new imperatives of the Second World War.

[5]

LOOK AWAY!
DIXIE'S LANDED!

AFTER WRITING the blockbuster novel of the decade, Margaret Mitchell adjusted her schedule to the overwhelming volume of letters and inquiries that crossed her desk. Even before her book sailed to the top of the bestseller list, Mitchell began answering fans' questions, responding to countless interviews, and negotiating film rights for her epic 1936 novel of the Civil War. For some of the Atlanta author's correspondents, *Gone with the Wind* prompted heartfelt appreciation for a story that resonated strongly with their own experiences. Others wrote about their interest in the upcoming movie, maybe hoping to convince Mitchell they had just the right smile to be Scarlett or were familiar enough with southern Negroes that, even if they were white, they might play Mammy or Pork. A few, of course, didn't really like the book, mostly for its more explicit presentations of sex and drunkenness. But the bulk of Mitchell's letter writers begged her to write a sequel, hoping to get the final word on whether Rhett and Scarlett would be reunited. Truth be told, Mitchell showed little interest in clearing up that mystery. Besides, her voluminous correspondence gave her little time for additional fiction writing. For the next ten years, indeed until her untimely death in 1949, Mitchell would write to readers, interviewers, scholars, and others about her one iconic work of fiction, reacting to effusive praise, responding to occasional criticisms, and often pushing back against misunderstandings regarding both herself and her novel.[1]

Among those misunderstandings, one stood out with particular force: Mitchell had no wish to be cast as some hidebound southerner wallowing in the hazy glow of old-time Dixie. Writing to an Atlanta journalist in 1939, she made her point this way: "I never knew any family that didn't [talk about the war] if they were Southerners who had any part in the War. But my family were not living in the past and unaware of the present, and the War was not their only topic of conversation." The inquiring journalist, Mitchell suspected, had fallen prey to the "Margaret Mitchell legend," a myth that cast the Georgia writer in a time warp where the sectional conflict of the nineteenth century eclipsed all other thoughts and experiences.[2]

In the 1930s, the "Margaret Mitchell legend" was hardly unique to Margaret Mitchell. "You still fighting the Civil War down there?" was, according to Virginia novelist Clifford Dowdey, a frequent refrain heard by southerners traveling north. The perception, in fact, was widespread that southerners, and the southern region more generally, bore the imprint of the past like nowhere else in the country. With most southerners still living off the land and agriculture often adhering to practices associated with the antebellum plantation system, many came to believe that the history of the South had inextricably merged with its present. Howard Odum, the premier sociologist of the Depression-era South, diagnosed the problem as a regional "time lag" particularly affecting the Southeast, where conditions resembled what "the whole nation was in the earlier decades to the extent that agricultural occupation and ways of life and thought predominate." The people of the South were also, as Dowdey noted, assumed to be unusually obsessed with their past: the good parts, the bad parts, and the imagined parts. "After the wreckage which followed Appomattox," argued Alabama writer Clarence Cason, "it was natural that the futility of the southern outlook should be balanced by an effort to glorify the era which had preceded Manassas.... The glories of the old South became an impregnable castle over which was flown the invincible banner of 'the Lost Cause.'" Others saw the imprint of the past, especially the specific past of slavery, playing out in more instinctive and unconscious ways, with particular effects on different types of southerners. Northern sociologist John Dollard believed that "the subservience of the Negro is obviously a heritage from slavery days," while southern historians Benjamin Kendrick and Alex Arnet argued that certain factory foremen as well as plantation overseers were "the spiritual if not the biological descendants of slavery-time overseers."[3]

Still, as Margaret Mitchell tried to affirm, the South was never the land that time forgot, although it may well have been a land that thrived on exploiting its never-to-be-forgotten past. Even in 1930, it was a complicated region with pockets of industry and commercial development and emerging signs indicating that modern ways of living, buying, and traveling had gained a solid foothold. Moreover, despite some unifying political tendencies and historical circumstances, there were many factors that cut against generalizations about "the South," perhaps none more extreme than the divide along racial lines. Yet both popular and academic thinking often blurred the region's past and present and depicted "the South" as a single coherent entity still residing in some kind of far-away, long-ago time unencumbered by either racial or geographic differences. Additionally, there seemed to be a steady consumer market in all regions for the sentimentalized portrayal of the southern plantation past—the "moonlight and magnolia" version of Dixie—so the old-timey South assumed a prominent presence in American popular culture. Film studios, publishing houses, advertising firms, radio broadcasters—most headquartered outside the southern states—had been releasing a steady flow of this kind of southern-themed material since the end of the nineteenth century.[4]

In short, this sense of the South's unique and enduring connection to its past was not new in the Depression years, but it did emerge with particular forcefulness, and it did have particular consequences, in the New Deal decade. Most notably, the economic crisis compelled an even stronger historical consciousness about the South's Civil War past, partly because of the window it opened onto an earlier moment of adversity and partly because it seemed to show the historical roots of contemporary southern woes. Over the course of the Depression decade, a growing number of southern whites drew from their backward-looking glances one overriding lesson: that northern and federal intervention had long ago been the source of southern suffering and would, if unchecked, be the source of suffering once again. In this way, southern whites revived and adapted a long-standing Lost Cause narrative that resurrected the demand for "states' rights," celebrated Confederate heroism, and repudiated various New Deal and politically liberal policies—especially pertaining to race—by casting them as renewed versions of the horrors of Reconstruction. Even more, this renewed defense of southern "traditions" increasingly merged with a growing anticommunist outlook: Lost Causers during the 1930s surveyed previous and current efforts to challenge the racial status quo through the prism of antiradical hysteria. This outlook dealt a significant blow not only to civil rights work in the 1930s, but also to the historical efforts to valorize the freedom struggle of the past.

THE LOST CAUSE HAD, of course, retained a strong hold on the imagination of white southerners ever since the cause had been lost. For the previous sixty-five years, white southerners, often with the assistance of white northerners, had used popular culture, history, politics, and commemorative work to flesh out a consoling narrative that bestowed honor on those who had fomented Civil War and were then forced to nurse the wounds of defeat. That narrative rested on a sentimentalized portrait of the Old South and its system of chattel slavery, an argument about the cause of the Civil War that downplayed the centrality of slavery, an account of the Confederacy that highlighted the brave and honorable deeds of its fighters, and a scathing indictment of northerners for their callous deployment of material and human resources in order to secure their wartime victory and subjugate the South in the postwar period. By the end of the nineteenth century, the Lost Cause not only told the tale of Confederate honor and wartime suffering; it also included an account of postwar oppression at the hands of "Negro rule" in Reconstruction and the eventual triumph against that oppressive system.[5]

These were all themes that took on new life in the 1930s, encompassing everything from the Natchez Pilgrimage tours (started in 1931) celebrating the city's antebellum gardens and mansions to the countless novels and films that showcased some aspect of the Confederate war effort. Thus the perfumed air of the Lost Cause wafted through Margaret Mitchell's depictions of old Georgia plantations and their kindly black slaves who served white masters with loyalty and devotion and enjoyed love and affection in return. It drifted, too, through films like *So Red the Rose*, a movie version of Stark Young's novel of the same name, which portrayed the white women of the plantation as the Confederacy's fiercest stalwarts and eventually as victims of untold Yankee cruelties. The Lost Cause left its mark as well on the popular Shirley Temple films of the 1930s, notably *The Littlest Rebel*, in which both Shirley and the slaves are left scratching their heads about what it even means to "free the slaves." And Lost Cause ideals likewise underscored biographer Douglas Southall Freeman's appreciative depiction of Robert E. Lee, a principled and "conscientious" leader, a man of good stock and deep Christian faith who treated slaves well and fought for his state, not to maintain black people in bondage. Writing in 1939, Freeman confirmed how much even "Northern and Western" readers had become Confederate "sympathizers," even "champions," ready to accept the belief that "the South fought its fight gallantly and, so far as war ever permits, with fairness and decency." Writing to the southern novelist Ellen Glasgow, Freeman suggested, "We Southerners had one consolation: If our fathers lost the war, you and Margaret Mitchell . . . have won the peace."[6]

The Lost Cause was not, nor had it ever been, simply the creation of writers and other creative artists. Although it had moved further away from its original core group of veterans and their descendants, it remained alive and well in the minds of many white southerners, many of whom drew on their own family stories and hand-me-down anecdotes to shape a larger worldview. For these men and women, ideas about the nobility of the Confederate cause undergirded their contemporary philosophies and beliefs. South Carolina journalist Ben Robertson fondly reminisced about his Confederate grandparents, about the stories they had told about battlefields and home-front struggles, not, he believed, to resurrect a "dead past" but to make the past "a part of the present," to be "a comfort, a guide, a lesson." Because his grandparents had never forgotten "Lee's surrender and the days of starvation in the South," they never "allowed any of us at their house to waste rations." For Robertson, in other words, every meal offered a chance to recall and reenergize the Lost Cause. Like Robertson, Philip Arnold, a Kentuckian who had moved to California, also saw in the South's Civil War past valuable lessons for the present. Reading Margaret Mitchell's work, Arnold was especially impressed by the writer's brief references to Robert E. Lee and explained that he advised "his son to imitate the fine character of Lee whom I admire above all men." Other *Gone with the Wind* fans, too, insisted the book was not an embellished rendering of the past but true to life. "Having read Gone with the wind," wrote Cornelia Arvanti from Knoxville, Tennessee, "I feel it is a true picture of the south at that particular period. . . . When my Grandmother was a little girl she lived on the outskirts of Savannah, Georgia . . . [and] told me about their saving a sack of potatoes because Mammy sat on them." Echoing the theme of the faithful "mammy," another reader likewise hoped the film producers would be able to "bring out the relation that really existed between fine white people and the loyal negroes" and to convey especially "the joyful memory of those who are old enough to have had a real 'mammy nurse.'"[7]

Among those who were particularly vigilant about upholding Lost Cause sensibilities were the white women who belonged to the United Daughters of the Confederacy (UDC), an organization founded by the female descendants of Confederate veterans in 1894 but still active in the 1930s. Dedicated to Confederate memorialization, the UDC in these years continued to give special attention to the leading men of the Confederacy: they promoted the Jefferson Davis Highway, raised funds for a statue of Davis in Montgomery, Alabama, and produced a national radio program on Robert E. Lee's birthday. They made a special effort, too, to convince national leaders to stop saying "Civil War" and instead adopt the phrase "War between the States," a term they preferred because it showed how secession proceeded "with all the dignity and weight of their State Governments back of them, after mature deliberation by conventions representing their entire populations." They also gave support to writers—like Mitchell and Freeman—who they believed helped win many northern converts to the Confederate cause. Although they balked at many of Scarlett

O'Hara's unseemly character traits, the UDC nonetheless sent Mitchell a message of appreciation for giving "a true portrayal of the relationship between the slaves and their masters such as has seldom been before presented."[8]

Yet even in the somewhat musty recesses of UDC convention halls, the Lost Cause was forced to adapt. Like many white southerners, UDC members initially gave considerable support to Franklin Roosevelt and the New Deal and often found themselves in an odd relationship with New Deal programs, even with New Deal principles. In 1933 UDC members worked to spread the fame of southern poet Sidney Lanier, proclaiming him "the Poet of the New Deal" for the way his work spoke to "the Brotherhood of Man." In 1934 the organization convened in New York for what they called their "New Deal" program. Here they assented to FDR's suggestion that they take up "the problems of this troubled time." By this point, too, state and local chapters of the organization had begun collaborating with specific New Deal agencies like the Civilian Conservation Corps (CCC) and the Civil Works Administration (CWA) and would later work with the Works Progress Administration (WPA) and the National Park Service (NPS). The Georgia division, for example, secured $29,000 from the CCC and CWA to defray costs for copying various Confederate records and repairing a home for aging veterans. In 1937 the president of the Alabama UDC attended the dedication ceremony for the Tennessee Valley Authority's Wheeler Dam, named in honor of "Fighting Joe Wheeler," a former Confederate general, Spanish-American War hero, and US congressman who worked to secure federal funding in the region. And in 1936, the UDC supported the production of a new Federal Theatre drama, a play named for the Confederacy's one and only president. Sometimes, these attempts to blend the UDC's sectionalism with the renewed federalism of the New Deal era sounded a discordant note. The reviewer for *Time* magazine found the Federal Theatre production of a play about Davis unsettling. Why, he wondered, had nobody "question[ed] the anomaly of employing Federal funds to present a waxworks glorification of an arch-enemy of the Union"? Theatergoers, too, may have felt uncomfortable with the apparent contradiction: following its twelve-day New York run, the president of the UDC concluded, "It was a mistake to produce Jefferson Davis in the North."[9]

The New York WPA production of *Jefferson Davis* may have been a bust, but it wasn't because the Lost Cause had no traction above the Mason-Dixon line. Indeed, during the 1930s some aspects of the Lost Cause message had a particularly powerful resonance for both northern and southern whites. More than anything, the Depression encouraged new regard for what was seen as white

Poster for the Federal Theatre production of John McGee's
Jefferson Davis. Although it was not one of the Federal
Theatre's more successful productions, *Jefferson Davis*
demonstrated the continued presence of the Confederate
president in the popular imagination and the efforts of the
United Daughters of the Confederacy to keep him there.
Federal Theatre Project Collection, Prints & Photographs
Division, Library of Congress.

southerners' distinct historical struggle to meet and overcome adversity. As
southerners, and Americans more broadly, battled for a measure of economic
security, the strivings of defeated southerners became newly relevant and stood
out in sharp relief. Journalist Ben Robertson was twenty-nine and living in New
York City in 1932 but found it comforting to think back on Confederate history.

He recalled his grandfather's ordeal in 1865, when he had to walk all the way back to his South Carolina home after being in a Civil War prison camp in the Hudson Valley. "During the depression of 1932," wrote Robertson, "I said to myself I need not worry too much if I lost my job—what my grandfather could do in 1865, I could do in 1932." Other white southerners urged Americans to look toward the Civil War generation for models that could be emulated in the present. Douglas Southall Freeman, famous biographer of Robert E. Lee, titled a radio address with this theme in mind. In "How a Great Leader Met Adversity," Freeman found in Lee's postwar career a model for struggling with difficult circumstances that seemed eminently relevant for Americans facing the hard times of the 1930s.[10]

When Freeman and Robertson told tales of Confederates—be it Robert E. Lee or a war-weary grandfather—struggling against adversity, they also held out a hopeful story line: the possibility that with the right spirit and gumption, Americans of the Depression could overcome their adverse circumstances, just like southerners of long ago. This was, in fact, a narrative that had considerable appeal beyond the South and offered a way to celebrate the fortitude of white men and women who had refused to let the Confederate loss turn them into second-class citizens. Perhaps nothing spoke quite as forcefully to that sentiment as Peggy Mitchell's book. True, the bulk of *Gone with the Wind* had been composed in the 1920s, but when it debuted in 1936 the reading public was deep in the throes of the Depression, hungry for a book that spoke to present-day tribulations. Mitchell believed her novel satisfied that demand. Identifying her book's central motif as "survival," Mitchell explained in a 1936 interview: "What quality is it that makes some people able to survive catastrophes and others, apparently just as brave and able and strong, go under. . . . We've all seen the same thing happen in the present depression." At the heart of this tale of survival stood Mitchell's female protagonist, Scarlett O'Hara, who, in her hard-fought quest, won the lifelong devotion of millions of female readers. "After all," wrote Marion Fritz of Menlo, Iowa, in a fan letter to Mitchell, Scarlett "wanted only what so many of us want now. Material security for our families that life may hold something but the endless drudgery of a bare existence." A reader in San Antonio, Texas, wrote to the casting director working on the film to describe a friend who would make the perfect Scarlett because she had such a personal connection to her ordeal. Scarlett, the friend insisted, "is no different from me in many respects, have I not shouldered responsibilities, smiled through insults and sneers for years? I too had everything . . . then suffering and sorrow as my father and mother were taken, insecure investments, bank failures, everything

Ann Rutherford and Evelyn Keyes play Scarlett O'Hara's sisters in a scene from *Gone with the Wind*. Depression-era audiences learned to sympathize with once-wealthy white southerners, like Scarlett O'Hara and her sisters, now forced to toil in the plantation fields. Photofest.

gone but this (meaning her home)." Summing up the book's appeal, a reviewer concluded: "The real stroke of genius is in the story of Scarlett's struggles to survive—it is the story of thousands of young (& older) women during the depression."[11]

Of course, as many critics have noted, Mitchell was hardly of one mind about "Scarlett's struggles to survive." In her inconsistencies, Mitchell spoke to the ambivalent feelings that many Depression-era Americans had about women of their own time, and perhaps even gave voice to some of the public hostility directed toward wage-earning women who were assumed to be taking jobs away from supposedly more deserving male breadwinners. Like those modern-day women, Scarlett received little praise for flaunting convention and was, in fact, punished for her transgressions, even those done in the name of survival. When Scarlett drives her own buggy through the dangerous mixed-race community of Shanty Town and is attacked by a black man, the plot line speaks not only to a long-standing hysteria about black men raping white women but also to an underlying resentment toward Scarlett, and women like her, who ventured beyond proper domestic boundaries. Despite Mitchell's intent, though, many readers, women especially, recognized the unjust social constraints imposed on Scarlett and saw in her struggles an echo of their own circumstances. "Why," one female reader in New York wondered, "should a woman always pay? Someone who has to work for theirself knows the fear Scarlett had of the future. Circumstances and people force us in to situations that our worst or our best comes out."[12]

Scarlett's central role as both survivor and sufferer speaks to a larger ambiguity that pervaded Depression-era writings about the southern Confederacy and the treatment of the Lost Cause. There was, on the one hand, the powerful resonance of loss that drew 1930s readers, men and women, to Mitchell's book. "Men broken by the depression," wrote Mississippi writer Edwin Granberry, "pour out their hearts to Miss Mitchell in sympathy for Ashley, who also was broken by change and upheaval of war and reconstruction." Yet, to simply succumb to the devastation ran counter to the "triumph over adversity" theme that was so pervasive in American culture. And so historians, like Douglas Southall Freeman, as well as novelists shaped their Confederate characters to be more than just victims, to show them struggling to rise above their circumstances, to make them relevant for the modern era and the current crisis. Like Mitchell, novelist Caroline Gordon also wrote about the dispossessed plantation aristocracy and their determination to make the best of a bad situation. In Gordon's 1937 novel *None Shall Look Back*, the survivors included former slaveholder Jim Allard, who reprimands his sister when she criticizes him for working in a store. "You'll see Allards doing lots of things you never thought to see before you're through with it," he explains. Although a reluctant convert to commercial capitalism, Jim Allard, like Scarlett O'Hara, casts his lot with the new economic order, making him emblematic of both the southern experience of defeat and a deeply American impulse to succeed.[13]

Yet in the 1930s, the success message could be a complicated one to peddle, especially given how tenuous success had become in these years of capitalist crisis. It was one thing, after all, to celebrate southerners' gumption, but celebrating their willingness to beat the Yankees at their own game, as Scarlett would put it, could also seem too much like joining forces with an economic system that was not only on the verge of collapse but also responsible for so much misery. Hence storekeeping held few, if any, charms for Gordon's characters, who did what they had to do just to get by. In a different way, Mitchell, too, questioned the worthiness of the new economic order, notably by making a woman the

foremost representative of emerging capitalism—Scarlett takes over her husband's store and starts a lumber mill—and holding up the old-fashioned Mela-
nie Wilkes as the true exemplar of female goodness. Scarlett's lust for economic
success thus taints the image Mitchell presents of postwar capitalism. Other
authors, especially those affiliated with the literary group known as Agrarians,
made their hostility to industrial capitalism, and their preference for the ways
and traditions of the Old South, explicit. Writers like Stark Young, Allen Tate
(husband of Caroline Gordon), and John Crowe Ransom pointedly ignored
the capitalist foundations of the Old South, not to mention its dependence on
racial exploitation, and helped craft an image of antebellum Dixie as a place
largely free of profit-seeking impulses. For these writers, the spirit of the Old
South was embodied in its dedication to humane and aesthetic values. Their
writings—which included historical novels as well as biographical portraits—
not only encouraged sympathy for struggling Confederates but also spoke to
anxieties and frustrations about the current crisis of capitalism and enshrined
an image of the Old South as a place of superior values and mores. This kind
of thinking had the power to encourage broad, even national, support for Lost
Cause ideas in the Depression decade. When members of Congress supported
a resolution to have a monument erected to Stonewall Jackson, the Confederate
commander was praised for what were seen as his typical Old South values: his
"high sense of honor and chivalry" and his "freedom from sordid ambition for
wealth or notoriety."[14]

In this way, the Lost Cause narrative of the 1930s merged almost seamlessly with another story line: an origin story about the source of the South's
Depression-era suffering. In this origin story, southern whites explained their
current poverty not by faulting their own weaknesses, or their own complicity
with exploitative practices, but by attributing blame exclusively to "the North"
and its presumably "sordid ambition." Often this story was told in a way that
blurred together the travails of black and white, all portrayed as people of "the
South" who had anguished and endured together since the Civil War days. Mississippi poet William Percy believed the troubles of the postwar era gradually
impressed on "ex-slave and ex-master" alike that "they were in great need of
one another—and not only economically, but curiously enough, emotionally."
The implication seemed to be that trying circumstances, inflicted by the North,
brought black and white together as "southerners" and that both races together
felt the burdens of "the Lost Cause." Similar tales of woe were told to Lorena
Hickok as she traveled southern back roads in 1933 and '34. It was also the story
North Carolina journalist Jonathan Daniels heard when he toured the South in

1937 and met a Mississippi state official who explained how the North set the slaves free but then "made the whole South slave." Depression-era culture frequently engaged in this kind of appropriation of the specific hurts of the black experience for downtrodden whites, even going so far as to cast white people as the real victims of "slavery." But white southerners also told a version of this story in which they merged black struggles and white struggles into a common portrait of "the South," depicting a region that had been brought to its knees by Yankee greed since the end of the Civil War. Journalist Ben Robertson reflected on his own South Carolina upbringing and found evidence of mutual needs and mutual sorrows, of white folks and black telling stories of hardship and seeking solace in the same types of songs and hymns, all of which made them uniquely "southern." My family and I, Robertson said, "have always been like the colored man in 'Old Man River' who when he was tired of living was also scared of dying." Robertson echoed the same sentiment voiced by Jonathan Daniels's Mississippi informant: "The Civil War gave the slaves their freedom, but the Southern white folks lost the war, so for thirty years after the surrender we all had to work like slaves in our country—the white and the black."[15]

Blaming the North was hardly a new feature in Lost Cause thinking, but the impulse to fault Yankees assumed particular urgency during the Depression, since it established just who bore responsibility for a portrait of misery that was becoming increasingly widespread. Pictures of southern poverty, in fact, became commonplace in the Depression years as both writers and photographers—many anxious to arouse public sympathy and increased funding—presented scenes of dilapidated dwellings, struggling sharecroppers, and barefoot and underdressed children. When the Agrarian writer Donald Davidson reviewed one such account, Margaret Bourke-White and Erskine Caldwell's photo essay *You Have Seen Their Faces*, he praised the pictures of the South's rural poor but lamented the "punily, sickeningly, incomplete" narrative because it failed to explain how all southerners, black and white, had been held, by the North, "in a bondage that is more subtle because the chains and indentures are not actually visible." The impulse to fault Yankees for southern misery even played out in a fiery debate over postage stamps. When Roosevelt encouraged the US Post Office to put the faces of Civil War leaders on its stamps, whites in Georgia reacted with outrage: putting William Sherman's countenance on a letter was an offense because he had devastated "this section of the South to such an extent that it has never fully recovered." Urging a boycott of the Sherman stamp, the Atlanta chapter of the UDC alluded to the way Sherman's March had been a kind of precursor to present-day miseries: "The only stamp to bear a likeness of Sherman," they argued, "should be a blackened chimney with a mother and her children grouped at its base homeless," an image that seemed as relevant to the 1930s as to the 1860s.[16]

Of course, not all white southerners clung to Lost Cause dogma, whether in its nineteenth-century gospel or its updated 1930s iteration. By the 1920s, there were already some southern writers and artists, including the aforementioned Caldwell, who had begun to question some of the foundational myths about the Confederacy. By the 1930s, others joined the ranks of these southern skeptics. These were men and women who had some exposure to interracial work, or who saw validity in the era's intensified black protest, or who simply felt ideologically and politically confined by the old-line mentality. Some of these folks also began, in the 1930s, to cast their lot, and their ballots, with Roosevelt and his more liberal wing of the Democratic Party as opposed to the old guard of white supremacist politicians, like the notoriously racist Mississippi governor and senator Theodore Bilbo. The Georgia writer Lillian Smith, for example, started a new literary journal in 1936 with the stated goal of rejecting the "sterile fetishism of the Old South which has so long gripped our section." Writer Katharine Lumpkin, a one-time darling of the Confederate veteran circuit, likewise found herself questioning the Lost Cause myth as she became more cognizant of the outrages perpetrated on southern blacks. Seeing the racial and economic turmoil that came in the wake of World War I, Lumpkin surmised that the South did not simply suffer from the strangulation of northern capital but had been complicit in creating its own poverty, which had caught blacks and some whites in a particularly oppressive grip. Over time, Lumpkin came to reexamine the "loyal slave" version of history and learned that "masses of ex-slaves . . . had volunteered to serve in the armies of Abraham Lincoln."[17]

Alongside the Lumpkins and the Smiths, there were more moderate Lost Cause critics, too—men and women who clung to racist assumptions but were now more critical of the way the old sensibilities kept white southerners trapped in political and economic stagnation. Prominent in this group was the liberal North Carolina journalist Jonathan Daniels, who embarked on a legendary journey across the South in 1937. Stopping off in Atlanta to spend some time with Margaret Mitchell, Daniels saw in the famous author a woman who presented a modern facade but remained trapped in the old regional mentality and its romanticized portrait of the plantation aristocracy. "Atlanta," Daniels wrote in his travel account, "has demonstrated that if the Lost Cause is gone with the wind, it still sells like Coca-Cola." Daniels did not object so much to Mitchell's stereotyped portrayal of southern slaves, but he did resent her worshipful tone toward the southern elite, and her ability to cash in on that worship.[18]

While no fan of FDR or the New Deal, William Faulkner likewise turned his attention in the 1930s to the mind-numbing power of the Lost Cause and its ability to obscure the complicated realities of the southern past. Several of Faulkner's characters—like the much-abused Rosa Coldfield of *Absalom, Absalom!* and the disgraced Reverend Hightower of *Light in August*—are tragically caught up in the myths and misplaced hero worship of Lost Cause romanticism. Even in *The Unvanquished*, most of which was serialized in 1934 in the *Saturday Evening Post* and is often judged to be one of Faulkner's unusual bids for mainstream attention, the Mississippi writer seemed to be doing more than just cashing in on the Civil War craze. In the final portion of the novel, the one section not serialized in the *Post*, Faulkner puts some unexpected critical distances between his central character, Bayard Sartoris, and Confederate romanticism when Bayard rebels against the expectations of southern "honor" by refusing to assassinate his father's killer.[19]

Writers like Faulkner, Lumpkin, and Daniels, fully cognizant of white southerners' own tendencies toward self-delusion and even self-destruction, pushed back against one of the prominent Lost Cause motifs of the 1930s: the tendency to fault Yankees for all of the South's post–Civil War woes. The "blame the North" strategy also lost some traction in the early years of the New Deal era as the North, at least in the eyes of some southern whites, seemed less blameworthy. Many of the region's working-class whites welcomed the initial intrusions of Roosevelt's government, especially when those initiatives promised improved conditions and benefits for the South's industrial sector. Some even hailed FDR for heralding a new era that would break the chains of "industrial slavery" and bring southern workers "industrial freedom." As late as 1939 a few southern leaders remained hopeful that FDR's administration would reverse the historical tendencies that kept their region "in hock to the remainder of the nation." As Florida senator Claude Pepper explained, perhaps this time the federal government had gotten it right and could provide the South with "A New Deal in Reconstruction."[20]

Still, over the course of the 1930s, plenty of southern whites came to believe, or at least promoted the belief, that the "New Deal" wasn't much different from the old. The more Roosevelt ramped up efforts in the South, the more he stirred up the outrage of southern elites and triggered the never-quite-dormant memories of the Lost Cause and especially the hostile narrative about the evils of

Reconstruction. Although he relied on powerful southern Democrats to shape and support New Deal legislation, Roosevelt also angered whites who resisted any tampering with long-standing southern practices such as the reduced wages paid in southern factories and the refusal to put black field hands on relief rolls for fear they would no longer be available for cheap, seasonal labor. Even during his first term, some political and economic leaders in the South had begun to resist New Deal directives, explaining their opposition to Roosevelt with respect to historic regional grievances. "The South," insisted the head of Alabama Fuel and Iron, "is worse off as a result of the Roosevelt Administration than it was as a result of the Civil War."[21]

In FDR's second term, the fight intensified. Frustrated at the limited effect New Deal programs were having, after 1936 Roosevelt doubled down on efforts to bring the South into line. Specifically, he began looking toward a new crop of liberal Democratic politicians—men like Senator Pepper of Florida and Lawrence Camp in Georgia—who might ease the way for more liberal New Deal reform. He undertook, too, a new and more highly publicized campaign that would signal his administration's interest in the economic uplift of the southern region. These efforts culminated in 1938 with the commissioning of a report on the southern economy, *The Report on the Economic Conditions of the South,* and with Roosevelt's efforts to aid several liberal southern white Democratic candidates running for office. Simultaneously, Roosevelt and the national Democratic Party also took some very cautious steps to encourage African American participation in the old party of Jefferson and Jackson.[22]

Despite attempts to break the stranglehold of tradition, Roosevelt, as well as liberal southerners, trod carefully in their work, trying to remain sensitive to Lost Cause attitudes. Claude Pepper in no way challenged the story line that held the North and the federal government responsible for all of the South's post–Civil War ills; he merely suggested that Roosevelt's legacy would be different. The authors of the *Report on the Economic Conditions of the South* also honored elements of the Lost Cause, even as they tried to push the South in a more "modern" and forward-thinking direction. For example, the document consistently employed the phrase "War between the States," never the supposedly offensive term "Civil War." The report also paid homage to a Confederate past, to "a population still holding the great heritages of King's Mountain and Shiloh." Perhaps most notably, the report refused to think about causes when it came to southern poverty, almost always phrasing the situation in the passive voice. Indeed, Roosevelt himself insisted, in his introductory letter, that the report would not explore "the long history of how this situation came to be—

the long and ironic history of the despoiling of this truly American section of the country's population." Instead, the report hewed closely to a simplified version of the origin story of southern suffering: "Ever since the War between the States the South has been the poorest section of the Nation."[23]

The report dovetailed with other efforts by Roosevelt to assuage southern white feelings regarding the Confederate past. Like other politicians on the national stage, FDR spoke in many tongues when it came to Civil War memory: he was fluent in the language of reconciliation, yet could also voice Lost Cause sentiments, even while bringing renewed attention to a pro-Union and pro-Lincoln perspective. FDR's speech at the seventy-fifth anniversary of the Battle of Gettysburg made much of Lincoln offering "solace for all who fought upon this field[,] . . . men who wore the blue and men who wore the gray," even though Lincoln really had only Union men in mind in his Gettysburg Address. Throughout the years of his presidency, Roosevelt also visited and honored Confederate shrines and heaped praise on men like Robert E. Lee and Stonewall Jackson. "We recognize Robert E. Lee," Roosevelt intoned at the unveiling of a Robert E. Lee memorial in Dallas, Texas, in 1936, "as one of our greatest American Christians and one of our greatest American gentlemen." By and large, though, Roosevelt seemed most comfortable depicting Confederates like Lee as symbols from a long-ago era; they were men who, while certainly noble, seemed to have diminished relevance for current problems and concerns. In the "greeting" Roosevelt sent for the dedication of Lee's home in Stratford, Virginia, he hailed "the memory of that very great gentleman, Robert E. Lee" and praised this "permanent memorial to a brave, young civilization for which modern America will always be grateful." By contrast, Roosevelt never used a quaint phrase like "gentleman" to talk about Lincoln, nor would he have dichotomized Lincoln's "young civilization" with "modern America." Rather, he spoke about the sixteenth president's "spirit," which demonstrated "that men and means will be found to explore and conquer the problems of a new time with no less humanity and no less fortitude than his."[24]

If FDR suggested that the Confederate spirit—as opposed to Lincoln's— had diminished relevance for the current crisis, this was confirmed in the central take-away point in the 1938 economic report. As Roosevelt explained in his much-quoted opening letter, the report affirmed his "conviction that the South presents right now the Nation's No. 1 economic problem—the Nation's problem, not merely the South's." Not surprisingly, calling the South a national "problem" hardly sat well with Lost Cause beliefs, especially in the apparent denigration of persisting southern "traditions" and with the insistence that the solutions to southern problems would come not from southern initiatives but from national ones. Consequently, the economic report, along with Roosevelt's political efforts to promote southern liberals in various senate and congressional campaigns, set the stage for a howling retrenchment to Lost Cause principles. Conservative politicians as well as a wide array of southern white writers loudly insisted on the superiority of the South's "way of life," on the correctness of "states' rights" codes, and on their version of the origin story, which put the blame for southern poverty squarely on the shoulders of Yankee, and especially carpetbagging, meddlers.[25]

Thus Virginia author Clifford Dowdey bristled when northerners asked him if southerners were "still fighting the Civil War": they had no choice but to keep the war going, he maintained, especially if Yankees were going to turn them into a "problem." Writing in the *Southern Literary Messenger* in 1939, Dowdey pushed back, reminding readers about Confederates' "courage and fortitude and stouthearted convictions as sources of strength for us to draw upon." Moreover, Dowdey called out the real source of the current calamity: "This section was pillaged by its conquerors and excluded from financial expression . . . until today the national President can say it constitutes the nation's number one economic problem." Dowdey's friend Margaret Mitchell heard "so many yells of 'states' rights' and 'Northern oppression' and 'sinister centralization of power' and so many bands playing 'Dixie' that I have wondered whether this was 1938 or 1861." Attributing this new sectional spirit to Roosevelt's support for southern liberals, Mitchell sympathized with her oppressed countrymen and saved her particular ire for northern critics who urged the South to just get over their history. Like Dowdey, she also zeroed in on the postwar Reconstruction era as the central moment of Yankee exploitation. The legacy of northern exploitation in the South, Mitchell argued, which dated back to Appomattox, meant the issues of the war had never really gone away. Perhaps, Mitchell suggested sarcastically, "when a section has been held in economic slavery for over seventy years that section should have the delicacy of feeling not to squawk."[26]

Because *Gone with the Wind* remained so prominently in the news, especially with highly publicized efforts to cast and begin production of the much-anticipated film, it emerged as a lightning rod for these efforts to strengthen the hand of the Lost Cause narrative, becoming a highly politicized work of popular culture. One reviewer, for example, called Mitchell's work "deeply significant as a national recognition of the undying traditions of the Old South," a point which stood clearly at odds with recent talk "about the South being 'the nation's Number 1 economic problem.'" This assessment, the writer claimed,

prompted a lot of "idiotic tomfoolery . . . that the romanticism and sentimen-
talism of the South was at fault for the depletion of her soil, the difficulties of
Reconstruction and poverty of her cotton belt." In fact, "the chivalry of the Old
South must be the foundation upon which that reconstruction and recovery are
built." Discussions about the possibility of federal involvement in southern state
elections prompted a North Carolina senator to reflect on the inherent truth
of Mitchell's novel: "The story," with its tragic "fall of Atlanta" and then "the
dread aftermath of Federal control which was worse than the war," he insisted,
"is not overdrawn."[27]

More than the economic report and more than Roosevelt's campaign on
behalf of southern liberals or election reform, it was the direct efforts to challenge white supremacy and the South's Jim Crow "tradition" that sent southern
writers, politicians, and other members of the white ruling elite back to the history books, and sometimes to Mitchell's novel, to take a stand on behalf of the
Lost Cause and especially the Confederate interpretation of Reconstruction.
This conversation reached a fever pitch in the debates over the lynching outrage, the murderous attacks on black men and women taking place with sick-
ening frequency, primarily in the South. Seeking to take advantage of some of
Roosevelt's seemingly more progressive views regarding race, members of the
NAACP had renewed their antilynching campaign and worked with political
representatives to craft and promote a law that would allow the federal government the right to prosecute lynchers in cases where a state had refused to do
so, while also imposing fines on local officials who were negligent in carrying
out their duties. Known as the Costigan-Wagner Bill because of its Democratic
sponsors in the Senate, the bill failed to overcome a Senate filibuster in 1935 and
then came before Congress again in 1937–38. Although the bill passed in the
House, it met intense opposition in the Senate and never earned FDR's support.
It also gave southern white politicians a new and vitriolic platform for rehears-
ing a viciously white supremacist narrative about the war and especially about
Reconstruction.[28]

In the debates on the antilynching bill, southern politicians returned to the
theme of Yankee culpability, using the history of "carpetbagger" interference
to insist that any type of federal meddling would lead to a frightening uptick in
black power and a ruthless campaign of terror against southern whites, especially southern white women. Senator Charles Andrews told of the way some
black people "were led by a horde of carpetbaggers into a philosophy of disrespect and contempt of the few masters who returned from the battlefields" and
how "many helpless female white children and widows of Confederate soldiers

were ravished and slain." Even the liberal Florida senator, Claude Pepper, believed the federal antilynching law would make the "New Deal" like the old one, leading to "a return to the shackles of reconstruction days upon the backs of our people." Reconstruction, Senator "Cotton Ed" Smith of South Carolina insisted, "brought into existence the theory and principle and practice that exslaves should be the legislators and judges, and that rapine and lust should have no check." Smith used this language to great effect in local political contests as well as in the federal legislature, accusing his more liberal opponent of forgetting the way Reconstruction had brought "black feet pressed on white heads [and] . . . the flowers of the solid South." This forgetfulness, he implied, would reopen the door to new federal meddling and racial upheaval.[29]

South Carolina state representative John Long, meanwhile, made his point in a different way: by urging his colleagues to raise the Confederate flag inside their chamber in the state capitol. Although Long, an ardent white supremacist, made no explicit mention of the lynching debate, it seems more than a coincidence that he introduced his resolution early in 1938, just after the debate had concluded. For Long and his colleagues, raising the flag likely symbolized the point made by US senator William Borah: that southerners had the right to challenge any law or policy, today or in the past, which promoted the idea that "the southern people are to be distrusted and are incapable of local self-government." Finally, as several senators implied, the federal law would again threaten the unity of white people by injecting "the same element of strife and contention that ran rife" during Reconstruction, an implicit reference to bringing African Americans into politics. This, in fact, may have been white southerners' chief point of concern: a fear that the Democratic Party might start to shift its gaze to northern black voters, which might in turn lead to more direct challenges to Jim Crow practices in the South and eventually undermine the white supremacist edifice. Southern white politicians' response, then, entailed a fervent reminder to their constituents about the horrors of Reconstruction in order to promote themselves as the champions of white supremacy committed to keeping their party racially "pure." The success these politicians had in beating back their liberal challengers at the local level offers a strong indication that, despite New Deal benefits, the Lost Cause narrative remained powerfully influential among southern white voters.[30]

Perhaps another reason behind the popularity of this reinvigorated Lost Cause message had to do with the new political overtones the debate assumed. During the 1930s, many southern leaders pushed the Lost Cause in a new and politically insidious direction by connecting it to the mounting anticommunist hysteria of the interwar years. White southerners, politicians as well as some writers and intellectuals, imagined the Lost Cause, as well as the white South's triumph over Reconstruction, as a defiant bulwark against the communist menace, especially as they increasingly linked "northern-led" communists of the Depression period with the antislavery and civil rights activists of the past—like abolitionists and carpetbaggers. This line of argument enhanced the contemporary relevance of "Old South" values, offering white southerners yet another reason to feel invested in their regional and political affiliations. Additionally, such thinking made it easier to portray radical activists of the twentieth century, some of whom had deep roots in the South, as the same kind of "outside agitators" who had haunted Dixie's past. Whether in the past or in the present, northern agitation was assumed to have a detrimental effect on southern race relations, especially in opening the door to that most deplorable of outrages: the threat of black men's sexual violence against white women.

The communist "threat," of course, was not wholly abstract for many white southerners during the 1920s and '30s. As the US Communist Party began to formulate a strategy focused on "self-determination in the Black Belt," party members turned their attention to working with African Americans, especially sharecroppers and factory workers, throughout the southern states. Although the plan to work both for a separate African American nation and for full social equality within the United States was problematic and contradictory, it none-theless focused US communists' attention on challenging racial oppression in Dixie. Some who aligned themselves with this program were homegrown radi-cals, both blacks and whites who had already committed themselves to fighting injustice. Others were "expatriates," men and women who because of their pro-gressive beliefs felt compelled to leave the South. Still others were the "outside agitators" of myth and legend: men and women of both races, many of whom made multiyear commitments to the fight against Jim Crow. By 1931, a small but determined communist presence appeared in the South, allowing the party to bring concerted attention to one of its first significant antiracist campaigns: the movement to free the "Scottsboro boys," nine young black men who had been pulled from a train in Alabama and falsely charged with raping two white women.[31]

The case—including communist efforts to defend the Scottsboro boys—quickly attracted attention, and in response a number of conservative southern whites deployed a particularly venomous stream of historical memory, spe-cifically about Reconstruction-era carpetbaggers, to condemn the communist "menace." "If one could just shut his eyes for a bit," wrote the editor of the *Jack-*

son County (Alabama) Sentinel, "he would think the years had dropped away and the Civil War had just ended and dark days of Reconstruction were in full bloom. . . . Seventy years ago the scalawags and carpetbaggers marched in the South with negro troops and said to the white people: 'The Negro is your equal and you will accept him as such.' Today in 1933, the Reds of New York march into the South . . . and again say, 'The Negro is your equal and you will accept him as such.'" Interestingly, the analogy obscured any notion of southern-bred radicalism, in either the 1930s or the 1860s, as even "scalawags," a term once used to describe southern supporters of Republican Reconstruction, were por-trayed as nonsouthern troublemakers. It also invested the "Reds of New York" with all the traditional horrors associated with the Reconstruction era: just as Reconstruction had presumably encouraged black men to rape white women, so would communists, in their defense of black men accused of rape, open the door to interracial sex.[32]

Offering an unusually sustained elaboration of this argument, the Agrarian writer and historian Frank Owsley made his case at the American Historical Association meeting in 1933. The communists' defense of Scottsboro, Owsley insisted, represented the "third crusade," the sequel to abolitionism and carpet-bagging, in that all three represented "the interference of the North—usually the Northeast—with the relationship between the whites and blacks of the South." Even more, each one showed how northern crusaders cloaked them-selves in a moralistic guise that obscured their real "motives of material gain." In each situation, Owsley insisted, northern activists aimed to gain power for industrialists, capitalist industrialists in the first two cases and "proletarian-industrialists" in the third. Owsley saw in all of this a particularly important, but apparently unlearned, lesson for "the Negro": he "should have learned . . . that . . . the relationship good or bad between himself and the white race of the South must be settled between them" with no outside interference. More ominously: the failure to learn this lesson would inevitably result in a vicious reaction from southern whites, who had in the past, and would in the future, seek violent retribution against African Americans.[33]

With outside northern agitators at the helm of these wrongheaded and misguided crusades, it was up to the South to push back. The Depression, as Owsley and others saw it, reflected capitalism's inherent weakness, including its inability to combat the threat of proletarian industrialism. Whatever form it took, though, industrialism "would face the same irrepressible conflict with agrarianism as existed under the old capitalistic industrialism." The Civil War, in effect, was being replayed, with "the South" taking up a timeless struggle against industrialism, this time in the form of communism. "The South," Owsley concluded, "is probably the greatest obstacle to Communism."[34]

Owsley thus made explicit a line of argument others only gestured toward. Ben Robertson heard this kind of talk when he encountered a group of unemployed South Carolina mill workers who, Robertson claimed, were afraid to join labor unions, especially when the delegates for those unions came from the North: "They remembered the carpetbaggers." Interestingly, Jonathan Daniels heard something similar in those same mill districts, only in this case from owners, not workers, who equated CIO leader John Lewis, a presumed henchman of the "Red Revolution," with John Brown and vowed to take their stand "in saving America" from this radical onslaught. Daniels heard these sentiments echoed again in the words of Agrarian writer Allen Tate, who railed against northerners pouring into the South to organize sharecroppers. "His voice," Daniels noted, "sounded of carpetbaggers and Reconstruction." The image of the communist-cum-Reconstruction-agitator may have even informed the work of William Faulkner, specifically in the writing of his 1932 novel, *Light in August*. In that book, Joanna Burden is "a foreigner whose people moved in from the North during Reconstruction." Granddaughter of a northern carpetbagger, she is described as "a Yankee" and "a lover of negroes." Like her ancestor, Joanna has a plan for Negro uplift, and specifically for reforming her protégé and lover, the mysterious and seemingly mixed-race Joe Christmas. And as with her ancestor, Joanna's plan, which involves meddling with southern race relations, ends in disaster for all concerned. In a sense, then, Joanna appears "as covert communist, racial renegade ... who yokes in her plan racial uplift and miscegenation." As some literary scholars have suggested, Faulkner himself "assented to this discourse in part because he viewed Reconstruction as not only a disaster but one in danger of being repeated."[35]

Over the course of the 1930s, as the communist presence in the South grew, as civil rights activists intensified their efforts to end lynching and other Jim Crow practices, and as Lost Causers retrenched further into a celebration of "southern" values against New Deal intrusions, southern whites girded themselves to push back against the abolitionist-carpetbagger-communist threat. Margaret Mitchell, never a friend of radical politics, believed communists had essentially found their new cause for southern rabble-rousing in her book. "The Communists," she wrote in a 1937 letter to her publisher, "have been using my book to sweep the Southern Negroes into the Communist Party even as the Abolitionists once used 'Uncle Tom's Cabin' to rally the Northern Anti-slavery sentiment." In 1939 Mitchell told her friend Susan Myrick "how happy" she was that "the Radical publications dislike 'Gone With the Wind.' I couldn't have held up my head if they had liked it." Over the next few years, Mitchell became an even more fervent anticommunist, working at one point with the notorious anticommunist journalist Westbrook Pegler and apparently keeping a "Red" file with material about southern "fellow travelers."[36]

Meanwhile, the figure of the communist–abolition agitator put in some noteworthy appearances in popular culture, including a Hollywood film directed by the Hungarian-born director Michael Curtiz. Before directing the film that would catapult him to ever-lasting fame, the 1942 motion picture *Casablanca*, Curtiz made a far less acclaimed movie in 1940 called *The Santa Fe Trail*. Having little to do with Santa Fe or the trail, the movie focused instead on John Brown (played by one-time Lincoln delineator Raymond Massey), his antislavery crusade in Kansas, and the efforts of both northern and southern men in the US Army to stamp out Brown's incendiary campaign. The film opens at West Point, where cadets from both the North and the South are training together "under a brilliant Commandant named Robert E. Lee." Aside from Jeb Stuart (Errol Flynn) and George Custer (Ronald Reagan), the film also introduces "Rader" (Van Heflin), a northern man who rants against southern slaveholders and their abuse of "Negro slaves" and reads from a book by John Brown that calls for breaking up the "American union as it now exists" and reorganizing it "on the great principle of emancipation." Rader seems to be cut precisely from the kind of cloth described by historian Frank Owsley: he proclaims abolitionist tenets and speaks an "inflammatory" and treasonous discourse but also has a very weak claim on moral principles. Though he upbraids Jeb Stuart for southerners' mistreatment of the enslaved, Rader abuses his own horse, while Stuart demonstrates a more humane approach to equine care. Eventually Rader is dismissed from West Point when Lee discovers that he has been asked by someone in the "abolitionist party" to distribute material to potential recruits to the antislavery cause. If Rader, then, is the radicals' front man, John Brown is abolitionism-communism's heart and soul: not only fanatical about the cause but even insincere about religion, making one wonder if even the Bible-toting Brown might have been a godless communist. At one point, soldiers come upon him transporting boxes marked "Holy Bibles" which turn out to contain guns. Like other "outside agitators," Brown knows nothing about the real nature of black-white relations. Indeed, a black family being sheltered by Brown eventually tell Jeb Stuart that they're not interested in John Brown's version of freedom and would rather go home to Texas. Finally, the film assigns the main responsibility for fighting the abolitionist menace, whether it is Rader or John Brown, to Jeb Stuart, the representative of all that is southern and emblematic of the Lost Cause. He is the one who challenges Rader's "treason"—Reagan's Custer is much more timid—and insists, despite objections from others, that Brown be hanged for his crimes.[37]

There seemed, then, to be something in southerners' DNA, particularly southerners of the old-timey Lost Cause type, which put them at the forefront of the anticommunist fight. Before titling their collection *I'll Take My Stand*, some of the contributors to the Agrarian manifesto had even thought of calling their book *Tracts against Communism*. A 1932 play "written for the Taylor Family Association"—as in Zachary Taylor—recounted an imagined relationship between Abraham Lincoln and a Confederate major who tells the sixteenth president that southerners dislike disunion but "can not brook the communistic attitude which seeks to imperil their personal prerogative." In 1939, the United Daughters of the Confederacy insisted that nobody was better fitted for "exterminating" communism than the "Daughters of the Confederacy, with their heritage of conviction and loyalty to the principles of the Founders."[38]

And then there was Cindy Lou Bethany, an extremely unlikely yet nonetheless effective soldier in the southern war against communism. Cindy Lou was the central character in Clare Boothe's 1938 popular Broadway farce, *Kiss the Boys Good-Bye*, a satirical take on the crazy Hollywood search for an unknown southern actress to play the part of Scarlett O'Hara in the film version of *Gone with the Wind*. In Boothe's play, the story revolves around casting "Velvet O'Toole" in the film version of *Kiss the Boys Good-Bye*. Having been brought to Connecticut to meet the film's producer, Cindy Lou comes to the home of Leslie and Horace Rand, where she encounters a bizarre and generally unpleasant assortment of characters. This includes her inhospitable hosts, the seasoned Hollywood actress who also wants the part, a newspaper editor, a dim-witted polo player, and Madison Breed, a left-wing journalist who constantly attacks Cindy Lou as the epitome of Ku Kluxism and southern fascism. Although nearly all the characters display despicable qualities, the play saves much of its sympathy for Cindy Lou, the victim of constant mocking from condescending northerners. "Look away! Look away! Dixie's landed!" one houseguest cracks when Cindy Lou appears in an elaborate southern belle getup. Ultimately, as one reviewer suggested, Cindy Lou "comes out on top because she is the only one carefully enough conceived to have much credibility." The play's dramatic turning point occurs when everyone in the Rands' home has turned against Cindy, deeming her an overly sentimental stereotype of the Old South and a bad actress to boot. But this Velvet wannabe wins over at least some of the

crowd when she finally confronts Breed, who has been opportunistically riling
up the Rands' black servants and delivering a constant spew of personal attacks
at Cindy and her family. Calling Breed a "damn Yankee pole-cat," she charges
into his ample stomach and knocks him off his feet. "You accept these people's
hospitality," Cindy Lou rants against Breed, "and then turn their own servants
against them! You take Mr. Wickfield's [the newspaper editor's] money here,
and aim to call a sit-down strike on his very own paper!" With this one act of
bravado, Cindy Lou wins the love of the dim-witted polo player and the coveted
movie role. In the end, good old southern values have apparently triumphed
over vituperative northern radicalism.[39]

One year later, though, Boothe's agenda had apparently shifted. As Nazi aggression was on the rise, Boothe may have been less inclined to champion the
Lost Cause, which had already become associated in some circles with fascist
tendencies, and more interested in proclaiming an anti-Nazi point of view. Having already earned success with her production The Women (1936), and now
married to Henry Luce, the extremely successful magazine mogul, Boothe took
a different tack altogether when she penned an introduction to the published
version of Kiss the Boys Good-bye in 1939. Now Boothe explained that her real
objective had been to present "a political allegory about Fascism in America,"
specifically by connecting fascism to "southernism" and in demonstrating "the
first coming of Fascism out of Dixie." Because this was an appealing type of fascism, one that disguised itself behind the kind of emotionalism and patriotism
of people like Cindy Lou Bethany, Boothe believed Americans had been admiring fascism for years: "'Southernism' is a particular and highly matured form of
Fascism with which America has lived more or less peacefully for seventy-five
years." Yet, for all her passion about this point, Boothe's message was apparently
missed entirely by critics and viewers. As one Chicago reviewer observed, "Both
critics and general public missed the point of the play, as Miss Boothe envisaged
that point." When she learned that Boothe's play was meant to be "a serious
expose" about southern fascism, Margaret Mitchell laughed out loud.[40]

In the time that elapsed between the first performance of Boothe's play and
its 1939 publication, the associations between anticommunism and the Lost
Cause may well have lacked their earlier potency. At the same time, world events
were encouraging writers and artists to showcase their personal abhorrence
of fascism. After The Santa Fe Trail appeared, actor Raymond Massey said he
hoped his performance as John Brown would remind audiences in 1940 of Adolf
Hitler. With US involvement in an antifascist war all but certain, Boothe and
Massey may have engaged in a kind of retrospective antifascism about their

earlier work. Additionally, like many non–Popular Front artists and pundits in the late 1930s and early 1940s, Boothe and Massey probably found the distinction between different forms of "totalitarianism" to be relatively minor. Nonetheless, both Boothe's play and Massey's film built on a discourse that equated abolitionism and other types of northern "meddling" in the South with communism and that saw particularly dire consequences for American values if such tendencies were left unchecked. Describing Reconstruction-era politics, Boothe herself wrote of "the carpet-bagger inspired Communism of the Negro" and speculated that it was this "Northern-agitated" movement that bore ultimate responsibility for encouraging the rise of "the Southern Fascist."[41]

Of course long before Boothe discovered "the Southern Fascist," many other writers, activists, and artists had pinpointed this phenomenon, making explicit connections between southernism, or really Jim Crow, with fascism. During the 1930s, as Hitler assumed and consolidated power in Germany, activists working in the South increasingly drew connections between the Nazi assault on Jews and Jim Crow's assault on African Americans. Black and white communists, as well as members and leaders of the NAACP, saw in southern lynchings, Ku Kluxism, and other forms of racial oppression a strong reverberation of the international fascist agenda. Even the NAACP's James Weldon Johnson made reference to "the Fascist South," while a black newspaper told of Hitler's rise to power with the headline "Adolph Hitler, KKK." As historian Glenda Gilmore puts it: "African Americans compared Jim Crow with Nazi oppression to unsettle white supremacy's place in a democratic system." Their work, too, was designed to make it difficult for white liberals to raise the cry against Hitler without also thinking about Jim Crow. It was, Gilmore maintains, an effective strategy that, for several years, allied American blacks and American Jews, while also providing a common frame of reference for one-time adversaries in the Communist Party USA (CPUSA) and the NAACP.[42]

So potent were the comparisons between Jim Crow and Nazi Germany, the analogy spread from left-wing to more mainstream circles during the 1930s, finding its way into the work of southern writers who worried that the economic crisis of the Depression may have been pushing the South's extremist tendencies to the surface. Clarence Cason, writing in 1935, saw "a peculiar type of Fascism . . . below the Potomac, although the southern states have not yet produced a Mussolini or a Hitler." Years later, southern writer W. J. Cash would develop a similar point in his notion of the South's "savage ideal," which he compared with "Fascist Italy," Germany, and Soviet Russia. Even *Gone with the Wind* producer David Selznick revealed some awareness that "an anti-Negro film"—*Birth of a*

Nation may have been foremost in his mind—would not play well in "fascist-ridden times." Writers like Cash and Cason rooted the South's fascist tendencies in its reaction to northern extremism during Reconstruction; like Boothe, they saw southern "fascism" as a response to northern "communism." Left-wing and civil rights activists, in contrast, were more inclined to locate the fascist impulse in the white South's long-standing commitment to racial supremacy, including its brutal system of chattel slavery. For communist writer Mike Gold, the "historic viewpoint" of American fascism of the 1930s was grounded in the idea that "Simon Legree should have conquered the emancipators of Uncle Tom." Gold likewise saw a natural link between a recent effort, on the part of southern white writers, "to glorify the southern case for Negro slavery" and their admiration for dictators like Mussolini. Like Gold, radical southern writer Grace Lumpkin also suspected that little separated the Agrarians' dedication to old-time southern values and modern-day fascism, a point she pressed in an interview with a fascist-leaning editor who had links to the Agrarian movement.[43]

Perhaps, then, it should be no surprise to find communists, Popular Fronters, and black and white civil rights activists more than ready to swing into battle against Mitchell's novel and Selznick's film, which they condemned not only for its racist caricatures and retrograde Lost Cause message, but for feeding into a current climate of political and social reaction. Quoting extensively from the novel's offensive characterizations of African Americans, George Schuyler, reviewing the book for the NAACP journal, *The Crisis*, suggested that "this slave-conscious South has not gone with the wind" but has been resurrected "from the ashes of defeat and today sits on the right hand of Uncle Sam in Washington," where it continued to make "an effective argument against according the Negro his citizenship rights and privileges." A civil rights group in Pittsburgh wrote to Selznick soon after he acquired the film rights: Mitchell's work, they insisted, was "a glorification of the old rotten system of slavery, propaganda for race-hatreds and bigotry, and incitement of lynching." The New York State Committee of the CPUSA argued that Mitchell's book "vilified and condemned . . . the historical struggle for democracy which we have come to cherish so dearly." Meanwhile, a black newspaper in Los Angeles took a more direct approach with a headline that proclaimed, "Hollywood Goes Hitler One Better." Never, they explained, could a film be made that repeated Hitler's lies about Jews in the way Selznick's film repeated "Ku Klux Klan slanders against Negroes."[44]

Still, neither communists nor the NAACP ever really managed to land an effective blow against *Gone with the Wind* and its Lost Cause message. Part of the problem had to do with the overall appeal of the film's story line, especially the strong identification many had, in this Depression moment, with suffering southerners and how strongly that image resonated for suffering Americans. An additional problem may have been a kind of "romance with the movies" attitude: a desire to accept the spectacle of the motion pictures, regardless of the message. A *New York Times* reporter thus noted that "occasionally some bewildered child Yankee" who has seen the film "remembers what he was taught in school and asks, confusedly, if it wasn't all right for us to have won the war." But unlike naïve children, "modern" consumers of Hollywood spectacles understood the magic of the movies and were willing to ride the tide of this popular culture moment: confused children notwithstanding, "nearly every one," the *Times* writer asserted, "has the right Confederate spirit!"[45]

Of course, it also helped that *Gone with the Wind* made the Confederate spirit more appealing and entertaining, not like the stodgy, tradition-bound spirit expressed in the far less successful *So Red the Rose*. While *So Red the Rose* had upset critics with its strong demonization of Yankee troops, *Gone with the Wind* kept its Yankee-bashing confined to the one straggler from Sherman's army who tries to steal Scarlett's jewels. And unlike the earlier film, *Gone with the Wind* was not above poking fun at those who worshipped and revered "the Cause," reflected in the cynical musings of both Scarlett and Rhett. The film even raises some questions about the efficacy of the slave system when Ashley Wilkes indicates, postbellum, that he would have freed his slaves if the war had not already done so.[46]

Other factors suggest how and why *Gone with the Wind*'s logical critics may have been neutralized. Surely, David Selznick's concerted campaign to offset black criticism of the film provides part of the explanation. In the years leading up to *Gone with the Wind*'s release, Selznick and his associates frequently corresponded with Walter White and various NAACP officials, as well as other black journalists, in an effort to placate their concerns. They agreed to tone down some of the more explicitly racist features of Mitchell's novel, especially in terms of anything that might show African Americans as angry or vicious toward whites. They also removed explicit mentions of the KKK and famously agreed to substitute words like "darky" and "colored" for the more offensive language used by Mitchell. Finally, they had many of the film's black actors speak out to praise the film and the way it implicitly revealed the progress African Americans had made since the Civil War. In the end, newspapers and individuals that had once been critical ended up offering, if not praise, then muted assent. Hattie McDaniel's Oscar win—the first for a black actor—for her artful portrayal of "Mammy" may have also discouraged some of the protests, especially since her award came soon after the film opened. Criticism persisted, of course, and there were those who continued to consider a boycott, but in the end the efforts to push back against this Lost Cause resurgence were mostly unsuccessful.[47]

Some indication of just how that happened can perhaps be gleaned in a letter that NAACP leader Roy Wilkins wrote in January 1940, soon after he and Walter White had gone to see a preview of the film. We expected, Wilkins explained, to "see some of the virulently anti-Negro material such as is contained in the book. We expected a second 'The Birth of a Nation.' However, there is very little direct anti-Negro material aside from a few uses of the word 'darky.' Of course, the whole theme, glorifying the South's civilization under slavery and the South's point of view in the Civil War is one with which Negroes cannot agree; but there is no good reason why we should advise colored people not to go to see the picture." Wilkins's letter suggests that he and White (and perhaps other civil rights leaders) may have believed they had scored a minor victory in not seeing the kind of vicious material they anticipated and that Birth of a Nation may have set the bar so low that anything less vicious registered as a victory. Interesting, too, are Wilkins's suggestions as to what might constitute "anti-Negro material": apparently it had little to do with the broad, historical story line or a bankrupt and false portrayal of chattel slavery, but instead involved something far more narrow: whether black characters might be considered likeable, perhaps. Indeed, it suggests that a film depicting black men and women in rebellion against their slave masters might have been perceived, even by the NAACP, as "anti-Negro."[48]

The communist attack also fell flat, although not for lack of trying. Surely some of the problem lies with the party's adherence to the Hitler-Stalin Nonaggression Pact and the way it blunted the CPUSA's message between August 1939 and June 1941, precisely the period when Gone with the Wind was in the news. During these months they backed away from a highly effective antifascist strategy, one that teased out the fascist strains in southern white supremacy and allowed them to make common cause with black civil rights activists. Since the new political agenda minimized anti-Nazi rhetoric, they focused instead on the problem of imperialist warmongering. Ben Davis, the black communist who reviewed the film for the Daily Worker, blasted the film's "Insidious Glorification of the Slave Market" and its chilling effect on the antilynching bill. But this focused critique took a convoluted turn: it showed the way the film reflected the merging of interests between northern "bluebloods" and southern "colonels"—in other words, the melding of US imperialist objectives—and how it would "incite a wave of war hysteria based upon the principles of lynch reaction against Negroes." Additionally, the content of Davis's review was over-shadowed by an internal personnel matter: the firing of the original film critic, Howard Rushmore, who, it was said, had not condemned the film strongly enough. Indeed, the *New York Times* even published a front-page article, as well as follow-up articles, about this internal politicking in the communist press, con-demning the suppression of Rushmore's speech rights while also noting that he no longer felt comfortable working in the climate of the Nazi-Soviet pact. The *Times* further suggested a split between Rushmore, "a tenth generation Ameri-can whose forebears fought in the War of Independence and whose grandfather was a Confederate soldier," and the presumably foreign-leaning hardcore com-munists, the "outside agitators" of long-standing myth who viewed southern race relations from an alien and fanatical perspective. Perhaps prompted by the *Times'* coverage, David Selznick even considered bringing a lawsuit "against various Communist organizations" in order to squash not simply the negative reviews written in the *Daily Worker* but also what he claimed was a larger "con-spiracy to damage us." No doubt the *Times,* as well as Selznick, saw this as an opportune moment to marginalize American communists, a group who had certainly been an unwelcome presence, from Selznick's perspective, in the mo-tion picture industry. Still, the fact that Selznick and the *Times* gave so much attention to the way communists reacted to *Gone with the Wind* suggests that communists must have amassed a surprising level of influence, especially in the fight against Jim Crow, over the course of the 1930s.[49]

Finally, it is important to note the consequences that may have resulted from all of this: the inability of US communists, along with the NAACP, to keep up a sustained and compelling critique of the film may well have had a decidedly det-rimental outcome. Several years after the film's debut, a black educator taking stock of *Gone with the Wind*'s effects reported that a white child in the South told a Negro maid that she "'would still be a slave' and 'Daddy would not have to pay you' but for the Yankees." Perhaps even more ominously, NAACP head Walter White apparently took the view that "whatever sentiment there was in the South for a Federal anti-lynch law evaporated during the *Gone with the Wind* vogue."[50]

Gone with the Wind must ultimately be counted as one of the most important stimulants to the Lost Cause tradition in the twentieth century. True, it did not perpetuate the Lost Cause in precisely the same guise it had taken in the late nineteenth or early twentieth century. But given the appearance of both the book and film in the midst of the hard times of the Depression, *Gone with the Wind* surely created a well of sympathy, across the country, for the southern white point of view. It underscored themes of Confederate honor and sacrifice while further contributing to a prevailing view about the mild and benign conditions of antebellum slavery. Even more, both book and film revealed how vital the "tragedy of Reconstruction" narrative had become to the Lost Cause, perhaps even more important than the story of the war itself. Increasingly, and especially during the 1940s, these distorted Reconstruction memories would be critical in helping southern whites formulate their arguments for beating back the civil rights challenges of the New Deal and post–New Deal eras.

[6]

YOU MUST REMEMBER THIS

"I REMEMBER EVERY DETAIL," Humphrey Bogart says to Ingrid Bergman. "The Germans wore gray, you wore blue." Here, indeed, was a familiar color scheme for an American war movie, only this was no Civil War film, but rather the most iconic movie of the World War II era, Warner Brothers' *Casablanca*. In this story of anti-Nazi resistance, set in the officially neutral but intensely divided North African city of Casablanca, where one-time lovers reconnect and ultimately part so that the war against fascism can continue, one would be hard pressed to find much besides this fleeting reference to the blue and the gray that summons up the usual elements of Civil War cinema. There are no idyllic plantations, no flags waving on the Gettysburg battlefield, no solemn appearances by Abraham Lincoln. Yet the classic Bogart-Bergman film of 1942 (released in January 1943) shares an unusual array of similarities with a film made two years earlier by *Casablanca*'s director, the Hungarian émigré Michael Curtiz. Like *Casablanca*, *Virginia City*, Curtiz's eminently forgettable movie from 1940, revolves around a wartime romance filled with intrigue, takes place in a divided city (Virginia City, Nevada), and situates a number of critical scenes in a bar swarming with spies where saloon singers croon patriotic hymns: "Battle Cry of Freedom" in *Virginia City*, the masterpiece of national anthems in *Casablanca*. Most importantly, the two films ultimately unite men once divided over both politics and a woman around a common cause: in *Virginia City*, Union and Confederate work together to fight gold bandits, while *Casablanca* brings together the seemingly indifferent Rick Blaine and the committed partisan Victor Laszlo.[1]

In many ways, *Casablanca* and *Virginia City* demonstrate how Civil War symbols and sentiments could be marshaled in the name of a new war and a new cause. *Virginia City*, not surprisingly, makes much of bringing Union and Confederate together, an important element in showcasing American unity on the eve of the Second World War. In both films, men discover how much more they have in common—in terms of fundamental beliefs—than what divides them. But

Casablanca also gestures toward another theme that assumed tremendous significance in the lead-up to the new global conflict: how the moral framework of the American Civil War, especially the fight against slavery, was put into service on behalf of the fight abroad. By the late 1930s, American politicians, as well as writers and artists, gave increasing attention to Abraham Lincoln and his refusal to tolerate a country that was "half-slave and half-free." These observations about Lincoln's domestic antislavery fight were deployed, almost seamlessly, as a critical moral imperative, pushing Americans away from indifference and into a more fervent support for the fight against Nazism and despotism across the globe.[2]

Casablanca is surely a film about breaking with indifference, and it references the Civil War theme in subtle but compelling ways. The film, of course, has one central African American character: Sam, the pianist in Rick's bar. With his knowledge of Rick's past and his access to Rick's inner sanctum, *Casablanca* allows Sam to emerge on a plane of greater racial equality than what had been dished up in previous Hollywood depictions of black characters. Thanks to Sam's presence, and sometimes his prodding, viewers become increasingly aware that Rick does indeed have a moral core and that he is no fan of Nazi bigotry. Nothing illustrates this quite so clearly as the moment when Rick's saloon-owning competitor in Casablanca asks if Rick's Café Americain, and Sam, are for sale, an offer that prompts Rick to answer in the voice of Civil War abolitionism: "I don't buy or sell human beings." Here viewers begin to glimpse the moral foundation beneath Rick's apparent disinterestedness, the ethical underpinning that will help Rick himself become a partisan. The link from the moral framework of the Civil War to World War II becomes even more palpable when we consider the author of these lines: Howard Koch, one of the film's main screenwriters, had cut his literary teeth writing about Lincoln for the WPA.[3]

Still, in at least one respect there is an awkward disjuncture between Curtiz's Civil War film and *Casablanca*. In *Casablanca*, the Germans, who wear the gray, and Bergman, who wears the blue, can never be reconciled. *Virginia City*, however, brings together men who had fought on opposite sides of a long and bloody war, with one side ostensibly committed to the principle of buying and selling human beings, the very opposite of the Lincolnian sentiments being expressed in the 1940s. In this regard, these two films tell us something else about what it meant to deploy the Civil War in the new era of global conflict. Much as American officials in the 1940s emphasized a unified home front, and the end of sectional division as a new war got under way, they also confronted the problem of how to bring together a racially and regionally divided nation in the Jim Crow era to fight a war that seemed to have as its central objective the destruction of a worldwide system of "slavery."

AS AMERICANS MOVED headlong into the cataclysm of war, officials in the government, as well as creative artists supporting the aims of FDR's administration, faced two critical challenges: (1) how to convince Americans to abandon the strong antiwar tendencies of the interwar period and participate in a new overseas conflict; and (2) how to project a vision of a unified home front, one that would include Americans with interests that often were in conflict due to racial and regional differences. The Civil War factored significantly into both of these challenges. In the first instance, the Civil War was often deployed as a vibrant historical memory that could help erase the troubled memory of World War I. As the scholar Ichiro Takayoshi has brilliantly demonstrated, few worked more diligently on this endeavor than the Lincoln playwright, and later FDR speechwriter, Robert Sherwood. Sherwood's efforts got an assist from various intellectuals, artists, and politicians, all of whom made compelling use of the Civil War in order to elevate the memory of a "good war," indeed a "necessary war," over negative assessments of the more recent conflict in Europe. Drawing on a moral framework associated with the conflict of the nineteenth century, Sherwood and others helped turn the cultural tide against a prevailing post–World War I isolationism.[4]

That isolationism remained on full display as the Depression decade drew to a close and as the military situation abroad intensified. A Gallup Poll conducted in 1939 found that 68 percent of the respondents believed the United States had been wrong to enter the European war of twenty years earlier. Even more, American culture was filled with ruminations about the futility of war, with many artists and writers using the Civil War as a vehicle for these meditations. Observers who remarked on the seventy-fifth-anniversary ceremonies at Gettysburg in 1938 highlighted the devastating consequences of the Great War and stressed the overriding goal of peace, even to the point of diminishing the martial accomplishments of Civil War veterans. Novels published at the end of the decade—for example, Hervey Allen's *Action at Acquila*—drew on the brutal details of Civil War battles to make a broader plea for understanding and reconciliation. In a *Saturday Evening Post* story, noted Civil War novelist MacKinlay Kantor told a tale of two men, veterans from the most recent war in France, who bring their older and increasingly forgetful relatives—one Union and one Confederate—back to Gettysburg for the 1938 reunion. As the younger men circle nervously around their own war memories and struggle with battlefield injuries, the old men imagine they fought together, on the same side, in the battle for Little Round Top. Both wars, for Kantor, prompt reflections about the terrors of battle and the seeming inevitability of forgetfulness. If reconciliation is the ultimate outcome, Kantor wonders, just what made all that carnage really necessary? Even the blockbuster movie of the decade, *Gone with the Wind*, put a wide-angle lens on wartime devastation, portraying thousands and thousands of soldiers seeking medical relief after the Battle of Atlanta and giving a visual accent to the antiwar attitudes of the late 1930s.[5]

Academic historians gave these reflections a scholarly veneer. These were the men who used phrases like "blundering generation" and "repressible conflict" to argue that nothing was inevitable in the drift toward Civil War. There was, historians Avery Craven and James Randall claimed, no fundamental cultural or economic difference that could not have been resolved with compromise and with a greater application of political restraint. James Randall made this argument in a 1940 lecture to the American Historical Association, suggesting that this basic truth about the Civil War continued to be relevant to the global wars of the twentieth century. "It may be seriously doubted," Randall argued in his "Blundering Generation" address, "whether war rises from fundamental motives of culture or economics so much as from the lack of cultural restraint or economic inhibition upon militaristic megalomania." Randall urged listeners to heed his plea to think soberly and realistically about avoiding the horrors of war in light of present-day events. "In the present troubled age," he explained, "it may be of more than academic interest to reexamine the human beings of that [Civil War] generation with less thought of the 'splendor of battle flags' and with more of the sophisticated and unsentimental searchlight of reality."[6]

Alongside scholarly and popular antiwar feelings and attitudes about the Civil War's futility, though, other crucial trends had also emerged over the course of the 1930s. One was that Depression-era Americans had been thinking a lot about slavery, although in ways that focused less on the racial bondage of the antebellum period and more on a new slavery that resulted from contemporary problems and had its most baleful effects on white people. Even movies that looked back at the Civil War, films like *The Littlest Rebel* and *The Prisoner of Shark Island*, drew the past and present together and portrayed white people as the real victims of political and economic oppression. Lincoln, too, figured prominently in the thinking and culture of the 1930s, with many artists and politicians celebrating Honest Abe for his forceful deployment of federal power in the name of democracy and humanitarianism. Lincoln, like Roosevelt, stepped in to free suffering white men. Those trends—the new antislavery battle and the emerging cult of Abraham Lincoln—would play a central role in reorienting Americans' ideas about war, and its necessity, as Americans saw an ominous new war on their horizon.

Working-class white Americans had emerged as some of the most forceful critics of the "new slavery," now understood by many as a particular problem of contemporary industrial exploitation. Workers, including union organizers, had been particularly vocal in condemning capitalist control of the labor market and bosses' abusive practices on the shop floor. This language of workplace slavery continued to resonate even in 1941, when the United States was emerging from the Depression and gearing up for war production. "The US," insisted one Cleveland worker, "is a land of slavery brutal and merciless," a place where steel shops routinely demanded that workers lift hundred-pound weights and expose themselves to burning hot steam. But as global war loomed, this language, once an indictment of employers' greed for profit amid Depression desperation, became an accusation hurled at employers for their apparent disavowal of national propaganda. "I don't want to be treated like the people in Germany are," an Iowa worker explained. "We are suppose [sic] to be a free country." Another Iowa worker, possibly female, also clung to the rhetoric of American freedom but wondered whether the employers in her Des Moines shop, with their callous disregard for workers' safety, were doing the same. "This isn't slavery," she insisted. "Abraham Lincoln done away with that."[7]

By the time this Iowa worker penned her complaint, it was 1943 and the United States was fully engaged in a war against Germany and Japan. By this point, too, official rhetoric had become increasingly insistent that "slavery" had assumed a new and even more urgent meaning: it did not refer to the kind of slavery that had turned generations of African Americans into bonded chattel, nor even to the economic slavery American workers endured during the Depression. Instead, Roosevelt and many of his supporters and propagandists argued, slavery denoted the despotic practices of foreign dictators. Roosevelt began to speak of the division in the world as one "between human freedom and human slavery." The Office of War Information (OWI), the administration's propaganda arm, visualized this concept in the form of a poster that proclaimed: "This world cannot exist half slave and half free." A Nazi-like figure brandishing a whip casts a shadow over a group of frightened—and apparently white—children and adults. William Allen White, the Kansas Republican newspaperman who often lent support to Roosevelt's policies, offered further elaboration: "Our great round earth," White intoned in a 1940 speech, has become "a little place, a veritable neighborhood that cannot live half slave and half free. I don't know in what form the dictator philosophy in the totalitarian state will meet us in our lives. . . . I only know that unless that beast is chained our lives will be marred and mangled by his claws." In short, White, like others, transposed a domestic crisis, the calamity of a nation divided by slavery and freedom, into an international one, with Americans being marshaled to fight abroad for the cause of freedom.[8]

Dramatist Robert Sherwood, Ichiro Takayoshi shows, seems to have been ahead of the curve when it came to making Lincoln relevant for the new war. Having struggled with his own antiwar feelings, Sherwood swung forcefully into the anti-Nazi camp with Hitler's invasion of Czechoslovakia in the fall of 1938. Notably, the switch came precisely at the moment when Sherwood was working on the launch of his new play about the life and career of the Civil War president. The events inspired Sherwood to look at Lincoln through the prism of world events, with the play giving particular emphasis to Honest Abe's own transformation from a man who dislikes slavery to a political leader who recognizes the necessity of taking a stand to halt its expansion. Speaking at a benefit performance for *Abe Lincoln in Illinois*, the playwright urged his listeners, who had gathered to donate funds for relief efforts in Central Europe, to heed the warning that "our civilization can not endure permanently—half Nazi—and half free." Raymond Massey, the actor portraying Lincoln in Sherwood's play, made a similar point. "If you substitute the word dictatorship for the word slavery throughout Sherwood's script," he observed, the play "becomes electric with meaning for our own time."[9]

The implication here was that the United States occupied the "free" side of this equation, while foreign despotism stood on the "Nazi" or "slave" side of the balance. This formulation had certain important, and interrelated, consequences. It laid out a path whereby a domestic struggle attained international relevance and, in its stark formulation of the divide, could underscore the moral necessity for the current war effort. Yet it could also make it harder to sustain a critique of America's domestic "slavery," since the inference seemed to be that no matter what economic or racial exploitation persisted in the United States, the general working out of the American democratic system tended toward "freedom." African Americans remained vigilant in resisting this erasure of US slavery throughout the World War II years, emphasizing the similarities between Hitler's racism and Jim Crow oppression, and imagining Lincoln as a stalwart supporter of racial justice. Finally, with Lincoln enlisted for this new cause of fighting slavery on "our great round earth," the message became even more insistent that the United States not only remained dedicated to free principles;

Actor Raymond Massey (center), director Elmer Rice (left), and playwright Robert Sherwood (right) on the set of Sherwood's 1938 play, *Abe Lincoln in Illinois*. Robert Sherwood's play reimagined Lincoln as a figure poised to take the battle against "slavery" into the global arena. Photofest.

it might even be the nation best suited to spearhead the global fight for liberty. This partly explains why workers affirmed the American commitment to freedom but faulted employers for discounting it. Indeed, even when Roosevelt referred to the actual practice of American slavery, he did so to confirm America's ultimate mission of emancipation. "It is an irony of our day," observed FDR on the seventy-fifth anniversary of the Thirteenth Amendment, "that three-quarters of a century after the adoption of the Amendment forever outlawing slavery under the American flag, liberty should be under violent attack." Had this been 1936, Roosevelt might well have been alluding to various workplaces and factories as sites where liberty was "under violent attack," but in 1940 he surely had something else in mind. Roosevelt's argument, in effect, seemed to be that America, under Lincoln's watchful eye, had learned to fight slavery and end it for good, while other despotic nations now worked actively to promote it.[10]

Increasingly, then, a heavy symbolic weight fell on Lincoln's shoulders: he became the central figure who accentuated the moral necessity of both the old war and the new one, and of taking the old war's principles into the newly emerging conflict. Artists and writers seemed to find Lincoln's message particularly inspiring in the months just before and just after Pearl Harbor. Asked by the conductor Andrew Kostelanetz ten days after the Japanese attack to produce a musical portrait of a great American, the composer Aaron Copland turned to Lincoln. The artist Marsden Hartley portrayed a strong and confident Lincoln in his 1942 painting *The Great Good Man*. Robert Sherwood played a vital role, even earlier, in putting Lincoln at the center of the new global encounter. "When I wrote the play [*Abe Lincoln in Illinois*]," Sherwood explained to poet Archibald MacLeish in May 1940, "I did so primarily for the purpose of expressing . . . 'the conviction that there are final things for which democracy will fight.' Lincoln, it seemed to me, was the supreme non-isolationist in his essential faith." Sherwood, though, did more than make Lincoln a symbol for military engagement. He also made him the emblem for America's mission to the world, a figure not just for democracy but for the spread of democracy everywhere. In the published version of his play Sherwood developed this theme with an anecdote. In the postscript he presented a story about a Jewish immigrant, the labor leader and newspaperman Baruch Charney Vladeck, who had come to the United States in 1908 from Russia and had learned the true spirit of America by studying the Gettysburg Address. To Vladeck, the essential point was not about nationalization or "Americanization," but about "liberation." Surely in referencing a Jewish American immigrant who praises Lincoln the liberator, Sherwood made a powerful statement about contemporary global politics. Driving the point home, Sherwood explained that Lincoln was "essentially a citizen of the world." Presumably his power as liberator made him, and by extension the United States, a force for good in international affairs.[11]

Sherwood did not stand alone in creating this global Lincoln. He often acknowledged the inspiration he had drawn from Carl Sandburg's biographical portrait, particularly *The Prairie Years*, and even had Sandburg pen the introduction to the published Lincoln script. Then, shortly before the film version of Sherwood's drama opened in January 1940, the next several volumes of Sandburg's Lincoln biography—*The War Years*—were published to immense critical acclaim. This capacious biographical account of a wartime president, appearing as it did on the eve of US involvement in another war, seemed destined to become a cultural force in the new global conflict. At the conclusion of this work, in his reflections on the meaning of Lincoln's assassination, Sandburg made his own case for understanding Lincoln as a figure of transnational importance.

"Often came the statement," Sandburg wrote, "that over the world the whole civilized Family of Man shared in regrets or grief for the loss of a common hero who belonged to humanity everywhere"; in a particularly timely passage, Sandburg even called Lincoln "a spokesman to be consulted in future world affairs." Sherwood, for his part, found these "passages . . . describing the effects of the assassination on men everywhere" to be the finest in the book. Called on repeatedly during the 1940s to reprise his thoughts about Lincoln—and to lend support to Roosevelt—Sandburg often reiterated the point about Honest Abe's global impact, particularly after the United States became an active participant. Noting how people everywhere "take Lincoln now for their own," Sandburg suggested that this worldwide love of Lincoln came from a yearning to see "something" about Lincoln "spread everywhere over the world." In characteristic Sandburg fashion, he left that "something" vague and unspecified, shrouded in a typical Lincoln "mystery that can be lived but never fully spoken in words." Sandburg gestured toward democracy and popular rule as the ingredients behind the "mystery." And yet, as was often the case with these assessments of the Lincoln mystique, the enigmatic language served an important function: by cloaking Lincoln's global appeal in mystery, Sandburg could also obscure the tension between the idea of promoting "government where the people have the say-so" and the implicitly imperialistic proposition of spreading American influence abroad. Neither Sherwood nor Sandburg said so explicitly, but by 1940 Lincoln had become well positioned for the work of cultural imperialism.[12]

Sandburg's readers agreed that this portrait of Lincoln was particularly relevant to global affairs and that the current crisis enhanced Lincoln's international stature. "In the present distracted condition of the world," Frank Riddleberger of Virginia wrote to the biographer a week after Pearl Harbor, "it seems to me this is a timely period in which to read" these volumes about Lincoln. The Civil War president "inspires in one a conviction that, after all, there is something vital about [democracy], that cannot be crushed . . . however many dictators may arise and fall in our world." Soldiers, too, told Sandburg how valuable they found his books, including one who later told the author that "on more than one occasion" he had read his works "in a foxhole under Japanese shelling in the jungles of Bougainville in the Solomon Islands." Private John Hulston likewise confirmed that his conversations with other soldiers revealed "that great numbers are more than slightly familiar with your works and several are extremely well informed." Not all readers appreciated the way Sandburg bent his historical message toward current events. F. E. Bredouw in Kansas City enjoyed the "hours of instructive pleasure" he got from Sandburg's storytelling but had little patience for the writer's continued support of Roosevelt, particularly his public endorsement of FDR's third presidential bid. "I am writing [Roosevelt's 1940 Republican opponent Wendell] Willkie to read your six volumes, remember the Lincoln stories, and be elected the next time he runs."[13]

Bredouw clearly saw how Sandburg's, and Sherwood's, portraits of Lincoln made for effective political strategy for the current American president, and how important it had become for Roosevelt to strengthen his own links to Lincoln as he roused the nation into war. Indeed, as we have seen, Roosevelt had already inspired countless writers and artists and New Deal supporters to see in his presidency a persistence of Lincolnesque qualities, with many insisting that the New Deal was a continuation of Honest Abe's deployment of federal power for humanitarian ends. By 1940, Roosevelt and his associates made the connections with Lincoln even tighter, especially on matters of global significance. Once again, Sherwood's work had been vital. The playwright started sending FDR timely Lincoln quotes and, in 1940, began working in the Roosevelt administration. At a press conference in 1941 Roosevelt even answered a reporter's question by pulling out his copy of *The War Years*, quoting from a passage where Lincoln tells a group of women how the nation needs to fully rouse itself about war with the South. Roosevelt found this a highly relevant analogy for his own time, when Americans, he believed, still thought conflict avoidable and perhaps still regretted American involvement in World War I. In his own way, Roosevelt could have been talking about the Rick Blaines of the world, using the Civil War to spur them into action. Asked what a newspaper headline on this topic might be, FDR responded: "President Quotes Lincoln— And Draws a Parallel." Still, the slavery "parallel" received more attention than any other. A cartoon appearing in the *New York Times Magazine* in 1942 showed Lincoln standing by Roosevelt, who pounds his fist on the map of the world. "You have a greater task than I had," Lincoln tells Roosevelt. "Slavery must be removed from the whole of the earth." A year later, Roosevelt used Lincoln to further press the case for bringing America's vision of freedom to the rest of the world. "The living memory of Abraham Lincoln," FDR stated in his address to the White House Correspondents Association, "is now honored and cherished by . . . men and women and children throughout the British Commonwealth, and the Soviet Union, and the Republic of China, and all of our sister American Republics, and indeed in every land on earth where people love freedom and will give their lives for freedom."[14]

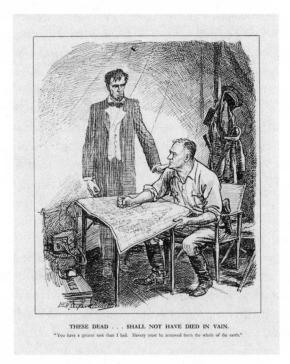

THESE DEAD . . . SHALL NOT HAVE DIED IN VAIN.
"You have a greater task than I had. Slavery must be removed from the whole of the earth."

Lincoln consults with FDR about war and slavery in a
1942 cartoon. This cartoon, from the February 8, 1942,
New York Times Magazine, shows Lincoln offering his
support for Roosevelt in his task to wipe slavery "from
the whole of the earth." Punch Limited.

THESE POWERFUL ANALOGIES—Lincoln, the fight against slavery—helped
build support for the Allies, but they were not without complications. If the
United States meant to wage war, Lincoln-style, in a fight against Nazi "slavery," what did this mean for the all-important task of building a united home
front and especially for cementing the loyalties of white southerners and African Americans, who certainly heard other types of references in these metaphors? In 1939 British prime minister Winston Churchill delivered a radio address exploring the link between Nazism and slavery, points not well received
by pro-Confederate southerners. "Britain," Churchill proclaimed, "may take
good heart from the American Civil War when all the heroism of the South
could not redeem their cause from the stain of slavery, just as all the courage and
skill, which the Germans show in war, will not free them from the reproach of

Naziism with its intolerance and brutality." These remarks outraged the president of the UDC, although she ultimately decided "the times are too troubled to start out on the errand of educating an English statesman." Nor was Churchill the first observer to make these connections. In 1938, *Time* magazine compared Spain's Francisco Franco, the leader of a "rightist revolution," to Robert E. Lee. Again, white southerners howled in reproach. Over the course of the Depression decade, several writers and dramatists, both black and white, likewise linked "southern identity" and fascism, including Clarence Cason, Clare Boothe, James Weldon Johnson, and Mike Gold. In 1941, the southern journalist Wilbur Cash published his groundbreaking meditation *The Mind of the South*, in which he challenged benign images of the courtly and cavalier South and saw evidence instead of something "savage" that made the region similar to despotic regimes like "fascist Italy," "Nazi Germany," and "Soviet Russia."[15]

Recognizing the prickliness of Lost Cause politics and seeking to ensure the support of leading southern Democrats for the fight abroad, Roosevelt and members of his administration repeatedly took steps to appease white southerners, offering small reminders of the Confederate past to underscore the importance of their contributions to the war effort. Several army posts named in honor of Confederate commanders were established in the southern states in the early 1940s, including Fort Polk in Louisiana, Camp Pickett in Virginia, and Fort Hood in Texas. UDC members attended White House garden parties, and on at least one occasion FDR hosted a reception for Confederate veterans. All of these symbolic acts not only encouraged Dixie's support for the Roosevelt administration's foreign policy but also acknowledged just how vital southern whites had already been in paving the way for US military intervention. In 1940–41, southern respondents to a Gallup Poll favored US involvement in the new war at a higher rate than the rest of the country. In May 1941, before Pearl Harbor, support for waging war against Germany and Italy was highest in eight of the former Confederate states. With the backing of federal money for a growing number of military installations in the region, the South, by World War II, had become well positioned to be the region most committed to military activity. In 1945, after a South Carolina captain raised a Confederate battle flag over ruins in Okinawa, a Chicago sociologist defended the action, suggesting "it was the tradition of the valor of the Confederates which gave him the courage" he displayed in the South Pacific. Indeed, it may have been precisely this southern enthusiasm for American defense that helped Robert Sherwood overlook any connections between Nazism and southern slavery. "I always forget the feelings of the South as regards Lincoln," Sherwood wrote in a letter to Walter Winchell.

"In quoting his cracks about the enemies of freedom, I always assume them to mean the Nazis, as indeed they do today."[16]

Southern historians also did their part to show the relevance of the Confederate past for the new international conflict. Lee biographer Douglas Southall Freeman appeared often in magazines and on the radio, offering his views about what the United States in the 1940s might learn from the South in the 1860s. In 1940, his message emphasized caution in attacking Germany based on his assessment of a too-hasty attack, by Lincoln, at Bull Run. Later writings by Freeman provided a more telling indication of how difficult it could be to make the Lost Cause story dovetail with the new wartime rhetoric. In 1942, the Virginia author contributed to a government-sponsored collection of twenty-eight essays, *There Were Giants in the Land*, designed to "help our own people and our friends in other lands" to see the "courage, ingenuity and sacrifice" used by Americans in the past "to meet the supreme crisis" of their generation. "Written at the suggestion of the Treasury Department," and with an introduction by Treasury Secretary Henry Morgenthau, the book was produced to showcase how Americans were, despite their initial reluctance, uniquely suited to meet the military and political challenges of the moment. The collection also spotlighted Americans' singular ability to forge unity out of diversity: it contained one essay each on a Catholic (Cardinal Gibbons), a German (Carl Schurz), a black American (Frederick Douglass), and even a female American (Julia Ward Howe), while Jews got two (Benjamin Cardozo and Joseph Goldberger).[17]

There Were Giants in the Land even contained one essay about a Confederate American: the chapter on Lee, written by Freeman. Lee, Freeman insisted, was a man the nation needed now. Yet even Freeman seemed to recognize that Lee might not offer the ideal model to emulate. Thus, much as the nation needed Lee, Freeman argued, "equally we need Lincoln." And Jackson. And Washington. And even Grant. Recognizing the challenges of facing the Nazi juggernaut, Freeman thought Americans might learn a lesson from the way Confederates faced adversity. Of course, as he noted, there remained "the all-embracing difference that the Confederacy lost inevitably whereas the nation today can win," an acknowledgment that the history of defeat—and an "inevitable" one at that—might not offer the best comfort at the present time. And then there was this problem: when Freeman advised Americans to learn from Lee's attentiveness to strong military preparations—including his recognition that "the Northern people would wage a long and hard struggle"—the analogy became further strained. "Change 'Northern' to 'German,'" Freeman suggested, and Americans would draw a valuable lesson for today. It is hard to imagine a clumsier metaphor at a time when Americans were being roused to fight the Nazi system of slavery.[18]

Because the messages tended to be more simplistic, with analogies suggested more than explained, Hollywood movies may have been more effective than historical profiles in linking the Confederate past to current military efforts. Several films appeared, starting in 1940, which spotlighted Confederate heroism, while also showing the profound respect Unionists bestowed on their foes. Michael Curtiz's *Santa Fe Trail* (1940) brought Jeb Stuart and George Custer together in a battle against extremist John Brown. Although they fought a common enemy, the Confederates were undoubtedly the more appealing actors, especially Errol Flynn's dashing Stuart, who ultimately wins the girl away from Ronald Reagan's whiny Custer. Curtiz's *Virginia City,* also released in 1940, opens with a dedication to seventy-three people who carried out "one of the most daring adventures in American history" in December 1864: an attempt by Confederates to smuggle gold out of Nevada to help their nearly doomed fight for independence. Again Curtiz asks audiences to cheer on Confederates but also eventually lets them rally to the side of the Union, when former adversaries fight together to prevent the evil bandit and his gang from stealing the gold. By the end, they have further cemented their bond around an agreement to use the gold to help rebuild the postwar South. Even more of a Confederate rabble-rouser was the 1943 Paramount movie *Dixie,* a film very loosely based on the life of Daniel Emmett and his career as a songwriter and minstrel performer. Starring Bing Crosby, the film careens toward one overriding objective: to show Emmett's ultimate success in writing the stirring and popular war song "Dixie." In a final scene that depicts a whole audience of southern white folks leaping to their feet and singing Emmett's song, the film suggests how everyone might benefit from a dose of the southern war spirit. Tellingly, black people appear only as background characters or as the hideously lampooned objects of Emmett's minstrel shows.[19]

None of these films garnered much critical acclaim, and more for artistic than for political reasons. More biting censure, particularly regarding the appeasement of Confederate and white supremacist sensibilities, came from African Americans. "We're surprised and disgusted at Paramount," wrote the entertainment columnist for the *Pittsburgh Courier,* "for making such a film [*Dixie*] that slurs a race of people who are fighting as hard as any others to create a free world with equality and justice for all." Indeed, with the United States now fully engaged in war, and with a million African American men serving in the armed forces, the black press and black political leaders lost no time in underscoring how detrimental these lovefests with the Confederacy could be for African American morale. The *Pittsburgh Courier* was itself at the forefront of the Double V campaign, launched in early 1942, which urged black Americans to support the war abroad while also fighting for racial justice at home, including in the military and in war-related industries. This work included pressuring Roosevelt to ban discrimination in defense industries and the government, efforts that ultimately culminated in FDR's Executive Order 8802. Although not a highly publicized feature of the Double V campaign, the work to expose public mollifications of pro-Confederate sensibilities also figured prominently in the wartime civil rights agenda. These efforts, in fact, had an especially important rhetorical significance, since they allowed black leaders to expose the hollowness of southern white claims of patriotism while highlighting the far less ambiguous patriotic contributions of African Americans, historically and in the present.[20]

In this spirit, black leaders and black newspapers undertook a concerted effort to attack Jim Crow and blatant manifestations of white supremacy in the South, especially when they were aimed at black soldiers. Reporting on violent attacks directed toward African American soldiers in southern states, the *Chicago Defender* made it clear how much this stemmed from an Old South kind of mentality. Understanding the depth of race hatred in Dixie, argued a *Defender* reporter, requires knowing something about the people there who "still bask in the spent glories of the Confederacy, revel in memories of slavery, feast on the traditions of the Rebellion and honor those departed soldiers who gave their lives for the 'Lost Cause.'" Southern whites' insistence on discriminating against black Americans at the workplace and in schools likewise revealed how the region's racial practices, steeped as they were in the Civil War era, undermined wartime unity. "A unified national war effort," *Defender* writer A. C. MacNeal argued, "is thwarted because one section of the country and a section of the American people refuse to forget the past and are willing to lose this war rather than give up social theories which precipitated the Civil War." So out of the mainstream was the white South, the *Defender* insisted, that "the rabid Southerner" believes "Abraham Lincoln is a tyrant and a despot whose memory rankles in their breast." This insistent coupling of current Jim Crow practices with the Confederate past surely offered a powerful line of argument: it clearly associated the region with treason and rebellion, not to mention the cardinal sin of hating Honest Abe. It also made clear that a real fight against "slavery" would have to target domestic as well as international conditions. With Lincoln and the battle against slavery so central to the government's campaign, African

Americans found an opening to advance the fight for racial justice, although it required some pushback to the vague and overly generalized formulations that FDR and his supporters relied on.[21]

Indeed, African Americans had to navigate a climate of complicated and conflicting political currents in the period just before and during US involvement in the war effort. On the one hand, it was apparent that federal officials recognized the importance of maintaining, even cultivating, black support and understood the risks of alienating African Americans at this highly charged moment. Thus, it seems noteworthy that the propaganda volume documenting the lives of historic Americans, *There Were Giants in the Land,* included not only an essay on a black American but one that was written by Angelo Herndon, a well-known black activist and communist. Herndon, who had been arrested, tried, and jailed in a notorious free speech case in Georgia nine years earlier, seems an unlikely collaborator for this government propaganda campaign. Yet his inclusion in the volume may have signaled an acknowledgment that a hard-hitting black perspective, one that really pushed the point about fighting slavery, would be more effective than a lukewarm celebration of black progress. Hoping to circulate the book globally, officials may have also been mindful of the message Herndon's essay could project to brown and black peoples in other countries. Herndon's essay, "Frederick Douglass: Symbol of Freedom," made no attempt to soften Douglass's staunch opposition to both slavery and slaveholders, and also placed Douglass's crusade at the core of the fight for democracy. Douglass, Herndon wrote, "helped to make America conscious of the fact that true democracy is not the exclusive privilege of any one race or group, but the right of all men of all races who would fight and die for it." In this way, Herndon firmly aligned Douglass with the current fight against slavery across the globe, although not with the vague, antitotalitarian gestures made by Robert Sherwood, or Raymond Massey, or even Carl Sandburg. Rather, Herndon made clear that Douglass, in fighting racial slavery in the United States, truly embodied what it meant to stand for a worldwide fight for democracy. "It is, in a sense, tragic," Herndon concluded, "that Douglass becomes meaningful to most Americans at a time when the new slavery which is fascism strives to engulf the democratic world. It is fortunate, however, that his vision applies with such startling clarity to the major problems of our time."[22]

The inclusion of Herndon's essay represented a significant acknowledgment by the US government of the black freedom struggle, yet the clarity Herndon ascribed to Douglass's antislavery fight could easily be obscured. As the antislavery language ramped up, black Americans registered skepticism about just what government officials meant and who bore responsibility for the spread of slavery. In June 1940, Richard Wright penned an article for *New Masses* and explained his confusion on hearing Secretary of State Cordell Hull refer to the Nazi program of conquest as a plan to force the conquered peoples into "an economic master-and-slave relationship." "The moment I heard those words," Wright explained, "I felt and thought that the Secretary of State was describing the policy of the United States towards its largest minority, the Negro people," not "the imperialist policy of the German High Command!" Wright was probably unusual in adopting such a cynical tone about the new antislavery war. Others in the black press did not reject the language of slavery as it was being applied to the international arena, although they took pains to give the language a direct and tangible connection to something historically linked to racial oppression in the United States. Recognizing that African Americans did not favor any type of imperialistic expansion, including by the British, the black writer Theophilus Lewis nonetheless believed that much was at stake for American blacks in the defeat of Nazi Germany. "The Nazis," Lewis wrote in April 1941, "have made it clear that after they win the war they intend to reduce the non-Aryan races to slavery." Perhaps recognizing the imprecision in the government's propaganda message, Lewis added: "They [Nazis] have stated emphatically that they are not using the word slavery in a figurative sense. They mean literally what they say." Others took a different tack: they assumed that when FDR insisted on fighting "slavery," he surely meant to fight slavery wherever he found it, even in the United States. Carl Murphy, the editor of the *Baltimore Afro American*, in April 1942 described Roosevelt as "a man with Lincoln's courage" who "has found us a people half free and half slave." By 1942 FDR certainly employed this phrase, but he used it to describe the world, not, as Murphy did, to characterize US domestic politics. Nonetheless, Murphy and others took the approach of expecting Roosevelt to make good on his pledge to fight slavery, including those who would deny "citizenship rights to colored persons" in the United States. Similarly *Chicago Defender* writer A. C. MacNeal tried to use the stark metaphors of "half-free and half-slave" to get American lawmakers to be more straightforward about where their true sympathies lay. The United States, he explained, must either explicitly support democracy for all people "or change the Constitution and repeal the Thirteenth, Fourteenth, and Fifteenth amendments and enact laws similar to Hitler's declarations and edicts which would mean that Negroes were to be returned to chattel slavery."[23]

The challenges associated with this new war on "slavery," and the question of how African Americans would, in the midst of a foreign war, pursue the fight both at home and abroad, took a Hollywood turn as well. By the end of the 1930s, African Americans were demanding a more influential role in the film industry, having already tried to insert the NAACP into some of the negotiations over offensive language and stereotypes in *Gone with the Wind*. Walter White wrote often to David Selznick, and Selznick himself, albeit half-heartedly, sought to win support from black leaders and the black press and to avoid the fiasco of black protest that had surrounded *Birth of a Nation*. Notably, in discussions over *Gone with the Wind* and other films, black activists failed to win concessions on historical content. No film spotlighted the oppressive nature of chattel slavery, or slaves' resistance to white masters, or the democratic triumphs won by African Americans in Reconstruction. Instead, the NAACP scored a more stylistic type of success with respect to things like language and the gradual inclusion of a wider range of black characters in contemporary settings.

The NAACP campaign continued in the 1940s, although it often bogged down in the division between black artists in Hollywood, who wanted the work and the recognition, versus those who found the constant portrayal of black men and women as slaves, servants, and buffoonish entertainers demeaning and disgraceful. American communists also remained active in pressing Hollywood to combat racism in cinema, often singling out movies that dealt with historical subjects like slavery, Civil War, and Reconstruction. Their influence in the arts had, however, become more tenuous due to the HUAC campaigns as well as the CPUSA's support for the Nazi-Soviet pact of 1939. In the 1940s, political wrangles over movies involved yet another participant: the Office of War Information and its newly created Bureau of Motion Pictures (BMP), organized to assess the impact various films might have on wartime goals. Hollywood was not required to take the BMP's suggestions, but, not wanting to anger government officials in the midst of conflict, they often tried to accommodate the bureau's advice. Significantly, the BMP offered black activists a new type of leverage with Hollywood, a vehicle for voicing disapproval for films that might offend blacks and undermine their support for the fight abroad. A particularly intensive battle was waged over one Civil War–themed film, a 1943 MGM movie, first titled *The Man on America's Conscience* and then finally released as *Tennessee Johnson*.[24]

The film, essentially a biopic of Lincoln's presidential successor, Andrew Johnson, was envisioned as an appropriate wartime film for its message of unity and democracy. Johnson was heralded as a prime defender of both: for his political campaign to ensure that even propertyless white men gained the right to vote and then for bringing the South back into the national fold after the Civil War. Arrayed against Johnson in these efforts is the Pennsylvania congressman Thaddeus Stevens, a man determined to inflict punishing blows on ex-Confederates and to undermine the democratic process by trying to impeach Johnson. The script promoted what was the almost universally accepted interpretation of Reconstruction, essentially the same story presented by the Dunning school and then rehashed by Claude Bowers in 1929: that it was an era of Yankee corruption and vengeance, black incompetence, and misery for white southerners. During the 1930s, this take on Reconstruction became even more firmly entrenched as it became intertwined with southern white reactions to New Deal measures and especially the antilynching bill that was debated at various points in the decade. At the same time, though, both blacks and communists had been pushing back, writing their own historical narratives that challenged the white supremacist agenda. Their work, most notably W. E. B. Du Bois's *Black Reconstruction* but also James Allen's *Reconstruction: The Battle for Democracy*, showcased this period as a moment of interracial democracy, spearheaded by men like Thaddeus Stevens, over the obstructions thrown up by racist and incompetent leaders like Andrew Johnson who ultimately managed to thwart democracy and restore control to southern whites. During World War II, when black men were called off to fight a war for freedom, left-wingers continued to find contemporary relevance in the Reconstruction saga. Communist Elizabeth Lawson wrote a short biography of Thaddeus Stevens, observing that all "he stood for is today menaced by fascism at home and abroad." And writer Howard Fast, inching toward communism and working for the OWI on the issue of integration in the armed forces, wrote a novel called *Freedom Road* that chronicled the postwar experience of a black Union soldier who actively participates in Reconstruction. Despite its radical bent, Fast's book earned widespread praise, including favorable reviews from mainstream newspapers. Indeed, the *Hartford Courant* was surprised and impressed by Fast's chronicle of "Negroes who participated in state constitutional conventions" and "were excellent statesmen, men who had educated themselves in much the same manner as Abraham Lincoln had and who wanted only to own a part of the land where they had formerly been slaves."[25]

In 1942, as *Tennessee Johnson* was in production, conditions thus seemed ripe for an intensified battle over these two interpretations of Reconstruction, not only because a Hollywood studio was actually planning to make a movie about Andrew Johnson but also because the Office of War Information had demonstrated an interest in more positive portrayals of African Americans, especially in film. As both communists and civil rights activists made clear, cinematic celebrations of Andrew Johnson would be counterproductive to that end. Yet

Tennessee Johnson forced activists to work on a challenging historical terrain: this was not a confrontation about casting blacks in demeaning roles as slaves or about prettifying portrayals of plantation life but about thornier problems of postwar democracy and black politics. With this in mind, Walter White and the NAACP hoped to convince OWI officials that the long-standing story of Reconstruction was actually a tale that glorified the Klan and supported "the subjection of the Negro," even if the film never explicitly made these points. The *California Eagle,* a black newspaper, also turned up the heat on Hollywood. The "parallel between these days and those of the Civil War is abundantly clear," the *Eagle's* editors maintained, especially with a new premium placed on the "battle against the enslavement of mankind," which includes "the liberation of the Negro people, whose complete freedom was sabotaged after the Civil War." In light of this, they insisted that the MGM film represented "a threat to the development of national unity, an insult to the Negro, aside from being a shocking corruption of history." Communists, too, joined the effort, with the *Daily Worker* publishing numerous attacks on the film, including one that called it "No. 1 on Hitler's Hit Parade." Government officials agreed that degrading portrayals of black Americans must be avoided, including BMP head Lowell Mellett, who told MGM that "the film, as currently planned, would be injurious to national war morale and especially that of the country's Negro population." Anxious to avoid the controversy, MGM took the somewhat unprecedented step of altering the film after production in the hope of making Stevens a little less villainous and removing any egregious antiblack material. The *California Eagle* scored this an important accomplishment in the fight against cinematic racism.[26]

Although wartime conditions opened a space for challenging white supremacist history on film, the story of *Tennessee Johnson* also reveals the limits of that challenge. In its final form, the film, directed by the German refugee William Dieterle, remained a heroic presentation of Andrew Johnson, portrayed as a poor working man who sticks to his pro-Union principles and ultimately becomes a national leader in one of the nation's most trying moments. Some of the changes tried to make Thaddeus Stevens seem genuinely concerned with the fate of the former slaves, although the essential hero (Johnson) versus villain (Stevens) plotline remained in place. The final version of the movie also includes virtually nothing about the black experience and shows virtually no black characters. If the goal was to placate potential protest over racial caricatures, the solution involved outright elimination of all black parts. Curiously, the OWI applauded *Tennessee Johnson* for showing that "neither white slavery nor Negro slavery is compatible with the American way of life." Yet if this is what it showed, it did so in classic Hollywood fashion: by showing white men, not African Americans, as the ones who were enslaved. The film begins with the young Andy Johnson cast as the "white slave," the poor indentured servant on the run from his employer, bound in chains that are later struck from his ankles. Later, as president, Johnson continues to hold on to the leg irons he used to wear, telling Stevens that he keeps these as a reminder of what it feels like to be chained and confined. Stevens, much as he claims to be the champion of the former slaves, has no idea what the leg iron is. Clearly, so fluid and flexible was the "slavery" metaphor that even Andrew Johnson could wear its shackles. Yet so determined were Hollywood and government officials to avoid black protests, and perhaps white southern objections too, that "Negro slavery" remained nonexistent.[27]

The battle over *Tennessee Johnson* illuminates how much the trope of "white slavery" remained a Hollywood staple, a visual theme that allowed for the cinematic erasure of black enslavement. It also reveals how difficult it was to dislodge the traditional Reconstruction narrative. Much as African American criticism seemed to carry some weight when it came to portrayals of blacks, it was difficult to push back against the essentially pro-Confederate attitudes about Reconstruction and especially about Thaddeus Stevens. Government officials came to believe that only avowed communists, not blacks, really cared about Reconstruction history. "The management of MGM," wrote OWI official Nelson Poynter to Walter White, "is completely upset because it feels the agitation of the negroes over the picture is directly a result of the communists." More specifically, they believed that Thaddeus Stevens "was a hero of the left-wingers rather than of the Negro people" or, as one of the scriptwriters contended, "Stevens was for chasing the Kulaks off their land and this is very appealing to the Communists." In the end, both Hollywood and the OWI apparently believed they could dismiss most of the historical criticisms of *Tennessee Johnson* as a lot of communist hot air, thereby clearing the decks for a film that continued to distort a more historically accurate version of the Reconstruction story. In this way, they helped keep the traditional, pro-Confederate, white supremacist accounting of Reconstruction alive and well, a point deeply regretted not only by communists but also by African American scholars. "This picture," wrote the black sociologist E. Franklin Frazier after attending a private screening of the final version of the film, "is just another distortion and falsification of history designed to appeal to the moral hypocrisy of white America. . . . The real issue between Andrew Johnson and Thaddeus Stevens was over the question whether the Negro was a human being and should become a citizen of the United States." It would take another twenty years or so before this argument gained much headway in American scholarship and even longer before it had any standing in American popular culture.[28]

Also indicative of the possibilities, and limitations, of the African American campaign to produce more accurate black history on film was the 1944 motion picture *The Negro Soldier*, an explicit propaganda effort designed to encourage black military participation and promote greater racial tolerance in the armed forces. Developed and produced in the army's film unit, headed by noted Hollywood director Frank Capra, *The Negro Soldier* drew together various government officials and Hollywood artists, mostly white but some black, who began their research and writing for the movie in 1942. This entailed compiling a list of "do's and don'ts" for portraying blacks on the screen, including the suggestions not to accentuate racial identity and not to play up "Lincoln, emancipation, or any race leaders or friends of the Negro." The final film, appearing in January 1944, was made by a white director, Stuart Heisler, and was based on a script by black actor and writer Carlton Moss.[29]

The Negro Soldier focuses primarily on a middle-class black church, filled with men and women who have either joined the military or have family members in the armed forces. A significant portion profiles one mother in the group who reads a letter she has received from her son about his experience in being trained and deployed to fight for Uncle Sam. The film also includes a historical interlude on black involvement in past American wars. This historical overview makes no mention at all of slavery or racial oppression. Remarkably, the section on the Civil War does not even include any images or discussion of black soldiers, although African American troops appear in every other war depicted in the film. In fact, the Civil War sequence consists only of a view of the Lincoln Memorial with Lincoln's words being read aloud, an interesting artistic decision given the earlier recommendation that references to the Civil War president be avoided. Presumably any footage of soldiers fighting during the Civil War would raise uncomfortable issues about the tenuous nature of North-South unity. Perhaps, too, because *The Negro Soldier* appeared during a global war that pitted the forces of freedom against the forces of slavery, a focus on actual US slavery would have presented an awkward reminder of Americans' less-than-stalwart antislavery history. Finally, the elevation of Lincoln points to Honest Abe's double role in 1944: as a symbol of racial identity and, implicitly, of racial justice; and as the foremost emblem of a country united in a worldwide struggle to promote freedom and crush slavery. The power of this visual image rested on its ability to appeal to different groups of viewers in these different and contradictory ways.[30]

'A SURVEY CONDUCTED in 1945 by the National Opinion Research Center found that Americans readily placed Abraham Lincoln among the top two of the "greatest men who have ever lived in the country." Outside the South, Lincoln was the clear winner, selected by 61 percent. Even among white southerners, Lincoln was chosen by 44 percent of respondents, coming second behind FDR, but slightly ahead of George Washington. Lincoln, in effect, emerged as a hero of national stature during the Second World War, the man who, coupled with Roosevelt, had led the nation, and ultimately the Allies, to a victory against fascism and despotism, sometimes referred to as "slavery." Writing years later, at the start of the Civil War centennial, southern novelist Robert Penn Warren detected that something in the way Americans thought about the Civil War had shifted during World War II. "We can remember," Warren wrote about his generation's most recent conflict, that "the Civil War, not the Revolution, was characteristically used in our propaganda, and that it was the image of Lincoln, not that of Washington or Jefferson, that flashed ritualistically on the silver screen after the double feature." Going further, Warren argued that the nation as a whole had learned in these years to take ownership of their Civil War legacy; no longer was "the custody of the War ... relegated to the Southerners."[31]

Lincoln's prominence in the spotlight could not help but make some Americans more reflective about the Civil War president's domestic antislavery crusade. Some, both black and white, pushed for Lincoln to be an even more forceful symbol in the new fight for racial justice. As African American leaders had persistently reminded anyone who would listen, "slavery" had to be understood as more than just a vague definition of foreign despotism: as a condition with historical specificity in the United States. Even more, both black and white activists had insisted that the racial oppression practiced by Hitler and the Nazis was not very far removed from Americans' own history of slavery and racial inequality. Wartime conditions, which placed a premium on securing black support for the war, meant that African American leaders also gained some leverage, especially from government propaganda officials and even in Hollywood, in seeing more dignified black characters appear in film and even in combating white supremacist assumptions about slavery and the Civil War. Thus, Angelo Herndon received official government sanction for his forceful portrait of Frederick Douglass's powerful antislavery crusade. And although no film in these years ever really exposed the problem of black enslavement, the OWI nonetheless insisted, in 1942, on Negro slavery's incompatibility "with the American way of life."

The new respect accorded to Lincoln's antislavery fight, both abroad and at home, no doubt helped shape new historical scholarship, loosening the grip of the "blundering generation" arguments and promoting instead more of a pro-Lincoln analysis that lauded the sixteenth president for his moral courage rather than criticize him for failing to find a compromise. Indeed, even among white scholars there was a more explicit recognition of Lincoln's antiracist views. Writing in the *New Republic*, the historian Arthur Schlesinger believed that Americans in 1944 were remembering Abraham Lincoln "more vividly than Washington or Columbus," partly because of his "simple and unpretentious" qualities but also because he tried to tackle many questions being confronted during the world war. Like Lincoln, Schlesinger wrote, "we too are defending free government against armed might. We too have resolved to end the doctrine of a 'master race.'" Lincoln was not simply a man opposed to "slavery," Schlesinger reminded readers; he opposed racism, the kind of racism that had a powerful foothold in the United States as well as in Hitler's Germany.[32]

American leaders came to realize, however, that promoting Lincoln internationally could also invite negative scrutiny. The determination to stand by Lincoln's principles on the world stage inevitably raised the troubling prospect that the rest of the world might wonder about Americans' own commitment to the president's antislavery legacy. In 1942, when he directed the government information office on "facts and figures," Archibald MacLeish registered alarm at the way various Axis powers had begun to spotlight the history of racial oppression in the United States in conversations with countries where black and brown people predominated. In a particularly powerful appeal to Brazilian blacks, Axis propagandists advanced the argument that "while the Brazilian Negro enjoys complete freedom, his fellow Negro in the United States is still a slave and the abolition of slavery after the Civil War was only a formal act." Concern about Americans' international reputation regarding race also gave added impetus to the landmark study of American race relations that was funded by the Carnegie Corporation and undertaken by Swedish scholar Gunnar Myrdal in the late 1930s and written after Pearl Harbor. This "is a day," wrote Carnegie administrator F. P. Keppel in the introduction to Myrdal's classic work, *An American Dilemma* (1944), "when the eyes of men of all races the world over are turned upon us to see how the people of the most powerful of the United Nations are dealing at home with a major problem of race relations." Indeed, in his single-minded focus on "an American Creed," referring to the nation's long-standing belief in democracy and equality of opportunity, Myrdal suggested that the tools were at hand for Americans to confront the problem of racial oppression. While racial moderates had often relied on Lincoln as a reference point for gradualism, Myrdal now referred to Lincoln as one of the foremost proponents of the creed, with its insistence on giving all classes, and people of all racial backgrounds, equal opportunities for success.[33]

Myrdal's approach in some ways anticipated the strategy employed by government officials in the postwar era, and especially during the early days of the Cold War. As the United States embarked more aggressively into global politics, US leaders became even more acutely aware of the way American racial practices were on display. They saw, too, how Soviets and others could exploit the unsavory aspects of the US racial past and how that compelled a new kind of response. Essentially, in order to be able to rejoice in the possibilities of the "American Creed," officials had to acknowledge moments in the past when that creed failed to deliver on its promise. As scholar Mary Dudziak has noted, this even included more forceful statements about the oppressive nature of chattel slavery. In a 1950 US Information Agency document, for example, the authors confirmed that the slave system had given rise to "a theory of racial inferiority" and a slew of unjust practices designed to subordinate "the Negro." Acknowledging the ugly side of slavery, officials could then point with pride to the struggle that brought slavery to an end and the way current race relations revealed undeniable indications of racial enlightenment and progress.[34]

Even Hollywood had a slightly harder time selling the old white supremacist version of the American past. In December 1946, Bowsley Crowther of the *New York Times* reviewed the newest Walt Disney film, *Song of the South*, a cinematic retelling of Joel Chandler Harris's "Uncle Remus" stories, and noted just how out-of-step Disney's paean to Old South values, especially its benign view of slavery, had become. Crowther condemned this "peculiarly gauche offense in putting out such a story in this troubled day and age. For no matter how much one argues that it's all childish fiction, anyhow, the master-and-slave relation is so lovingly regarded . . . that one might almost imagine that you figure Abe Lincoln made a mistake." Several years earlier, when the film everyone was writing about was *Gone with the Wind*, *Times* reporters had encouraged people to have "the right Confederate spirit," and the only ones lambasting Selznick's film for implicitly rebuking Lincoln's antislavery wisdom were communists. Selznick had been so incensed by this critique that he even considered bringing a lawsuit against the *Daily Worker*.[35]

None of this heralded the ultimate demise of the Lost Cause. Confederate heritage groups continued to meet and pay tribute to southern soldiers and officers. Civil War battlefields, since 1933 under closer government supervision, continued to publicize a pro-Confederate perspective, especially at National Park Service sites in the South. Even more, the Lost Cause demonstrated, as it had before, its remarkable ability to adapt to new circumstances and to assume a life that took it far beyond that of the traditional keepers of the memory flame. White southerners, as well as some white northerners, turned to the Confederate past during a new postwar era of heightened civil rights activism. They turned to Confederate slogans and Confederate symbols to combat intensified black protest as well as the new type of racial liberalism that was being articulated by figures like Arthur Schlesinger, Gunnar Myrdal, and even Bowsley Crowther. When the Ku Klux Klan began staging a revival in 1945, it adopted the Confederate flag for the first time as one of its public symbols. The flag came even further into prominence in 1948, when a number of conservative white southerners broke with the Democratic Party over civil rights issues and formed themselves as "Dixiecrats." Besides displaying flags, Dixiecrats also harked back to Civil War language with their insistence on maintaining "the integrity of the states and the basic rights of the citizens" against the "totalitarian" agenda of federal officials. Evidence suggests, too, that the Dixiecrat movement helped inspire a Confederate flag "fad" of the late 1940s and early 1950s, including the increased adoption of Confederate flags by southern military outfits and the raising of the Confederate banner, in 1947, at the University of Mississippi.[36]

The politics of the Cold War era shaped the way artists and writers, men and women who had done much to reimagine the Civil War during the 1930s and early 1940s, would pursue their postwar careers. Howard Koch, the playwright who had imagined Lincoln reincarnated as a 1930s labor leader and later wrote antislavery lines for *Casablanca*, was accused of "slipping Communist propaganda" into films at Warner Brothers. Placed on the Hollywood blacklist, he moved abroad and wrote under a pseudonym. Carl Sandburg, a far more successful Lincoln delineator, spent most of the 1940s writing a novel for Metro-Goldwyn-Mayer, a grand, sprawling patriotic book that would eventually form the basis for a "landmark patriotic movie." Sandburg's stature as a leading Lincoln scholar, one who had put his scholarship into service for Roosevelt and his administration, led Hollywood executives to think of him as the ideal writer for this nationalistic venture. In the end Sandburg seemed stymied by the move from the historical to the fictional, and the book, *Remembrance Rock*—a critical failure—never became a film. When the country became engulfed by the hysteria of anticommunism, Sandburg retreated into reminiscing and autobiographical writing.[37]

Margaret Mitchell, for her part, fully embraced the anticommunist tide, pushing her Lost Cause principles more thoroughly into line with a right-wing agenda. Ever resentful about left-wing assaults on her magnum opus, Mitchell's hostility became increasingly intense in the 1940s, even toward liberal New Dealers, not to mention socialists and communists, both at home and abroad. Bristling at some reviews *Gone with the Wind* had received in the Yugoslavian press, Mitchell was outraged at being portrayed as an apologist for "Negro slavery." American as well as international communists, Mitchell believed, "are bending all efforts to smearing the South and Southerners, because they know we are one of the strongholds of Conservatism and are likely to resist Communism more fiercely" than any other section. A few years before her death in 1949, Mitchell even assisted the notorious right-wing journalist Westbrook Pegler in an attempt to find a familial connection between Franklin Roosevelt and Rufus Bullock, the Reconstruction governor of Georgia, perhaps hoping to demonstrate that the president's "carpetbagging" tendencies were genetically preordained.[38]

With the end of federal funding for the Federal Writers' Project, Negro Affairs editor Sterling Brown sought other employment. In 1940 he was working at the Library of Congress as a senior editorial assistant, having received a significant pay cut. He soon left that post and returned to his professorial duties at Howard University, while also accepting visiting professorships at schools such as Vassar, New York University, and the University of Minnesota. His literary output slowed considerably in the 1940s, although he had plans to write a book about black people's experiences in the mid-twentieth-century South. Titling his book *A Negro Looks at the South*, Brown secured a Rosenwald Fellowship for the project in 1942. That year, Brown was also interrogated by FBI agents about contributions he made to communist front organizations and subscriptions he held to left-wing publications. Despite being cleared in 1942, Brown seems to have been the subject of FBI scrutiny as late as 1953. *A Negro Looks at the South* never appeared in print during Brown's lifetime; it was published posthumously in 2007.[39]

Although Howard Fast garnered considerable praise for his 1944 Reconstruction novel, *Freedom Road*, plans to turn the book into a movie were scratched amid the McCarthyite wave of the postwar years. Having joined the Communist Party the same year *Freedom Road* was published, Fast later refused to cooperate with the House Un-American Activities Committee and spent three months in a federal prison in 1950. While there, he became inspired to write a novel about slavery and devoted himself single-mindedly to the research. Blacklisted from all the major publishing houses, Fast self-published the book in 1951, then gradually saw it grow in popularity during the 1950s. Still, Fast understood that any work he hoped to sell in these years would have to tread carefully around potentially subversive topics. Asked by a *New York Times* advertising censor whether the new book contained "anything about the overthrow of the government by force and violence," Fast could truthfully reply, "Not this government. Ancient Rome." The book, Fast recalled, represented his second attempt to tell "the story of a slave": first in *Freedom Road* and now in *Spartacus*, a fictional account of an actual slave uprising led by a Roman gladiator, later (in 1960) turned into a lavish Hollywood film. Channeling his long-held political beliefs, Fast seemed determined to keep telling the story of slavery as well as the slaves' ongoing fight for freedom. Yet in the second telling Fast surely grasped how in this time of intense political backlash it would be easier, especially for a known communist, to tell a story about white men's antislavery resistance in a long-ago past rather than explore the struggles of black men and women in more recent times.[40]

$\left[\begin{array}{c}\textbf{CONCLUSION}\end{array}\right]$

THIS WAR AIN'T OVER

I BEGAN THIS BOOK in the age of Obama and finished it in the time of Trump. That transition reveals the way the Civil War has continued to resonate in our cultural and political imagination, whether in 2012, 2017, or 1936.

In 2008, liberals and progressives cheered the advent of the first black president and channeled Barack Obama's message of hope with an idealistic rhetoric that often pivoted back to the Civil War. *New York Times* columnist Thomas Friedman declared November 4, 2008, the day "the American Civil War ended": that war could not truly be over, he explained, "until America's white majority elected an African-American as president." Abraham Lincoln, not surprisingly, basked in the new light emanating from the Obama White House. A week after the election, the *New Yorker* showed the Lincoln Memorial lit up by the glow of a luminous "O." Obama himself invoked the sixteenth president when he was sworn into office in 2009, retracing a part of Lincoln's inaugural route and using the same inauguration Bible. Indeed, it's hard to disentangle Stephen Spielberg's 2012 movie, *Lincoln*, which focuses on the campaign to pass the constitutional amendment that would end racial slavery, from the optimistic rhetoric about a "postracial" America that surrounded the Obama presidency.[1]

Still, in the waning years of the Obama administration we were reminded that the Civil War was no lopsided victory for the champions of racial justice, just as Obama's victory hardly signaled an end to American racism. Indeed, there were indications that Confederate symbolism might, as it so often has, offer a rallying point for a racist backlash, for calling attention to the grievances some white Americans felt at being denied a free and unencumbered path to white supremacy. Nothing made this clearer than the use of the Confederate battle flag by Dylann Roof, a white supremacist killer who, in June 2015, murdered nine black worshippers at a historic black church in Charleston, South Carolina. Roof's actions prompted a national conversation, perhaps less about underlying problems of racism and more about the offensive nature of

Confederate iconography, eventually leading to flags and other symbols coming down in South Carolina, Mississippi, Louisiana, and elsewhere. Donald Trump's rise to power in 2016 opened the door ever more widely to white people's sense of grievance and, not surprisingly, kicked the debate over Confederate symbolism into high gear. By the summer of 2017 Americans bore witness to the appalling spectacle of violent white supremacists and neo-Nazis marching on Charlottesville, Virginia, insistent that the city's plan to remove a statue of Robert E. Lee was emblematic of "white genocide" and a pattern of replacing "our people, culturally and ethnically."[2]

A crucial difference between the New Deal era and both the Obama and Trump years may be how race has emerged front and center in today's discussion over Civil War symbols, usually (although not always) unencumbered by any nostalgic glow and despite efforts to push it to the background. During the 1930s, the sentimental power of the Lost Cause continued to obfuscate Confederate racism. In the 1930s, it was still possible to dress the Confederacy in a romantic cover, in the tattered dresses of Scarlett and her sisters, or to hide it behind the tearstained face of Shirley Temple pleading with Lincoln to spare the life of her Confederate father. There was, of course, vigorous protest from left-wing activists and African Americans who worked tirelessly to puncture the sentimental veneer and expose the base inhumanity that lay at the heart of the Confederate project. Margaret Mitchell, proclaimed black critic George Schuyler, "spurts the familiar southern white venom against Negroes and Yankees" in her portrayal of the South in the Civil War and Reconstruction eras. As this book has suggested, though, numerous factors worked to keep the anti-Confederate counternarrative tamped down. For one, the devastation of the Depression encouraged many white Americans in both the North and the South to feel compassion for the travails of white southerners—to find in Scarlett O'Hara, for example, a symbol for suffering, and survival, not an emblem of white domination. Even the language of slavery tended to situate white people as the nation's true bearers of suffering, past and present, whether it was the shackled Doctor Mudd in *The Prisoner of Shark Island*; the chain gang prisoner James Allen in *I Am a Fugitive*; or the oppressed coal miners who figured in performances on the Federal Theatre stage. Then, too, those who set themselves up as gatekeepers, ever vigilant against "un-American" influences in the nation's culture, tended to make left-wingers and black activists, not those peddling Confederate romance, the objects of scrutiny. A play celebrating Jefferson Davis, a man who committed an act of political treason against the United States, attracted no attention from patriotic politicians, yet a folksy tribute to

Abraham Lincoln made the men behind the House Un-American Activities Committee sit up and take notice. In the 1930s and '40s, US military bases were named to honor Confederate leaders, but none was given the name of any African Americans affiliated with the US Army or Navy. In some quarters, in fact, southern white attitudes were repurposed to fit an anticommunist agenda. As the UDC put it, few people were better prepared than the Daughters when it came to "exterminating" communism.[3]

Still, if Americans remained inconsistent, at best, when it came to honoring men and women who comprised the committed vanguard in the fight against slavery, they did show an increasing inclination in the 1930s, the 1940s, and beyond to heap praise and honor on Abraham Lincoln. By the 1930s, Lincoln's star was already on the rise, and not just on the silver screen. More white southerners showed a willingness to put Lincoln in their pantheon of heroes, sometimes just below and sometimes right next to Robert E. Lee. Additionally, his long-standing appeal as a figure of healing and reconciliation gained added luster in the New Deal years, especially as he became increasingly emblematic of the expansive-but-humanitarian style of government that was a hallmark of FDR's administration. So powerful, in fact, did Lincoln's image become that he seemed to obscure all other memories that had once clustered around the Union cause. Lincoln, in this regard, was far more than a Union man; he was the face of 1930s Americana, linking past and present like no other Civil War figure. Indeed, the United Daughters of the Confederacy may have doubled down in its efforts to celebrate Jefferson Davis in the Depression decade precisely because they felt the imbalance between the nation's swelling homage to the Union commander in chief—the "passionate addiction" observed by Alfred Kazin—and the scant regard shown the Confederate leader. Kazin's "addiction," though, was really a series of multiple "addictions": Lincoln managed to absorb a wide range of Civil War memories, including the liberal views of Carl Sandburg, the conservative values of anti–New Deal Republicans, and the emancipationist tendencies of African American artists, activists, and regular folk.[4]

Lincoln's adaptability made him the ideal figure for navigating Americans' transition from the Depression to the Second World War. Honest Abe not only fought economic devastation at home; he could also fight Nazis abroad. He had helped to smash chattel slavery, and he could also crush "slavery": that is, the subjugation that people, primarily white, experienced under the heel of totalitarian rule. As the central figure in the fight against southern feudalism, a system that even FDR thought resembled "the Fascist system," Lincoln's mission seemed eminently adaptable to the global war of the 1940s. And as America's foremost figure in the fight against slavery, Lincoln extended a hand of compassion and comradeship to those under the Nazi heel. In this way, Lincoln also increasingly became the friendly face of American imperialism, a symbol of American intentions to offer help, not wreak havoc, in a world in turmoil.[5]

Lincoln would continue to play this role in the Cold War era as the Nazi heel became the Soviet bludgeon and as the "enslaved" became those caught behind the iron curtain. But in the post–World War II years it also became ever more challenging to avoid the links between colonial oppression and slavery, so sometimes the "enslaved" were not just white people but the men and women who had once been colonial subjects and now invoked Lincoln to demand independence from the political and economic tyranny of the world's dominant powers. Once again, Lincoln became the bearer of conflicting messages. During the celebration of the 150th anniversary of Lincoln's birth, in 1958, the United States Information Agency plotted a campaign that would make Lincoln and his association with American democracy known around the world, including in a number of African countries. But as historian Kevin Gaines notes, many African leaders had already formulated their own message about Lincoln, drawing on his emancipation crusade as a source of inspiration in the ongoing anticolonial struggle. These African leaders, Gaines observes, never intended to be the passive recipients of Lincoln's (or American) goodwill, but the active instigators of a liberation agenda that found encouragement in the sixteenth president. In this way, African leaders borrowed a page from the playbook of American civil rights activists who, as Scott Sandage has argued, "refined a politics of memory" that allowed them to make strategic use of Lincoln as a weapon in the fight for racial justice. In 1963, at the historic rally at the Lincoln Memorial, Martin Luther King Jr. expanded on the message first delivered in 1939, at Marian Anderson's famous concert, and urged the nation's leaders to fulfill the vision of the hundred-year-old Emancipation Proclamation and make good on the "bad check" that had been issued to black Americans. Ghanaian leader Kwesi Armah likewise celebrated Lincoln, not only to press the case for racial equality but also to defend his country's path of national independence.[6]

Thus at least through the early 1960s, Lincoln remained a forceful icon for black and white activists who came together in a reinvigorated civil rights movement. But while Lincoln continued to gain traction, so, too, did the Confederate flag. "The height of the civil rights movement," explains historian John Coski, "saw Confederate flags used routinely by the segregationist resistance." White protesters regularly used Confederate symbols to express their opposition to a federally mandated program that sought, albeit in a largely piecemeal fashion, to break down features of the long-standing Jim Crow system. At a rally held in St. Augustine, Florida, on June 21, 1964, seven hundred protesters held the flag of the Confederacy high as they cheered prosegregation speakers. That flag also found a prominent place in American wars of empire, from the Spanish-American War down to present times. Thus, even as Lincoln might become the benign face of cultural imperialism, the Confederate flag found its own champions abroad, especially among southern white soldiers who hoped to tap the militaristic—and racist—spirit of the South in the fight against nonwhite colonial subjects in places like the Philippines, Korea, and Vietnam. "The Confederate flags," opined the *Chicago Defender*, "seem more popular in Vietnam than the flags of several countries."[7]

The *Chicago Defender*, like others in the black community, registered their opposition to such flagrant use of a racist symbol. Today others have added their voices to this opposition, recognizing, at long last, how much hate and brutality has been practiced under the cover of these "historic" emblems, be they monuments, flags, songs, or movies. Yet even today, even after the violence of Charleston and Charlottesville, many still justify their use through the neutral language of heritage and ancestor worship. Others return to Confederate symbols precisely because of their effectiveness in combining something "historic" and "cultural" with a message of white supremacy. "As long as we have a politics of race in America," argues historian David Blight, "we will have a politics of Civil War memory." That sentiment seems an apt, albeit tragic, summation of our current times, and of the New Deal era.[8]

[NOTES]

Abbreviations

BUL/BU	Frederick Lauriston Bullard Collection, Howard Gotlieb Archival Research Center, Boston University
DOS	David O. Selznick
DWG	D. W. Griffith
DWG/MOMA	D. W. Griffith Papers (microfilm ed.), Museum of Modern Art
FTP/LC	Federal Theatre Project Collection, Library of Congress
MM/UGA	Margaret Mitchell Family Papers, MS 905, Hargrett Rare Book and Manuscript Library, University of Georgia
NPS/NARA	National Park Service Central Classified Files, 1933–49 (RG 79), National Archives and Records Administration
Producing GWTW	*Producing "Gone with the Wind,"* online collection at the Harry Ransom Center, University of Texas at Austin, at http://www.hrc.utexas.edu /exhibitions/web/gonewiththewind/ (accessed May 17, 2017)
ROSE/LPA	Billy Rose Theatre Division, New York Public Library for the Performing Arts
SAND/ILL	Carl Sandburg Papers (Connemara Accession), 1898–1967, Rare Book and Manuscript Library, University of Illinois at Urbana-Champaign
SELZ/UT	David O. Selznick Papers, Harry Ransom Center, University of Texas at Austin
SHER/HARV	Robert E. Sherwood Papers, Houghton Library, Harvard University
SVB	Stephen Vincent Benét

Introduction

1. Irwin Silber, *Songs of the Civil War.*

2. Sandburg, *The People, Yes*; Mitchell, *Gone with the Wind*; *Gone with the Wind* (film).

3. Woodward, "The Mississippi Horrors"; Ritterhouse, *Discovering the South*, 4. My notion of "usable history" draws from scholarship on collective memory and historical memory including Halbwachs, *On Collective Memory*, and Thelen, "Memory and American History."

4. Alfred Kazin, "What Have the 30s Done to Our Literature?," *New York Herald Tribune*, December 31, 1939.

5. National Emergency Council, *Report on Economic Conditions of the South*.

6. Hudson and Painter, *The Narrative of Hosea Hudson*, 95.

Chapter 1

1. Rubin, "General Longstreet and Me," 23–25.

2. On Hoover's efforts to deal with the crisis see Kennedy, *Freedom from Fear*, 70–103; Kasson, *The Little Girl Who Fought the Great Depression*, 11.

3. Leuchtenburg, *Franklin D. Roosevelt and the New Deal*, 1; Green, *The Uncertainty of Everyday Life, 1915–1945*, 74; Ed Paulsen and Mary Owsley quoted in Terkel, *Hard Times*, 32, 50.

4. Kennedy, *Freedom from Fear*, 141; Alston, "Farm Foreclosures in the United States," 886; Mintz and McNeil, "The Farmer's Plight"; Oscar Heline and Harry Terrell quoted in Terkel, *Hard Times*, 218, 241.

5. McElvaine, *The Great Depression*, 81–82; Wall, *Inventing the "American Way,"* 20; Franklin Roosevelt, "The Forgotten Man," radio address, April 7, 1932, at http://newdeal.feri.org/speeches /1932c.htm (accessed August 13, 2012).

6. Wall, *Inventing the "American Way,"* 15–33.

7. *Saturday Evening Post* quoted in Kammen, *Mystic Chords of Memory*, 503.

8. Kennedy, *Freedom from Fear*, 79; Roosevelt, "The Forgotten Man," radio address; Leuchtenberg, *The Perils of Prosperity, 1914–1932*, 247, 266; Kennedy, *Freedom from Fear*, 90.

9. The extensive literature that examines the South's Lost Cause includes Foster, *Ghosts of the Confederacy*; Gallagher and Nolan, *The Myth of the Lost Cause and Civil War History*; Brundage, *The Southern Past*; and Janney, *Burying the Dead but Not the Past*. On adapting Lost Cause thinking to include the "victory narrative" over Reconstruction, see Blight, *Race and Reunion*, 264.

10. Letter of Virginius Dabney to Frederick Lauriston Bullard, September 28, 1946, box 3, file 29, BUL/BU; UDC, *Minutes of the Thirty-Seventh Convention, Held in Asheville, North Carolina* (1930), 64–65; 1936 interview with Margaret Mitchell by Medora Perkerson, PBS, http://www .pbs.org/wnet/americanmasters/episodes/margaret-mitchell-american-rebel/interview-with -margaret-mitchell-from-1936/2011/ (accessed May 8, 2017).

11. An excellent account of the Lost Cause and southern politics is Blair, *Cities of the Dead*.

12. On "loyal slave" and "mammy" worship see Blight, *Race and Reunion*, 284–91; UDC, *Minutes of the Thirty-Eighth Convention, Held in Jacksonville, Florida* (1931), 298; Daniels, *A Southerner Discovers the South*, 191.

13. For an insightful analysis of the Agrarians, and especially their relation to fascism and communism, see Brinkmeyer, *The Fourth Ghost*, 24–70; Twelve Southerners, *I'll Take My Stand*; Allen Tate, "Ode to the Confederate Dead," in *Selected Poems*; Young, *So Red the Rose*.

14. Dollard, *Caste and Class in a Southern Town*, 36; for more on Charles Francis Adams's tributes to Robert E. Lee see Nina Silber, "When Charles Francis Adams Met Robert E. Lee."

15. Editorial, *Chicago Defender*, May 30, 1931; *Chicago Defender*, September 26, 1931, and January 2, 1932, has coverage of different Emancipation Day programs. For more on Emancipation Day activities see Blair, "Celebrating Freedom," and Wiggins, *O Freedom*.

16. Interview with Elizabeth Sparks in Perdue, Barden, and Phillips, *Weevils in the Wheat*, 273.

17. Barber quoted in "Emancipation Celebration Is Laudable Custom," *Pittsburgh Courier*, January 16, 1932; Editorial, *Chicago Defender*, February 2, 1929; "Weakness Inherited," *Pittsburgh Courier*, October 17, 1931; "DePriest's Brilliant Plea for Slaves Hits Congress," *Pittsburgh Courier*, April 2, 1932.

18. Numerous books have recounted the way the Civil War was remembered in the years

between 1865 and 1920, including Blight, *Race and Reunion*; Nina Silber, *The Romance of Reunion*; and Blair, *Cities of the Dead*. Several recent works have challenged the notion that a Confederate bias dominated postwar memories, including Janney, *Remembering the Civil War*, and Gannon, *The Won Cause*.

19. Nina Silber, *Romance of Reunion*, 159–96.

20. On the *Century*'s "Battles and Leaders" series, see Blight, *Race and Reunion*, 173–81.

21. For more on the making and showing of *The Birth of a Nation*, including an excellent discussion of Griffith's influences, see Stokes, *D. W. Griffith's "The Birth of a Nation."*

22. Stokes, *D. W. Griffith's "The Birth of a Nation,"* 227–31.

23. "War Dead Honored in Services Here," *New York Times*, May 27, 1929; Brown, *The Public Art of Civil War Commemoration*, 158.

24. *Abraham Lincoln*, film; cable to DWG from John Considine, undated, reel 17, DWG/ MOMA.

25. Review of *Abraham Lincoln* in *National Indorsers of Photoplays: Their Monthly Publication* (October 1930), reel 18, DWG/MOMA; David Belasco, "America Never Knew This Abraham Lincoln," *Philadelphia Public Ledger*, October 5, 1930, reel 17, DWG/MOMA.

26. George Matthew Adams, review of *Abraham Lincoln*, in *Chicago Evening Post*, September 19, 1930, in Abraham Lincoln scrapbook, reel 32, DWG/MOMA.

27. Hemingway, *The Sun Also Rises*, 116; cummings, "Poem, or Beauty Hurts Mr. Vinal"; Sandburg, *Abraham Lincoln: The Prairie Years*, 1:59; cable to DWG from John Considine, July 27, 1930, reel 17, DWG/MOMA.

28. On Bowers and the politics behind *The Tragic Era*, see Kyvig, "History as Present Politics."

29. Bowers, *The Tragic Era*, vi, 283, 351.

30. Kyvig, "History as Present Politics"; Bowers quoted in ibid., 29.

31. Letter of SVB, December 28, 1927, in Fenton, *Selected Letters of Stephen Vincent Benét*, 147; Benét, *John Brown's Body*, 33; for biographical information on Benét see Fenton's introduction to *Selected Letters of Stephen Vincent Benet*.

32. Benét, *John Brown's Body*, 43; on Benét's suggestions of Sally Dupre's black ancestry see Carton, "Crossing Harper's Ferry," 851.

33. Letter of SVB, November 5, 1927, in Fenton, *Selected Letters of Stephen Vincent Benet*, 143–44; Benét, *John Brown's Body*, 366.

34. Letter to DWG, September 11, 1928, reel 16, DWG/MOMA; on Mitchell's debt to Benét see Haskell, *Frankly My Dear*, 136, and SVB, letter to MM, July 1936, in Fenton, *Selected Letters of Stephen Vincent Benet*, 286–87; Arnett and Kendrick, *The South Looks at Its Past*, 39; Janney, "Written in Stone."

35. Locke, *The New Negro*, 4–5.

36. French, *The Rebellious Slave*, 182–93; Fisher, "Nat Turner," 305; introduction to Bontemps, *Black Thunder*.

37. On Scottsboro and the communist response see, for example, Gilmore, *Defying Dixie*, 118–28.

38. On the mammy monument and the responses see McElya, *Clinging to Mammy*, 116–60.

39. On the work of the John Brown Memorial Association see *John Brown in Bronze, 1850–1859*; W. E. B. Du Bois, "John Brown," 260; Janney, "Written in Stone."

40. Janney, "Written in Stone," 130–31; *Pittsburgh Courier*, October 24, 1931.

41. J. Max Barber, "Daughters of the Confederacy and John Brown," *Pittsburgh Courier*, October 24, 1931; Janney, "Written in Stone," 135.

Chapter 2

1. A considerable corpus of scholarship examines some of these different ways of remembering. Historian John Bodnar distinguishes between official and vernacular forms of remembrance in identifying the memories that become codified on the national scene and how those memories are interpreted and understood by specific groups. See Bodnar, "The Memory Debate," 13–14. For many, the founding document in memory studies is Halbwachs, *On Collective Memory*, which includes Halbwachs's distinction between collective memory (how various groups rely on memory for their collective identity) and historical memory (memory conveyed through historical records and documents). In a recent essay, I encourage scholars to also think about the "imagined reconstitution of the nation" as a way to understand how various forces have conspired to give Americans images of the nation as it was reconstituted after the Civil War. See Nina Silber, "Reunion and Reconciliation, Reviewed and Reconsidered."

2. Reardon, *Pickett's Charge in History and Memory*, 201.

3. Nguyen, *Nothing Ever Dies*, 13.

4. For a good overview of the New Deal arts programs see Adams and Goldbard, *New Deal Cultural Programs*, http://www.wwcd.org/policy/US/newdeal.html.

5. For more on the New Deal's historical sensibilities see Kammen, *Mystic Chords of Memory*, 407–80; Susman, "The Culture of the Thirties," in *Culture as History*; Marling, *Wall to Wall America*, 208–10; Peterson, *John Brown*, 136–39. John Steuart Curry's John Brown murals in Kansas were not done under the auspices of Federal One.

6. On the New Deal's move toward cultural pluralism see Wall, *Inventing the "American Way,"* 63–65; on Howard Odum and southern regionalism see O'Brien, *The Idea of the American South, 1920–1941*, 66, and Odum, *Southern Regions of the United States*.

7. Reader's report for "Daughters of Dixie," box 175; reader's report for "Jefferson Davis Highway," box 230; John McGee, playscript for *Jefferson Davis*, box 682; all in FTP/LC; "Theatre: Double-Jeopardy," *Time*, March 2, 1936.

8. Playscript for *Frederick Douglass*, box 651 in FTP/LC; Ronda, *Reading the Old Man*, 113; promotion notes for *Battle Hymn*, box 979, FTP/LC.

9. Conkle, *Prologue to Glory*.

10. Excellent scholarship on the controversies in the Federal Writers' Project can be found in Sklaroff, *Black Culture and the New Deal*, and Stewart, *Long Past Slavery*.

11. "Like a Shadow That Declineth," interview with Bill Holmes in Terrill and Hirsch, *Such as Us*, 12–13; Effie Cowan and Mrs. Ernestine Weiss Faudie [Mrs. Ernestine Weiss Faudie], Texas, Manuscript/Mixed Material, Library of Congress, https://www.loc.gov/item/wpalh002243/ (accessed May 4, 2017); Capt. H. C. Wright [Capt. H. C. Wright], Texas, Manuscript/Mixed Material, Library of Congress, https://www.loc.gov/item/wpalh002444/ (accessed May 4, 2017).

12. For scholarship on the problematic nature of the FWP slave interviews see, for example, Stewart, *Long Past Slavery*; Yetman, "The Background of the Slave Narrative Collection"; Woodward, "History from Slave Sources"; and Musher, "Contesting 'The Way the Almighty Wants It.'" Appraisal sheet for Arkansas narrative, box 893, Federal Writers Project: Slave Narrative Project, Works Progress Administration Records, Library of Congress; William Sherman quoted in Stewart, *Long Past Slavery*, 222.

13. Quotes from Sklaroff, *Black Culture and the New Deal*, 81, 100, and Stewart, *Long Past Slavery*, 33–34, 84.

14. Sklaroff, *Black Culture*, 96, 102; Writers' Program of the Work Projects Administration in the State of Alabama, *Alabama*, 184; Du Bois, *Black Reconstruction in America*, 35, 725; appraisal sheet for Alabama narrative, box 891, Federal Writers' Project, Works Progress Administration Records, Library of Congress. On historians and the "objectivity" problem, see Novick, *That Noble Dream*. Analysis of the implicit Lost Cause bent in the slave narrative interview guide can be found in chapter 3 of this volume.

15. Senator Rush Holt quoted in 76 Cong. Rec. 8399–8400 (1939); Sklaroff, *Black Culture*, 62–72; Fraden, *Blueprints for a Black Federal Theater, 1935–1939*, 107–8; "Theatre Project Faces an Inquiry," *New York Times*, July 27, 1938; Thomas quoted in Jones, *Roosevelt's Image Brokers*, 37; Matthews, *The Federal Theatre, 1935–1939*, 211; Stewart, *Long Past Slavery*, 232; statement of Henry Alsberg, box 31, FTP/LC.

16. More on the changing oversight of Civil War battlefields can be found in Smith, *The Golden Age of Battlefield Preservation*; Zenzen, *Battling for Manassas*; Albright, *Origins of National Park Service Administration of Historic Sites*; and Unrau and Williss, *Administrative History*, https://www.nps.gov/parkhistory/online_books/unrau-williss/adhi.htm.

17. Albright, *Origins of National Park Service Administration*.

18. On the CCC role see Paige, *Civilian Conservation Corps and the National Park Service, 1933–1942: An Administrative History*, https://archive.org/details/civilianconservaoopaig.

19. James McConaghie, "Superintendent's Annual Report for the Year 1936–1937," written July 30, 1937, box 2493, NPS/NARA.

20. *Baltimore Sun*, May 15, 1938; *Christian Science Monitor*, April 1, 1938; reference to this as the "final reunion" can be found in at least one newspaper report that is quoted in Roy, *Pennsylvania at Gettysburg*, 4:134.

21. Murray, *On a Great Battlefield*, 34–35. I am indebted to John Heiser, historian at Gettysburg National Military Park, for helpful information on the Eternal Light Peace Memorial.

22. Hearings before the Committee on Military Affairs, House of Representatives, 75th Cong., 3rd sess., March 8, 1938; Roy, *Pennsylvania at Gettysburg*, 4:113, 110; Josiah Waddle and G. B. Doug [Josiah Waddle], Nebraska, 1936, Manuscript/Mixed Material, Library of Congress, https://www.loc.gov/item/wpalhoo1093/ (accessed May 4, 2017); John Young quoted in Hearings before the Committee on Military Affairs, March 8, 1938.

23. The poem originally appeared in the *Gettysburg Times*, December 30, 1935, and was found on *The Blog of Gettysburg National Military Park*, posted March 26, 2015, https://npsgnmp.wordpress.com/2015/03/26/fighting-today-for-a-better-tomorrow-the-civilian-conservation-corps-at-gettysburg/#_ftn32 (accessed May 2, 2017); Roy, *Pennsylvania at Gettysburg*, 171, 162, 217.

24. Roy, "Gettysburg as It Is Today," 20.

25. *Omaha Evening World* quoted in Roy, *Pennsylvania at Gettysburg*, 448; speech of Dr. Henry Hanson in ibid., 241; *New London Day* quoted in ibid., 456; clippings from *Hartford Courant* for June 28, 1938, and *Tucson Star*, July 1, 1938, SH 28, box 595, Paul L. Roy Collection, Gettysburg National Military Park; "Ceremonies at Antietam," May 31, 1938, *New York Times*.

26. On the growing popularity of the "needless" war doctrine in the 1930s see Bonner, "Civil War Historians and the 'Needless War' Doctrine"; Craven, *The Repressible Conflict*, 24; *Fort Worth Morning Star* quoted in Roy, *Pennsylvania at Gettysburg*, 453; Craven, "Coming of the War between the States," 305; clipping from *Kansas City Star*, July 3, 1938, in SH 28, box 595, Paul Roy Collection, Gettysburg National Military Park.

27. For more on the transfer from the Sons of Confederate Veterans to the NPS, see Zenzen, *Battling for Manassas*; SCV quoted in ibid., 14–15; deed in box 2596A, Manassas, 0.21–201.15, NPS/NARA.

28. "The Battle of Manassas," box 2596A, Manassas, 0.21–201.15, NPS/NARA; Kammen, *Mystic Chords of Memory*, 456; information and photographs regarding the dedication of the Longstreet monument site can be found at http://gettysburgsculptures.com/soldiers_sailors _of_the_confederacy_monument/the_1941_proposed_location_of_the_longstreet_memorial (accessed May 4, 2017). As Jennifer Murray notes in *On a Great Battlefield*, the money for this Longstreet monument failed to materialize, so no memorial was raised to this Gettysburg commander until 1998. It seems worth noting, too, that when referring to the conflict the NPS almost always used the phrase "War between the States"—the preferred terminology of Confederate groups—rather than "Civil War."

29. Nguyen, *Nothing Ever Dies*, 13; Kasson, *The Little Girl Who Fought the Great Depression*, 71–72.

30. For more on Hollywood and the challenges of presenting Civil War– and southern-themed films, including issues related to the Production Code, see Cripps, "The Myth of the Southern Box Office"; Stokes, "The Civil War in the Movies"; Ellen Scott, "Regulating 'Nigger'"; Chadwick, *The Reel Civil War*; Bernstein, "A 'Professional Southerner' in the Hollywood Studio System."

31. Stark Young to Leonidas Payne, February 10, 1933, and Young to Andrew Lytle, November 8, 1935, in Pilkington, *Stark Young*, 460, 646, 654.

32. Janney, *Remembering the Civil War*, 293–94; UDC, *Minutes of the Forty-Second Convention, in Hot Springs, Arkansas* (1935), 84; Draper, "Uncle Tom, Will You Never Die?"; *Bulletin for the Society for Correct Civil War Information* 2 (November 19, 1935): 8.

33. *New York Times*, November 28, 1935; *Variety*, December 4, 1935.

34. Bernstein, "A 'Professional Southerner'"; Young to Margaret Mitchell, March 17, 1939, in Pilkington, *Stark Young*, 802; Mitchell quoted in Pyron, *Southern Daughter*, 144; John Alexander to editor, *New York Times*, January 29, 1939; UDC, *Minutes of the Forty-Third Convention, in Dallas, Texas* (1936), 157; Mrs. C. H. Howard to David Selznick, June 29, 1938, in *Producing GWTW*).

35. Excellent analysis of Trotti's work as a "professional Southerner" can be found in Bernstein, "A 'Professional Southerner.'" *Judge Priest* (film); *Steamboat Round the Bend* (film); Trotti quoted in Bernstein, "A 'Professional Southerner,'"130. For more on John Ford's film versions of the South see Telotte, "The Human Landscape of John Ford's South."

36. *Motion Picture Herald*, February 9, 1935; Mary Elmore to David Selznick, July 1, 1938, and Mamie Hall to David Selznick, November 17, 1938, in *Producing GWTW*.

37. Draper, "Uncle Tom, Will You Never Die?"; Minnie Richardson to Charles Richards, August 9, 1938, in *Producing GWTW*.

38. *So Red the Rose* (film); Draper, "Uncle Tom Will You Never Die?"

39. *New York World Telegram*, October 26, 1935, in *So Red the Rose* clippings file, ROSE/LPA; "Scarred by History: Clarence Muse," in Manchel, *Every Step a Struggle*, 251; *Beverly Hills Liberty*, undated clipping, clippings file, ROSE/LPA; Howard, Bridges, and Boodman, *Gone with the Wind: The Screenplay*, 107; Cripps, "Winds of Change," 144–45.

40. Cripps, "Langston Hughes and the Movies."

41. Jackson, *Hattie*, 47–49; for more on the premiere see Pyron, *Southern Daughter*, 373–80. An excellent compendium on the making of *Gone with the Wind* and the premiere, including many documents and images from the Selznick collection, is Wilson, *The Making of "Gone with the Wind."*

42. Quote from Edna Carroll in Partington, *My Reminiscences of the GAR*, 28–29; Selznick letter of October 30, 1939, quoted in Selznick, *Memo from David O. Selznick*, 235; Pyron, *Southern Daughter*, 374.

Chapter 3

1. Beasley and Lowitt, *One Third of a Nation*, 56–57, 62, 49, 223.

2. Terrill and Hirsch, *Such as Us*, 52; Jacqueline Hall Interview with Paul Green, May 30, 1975, Southern Oral History Project, Documenting the American South, University of North Carolina, http://docsouth.unc.edu/sohp/B-0005-3/B-0005-3.html (accessed December 29, 2016); Beasley and Lowitt, *One Third*, 148.

3. Beasley and Lowitt, *One Third*, 23; Markowitz and Rosner, "Slaves of the Depression," 76; Beasley and Lowitt, *One Third*, 186.

4. Freeman, *R. E. Lee*, 1:95; Randall, *The Civil War and Reconstruction*, 47, 66; Reddick, "Racial Attitudes in American History Textbooks of the South," 233.

5. Writers' Program of the Work Projects Administration in the State of Alabama, *Alabama*, 52; Gordon, *None Shall Look Back*, 45–46.

6. Daniels, *A Southerner Discovers the South*, 211; Dowdey, *Bugles Blow No More*; Mitchell, *Gone with the Wind*, 312, 319, 19, 462; Williams, *Playing the Race Card*, 214; for more on Scarlett's appropriation of black suffering, see Adams, "Local Color."

7. Du Bois, *Black Reconstruction*; Brundage, *The Southern Past*, 138–82; Schuyler, "Not Gone with the Wind."

8. Interview with Parker Pool in Slave Narratives: A Folk History of Slavery in the United States from Interviews with Former Slaves: Typewritten Records Prepared by the Federal Writers' Project, 1936–1938 (Washington, DC, 1941), https://memory.loc.gov/mss/mesn/112/112.pdf (accessed December 29, 2016). I have chosen not to use the contorted "dialect" language often found in these interviews. *Chicago Defender*, May 25, 1929; June 1, 1929; June 8, 1929; and September 23, 1933; "Slavery in Arkansas," *Time*, December 7, 1936, 19; Baker and Cooke, "The Slave Market."

9. "Does It Mean Slavery?," editorial in *Chicago Defender*, September 22, 1934; "Protest Slave Scale of Wages in Works Plan," *Chicago Defender*, June 1, 1935; "Re-Enslaves Farm Workers in the South," *Chicago Defender*, September 19, 1936; Enoch P. Waters, "Abraham Lincoln and Frederick Douglass," *Chicago Defender*, February 15, 1936.

10. Bryant Simon documents the way South Carolina mill hands employed the language of slavery in the first half of the twentieth century, arguing that while there were "racial overtones," their use of the term *slavery* "was more of a descriptive term referring to class issues rather than to gender or racial concerns." He does argue, however, that labor leaders more often talked about links between white workers and black slaves. See Simon, *Fabric of Defeat*, 48, 257n42.

11. Markowitz and Rosner, "Slaves of the Depression," 113, 1. For more on "wage slavery" see Stanley, *From Bondage to Contract*, 84–97; on "white slavery," see Roediger, *The Wages of Whiteness*. Hugh Grant Addams of Australia quoted in Dumenil, *The Modern Temper*, 60.

12. Hall et al., *Like a Family*, 297. For more on how South Carolina mill hands used the language of slavery see Simon, *Fabric of Defeat*, 48–49. Analysis on how Depression-era workers thought about slavery can also be found in Markowitz and Rosner, "Slaves of the Depression," 7–8.

13. Insightful analysis of the emerging labor movement in the New Deal era can be found in Fraser, "The 'Labor Question.'"

14. Terrill and Hirsch, *Such as Us*, 181; Rosner, "Slaves of the Depression," 72, 76, 28; quoted in Foner, *The Story of American Freedom*, 200.

15. Simon, *Fabric of Defeat*, 257n4. Here Simon argues that ordinary white mill hands did not think much about interacialism in their references to slavery but that labor leaders did. Simon, *Fabric*, 112. The authors of *Like a Family* see evidence of some racial empathy in the frequent

references to Old Testament analogies. See Hall et al., *Like a Family*, 296; Rosner, *"Slaves of the Depression*," 27; "Emancipation Day Marked in Harlem," *New York Times*, January 3, 1938; *Chicago Defender*, September 22, 1934.

16. La Touche and Robinson, "Ballad for Americans" (1939); Denning, *The Cultural Front*; Kazin, *American Dreamers*, 155–208; Gilmore, *Defying Dixie*, 157–200; Kazin, *Dreamers*, 178.

17. Angelo Herndon, "You Cannot Kill the Working Class" (1937), http://www.historyisa weapon.com/defcon1/herndoncannotkill.html (accessed December 30, 2016); Hudson and Painter, *The Narrative of Hosea Hudson*, 95; Allen, *Reconstruction*, 14.

18. On Mike Gold see Wald, *Exiles from a Future Time*, 40–71; Gold, *Jews without Money*; Gold, *Change the World*, 22, 38, 34.

19. Typescript for Michael Gold and Michael Blankfort, *Battle Hymn*, first produced by the Experimental Theatre, part of the Federal Theatre Project (1936) in ROSE/LPA. On reception by the *New York Post* see Flanagan, *Arena*, 76–77.

20. Caldwell and Bourke-White, *You Have Seen Their Faces*, 21, 11; Graham, "American Document"; Costonis, "Martha Graham's American Document"; Anderson, *Art without Boundaries*, 170–74; "Martha Graham Offers New Dance," review in the *New York Times*, October 10, 1938.

21. Caldwell and Bourke-White, *You Have Seen Their Faces*, xiv. My interpretation here about the whitening of slavery draws on Gary Gerstle's analysis about the whiteness of "the common man" in New Deal rhetoric. See Gerstle, *American Crucible*, 180–82.

22. Koch, *The Lonely Man* (1937), typescript of play, prologue page 2, act 1, scene 1, p. 7; act 2, scene 1, p. 15, in ROSE/LPA. On Koch's political leanings, see John Houseman, introduction to Koch, *As Time Goes By*, xv–xvi.

23. Filene, *Romancing the Folk*, 64–65; Berlin, Favreau, and Miller, *Remembering Slavery*, xiii–lii.

24. Berlin, Favreau, and Miller, *Remembering Slavery*, xiii–lii; scholarship that evaluates the slave narratives includes Yetman, "The Background of the Slave Narrative Collection"; Woodward, "History from Slave Sources"; and Musher, "Contesting 'The Way the Almighty Wants It.'" A good analysis of the federal efforts to interview former slaves is Stewart, *Long Past Slavery*. Stewart also discusses the publication history of the ex-slave project in *Long Past Slavery*, 261n11.

25. Musher, "Contesting," 11; memorandum, "Ex-Slave Stories," from Alan and Elizabeth Lomax to Henry Alsberg, n.d., entry 21, box 1, file "Ex-Slaves Correspondence," 1, Record Group 69, National Archives and Records Administration.

26. Interview with Rachel Adams of Athens, Georgia, by Sadie Hornsby, undated, in Rawick, *The American Slave*, 7; interview with "Aunt Millie" Bates, Union, South Carolina, by Caldwell Sims, in *Federal Writers' Project: Slave Narrative Project*, vol. 14, *South Carolina*, part 1, Abrams-Durant, 1936, Manuscript/Mixed Material, Library of Congress, https://www.loc.gov/item /mesn141/ (accessed May 15, 2017), 46.

27. Interview with Rev. W. B. Allen, ex-slave, Columbus, Georgia, July 28, 1937, in *Federal Writers' Project: Slave Narrative Project*, vol. 4, *Georgia*, part 1, Adams-Furr, 1936, Manuscript/ Mixed Material, Library of Congress, https://www.loc.gov/item/mesn041/ (accessed January 2, 2017); interview with Hannah Austin, Georgia, by Minnie B. Ross, undated, in *Born in Slavery: Slave Narratives from the Federal Writers' Project, 1936–1938; Georgia Narratives*, vol. 4, part 1, https://memory.loc.gov/cgi-bin/ampage?collId=mesn&fileName=041/mesn041.db&rec Num=22&itemLink=S?ammem/mesnbib:@field%28AUTHOR+@od1%28Austin,+Hannah %29%29 (accessed December 11, 2015).

28. Sklaroff, *Black Culture and the New Deal*, 81–112, 114; Dollard, *Caste and Class in a Southern Town*, 89; Wall, *Inventing the "American Way*," 75–76.

29. Wall, *Inventing the "American Way,"* 39; FDR quoted in Chadwick, *The Reel Civil War*, 179. On the New Deal's indebtedness to white southern Democrats and their acceptance of Jim Crow discrimination, see Katznelson, *Fear Itself*, 133–94.

30. Representative Frank Dorsey quoted in 74 Cong. Rec. 1940 (1936); Representative William Connery quoted in 74 Cong. Rec. 8537 (1935).

31. For more on the focus on male workers during the Depression and in New Deal legislation see Harris, *Out to Work*, 250–72; Gerstle, *American Crucible*, 176–78. Special thanks to Susan Ware for encouraging me to address the gendered component of this problem.

32. Du Bois, *Black Reconstruction*, 8–9, 635.

33. Craven, *The Repressible Conflict, 1830–1861*, 24.

34. Lichtenstein, "Chain Gangs, Communism, and the 'Negro Question,'" 638.

35. Rodimtseva, "On the Hollywood Chain Gang."

36. *I Am a Fugitive from a Chain Gang* (film); the phenomenon of whites appearing in situations historically associated with black oppression is also discussed in Rogin, *Blackface, White Noise*. My analysis of LeRoy's film also draws on Duck, "Bodies and Expectations."

37. *I Am a Fugitive from a Chain Gang* (film); Rodimtseva, "Hollywood Chain Gang."

38. *I Am a Fugitive from a Chain Gang* (film); Duck, "Bodies and Expectations," 85.

39. More about the changing cultural phases of the 1930s can be found in Dickstein, *Dancing in the Dark*. Some discussion of Hollywood production codes and representations of race can be found in Rodimtseva, "Hollywood Chain Gang." Concern about making films that would appeal to white southern audiences is discussed in Cripps, "The Myth of the Southern Box Office."

40. *The Littlest Rebel* (film); duCille, "The Shirley Temple of My Familiar."

41. Williams, *Playing the Race Card*, 44.

42. For more on Ford's life and career see Gallagher, *John Ford*. On Hollywood and "racial intimacy" see Osterweil, "Reconstructing Shirley."

43. *Judge Priest* (film); Eisenberg, "John Ford," 13; analysis of Judge Priest, including its approach to race, can be found in Bernstein, "A 'Professional Southerner' in the Hollywood Studio System," 173–74.

44. *Judge Priest* (film); on the links between Will Rogers and the New Deal see May, *The Big Tomorrow*, 45.

45. *Prisoner of Shark Island* (film); clippings file, *Prisoner of Shark Island*, ROSE/LPA.

46. *Jezebel* (film); Adams, "Local Color"; *Jezebel* trailer, YouTube, https://www.youtube.com/watch?v=TxXUbXhN7H0 (accessed March 15, 2018).

Chapter 4

1. McElvaine, *Down and Out in the Great Depression*, 48; Levine and Levine, *The People and the President*, 50, 87.

2. In his seminal essay on the uses and abuses of the Lincoln image, "Getting Right with Lincoln," David Donald noted how critical the 1930s were in shifting the discussion. See Donald, "Getting Right with Lincoln." The phrase "imaginative repository" appears in Long, *Rehabilitating Bodies*, 12. Long uses this concept to describe Walt Whitman's use of Civil War images to envision the possibility of healing and rehabilitation for damaged bodies.

3. Donald, "Getting Right with Lincoln"; thanks to Tom Brown for suggesting the phrase "getting left with Lincoln." Where Donald emphasized the political usage of Lincoln in post–Civil War America, my focus here is more on Lincoln's cultural power. "Invoke Lincoln Spirit in Fight for U.S. Liberty," *Chicago Daily Tribune*, February 13, 1936; Representative Frank Dorsey quoted in 74 Cong. Rec. 1940 (1936). On the Rivera mural see Scott, "Diego Rivera at Rockefeller

Center." The mural that replaced Rivera's, Jose Sert's *American Progress,* also gives prominent attention to Lincoln.

4. *Los Angeles Times,* May 28, 1939; *Boston Globe,* February 12, 1939. *The Littlest Rebel* (film). The scene between Temple and Lincoln was, apparently, a highlight of the movie, with one theater owner in Detroit proclaiming that whoever "included the apple incident between Lincoln and Shirley deserves a medal" (*Motion Picture Herald,* April 11, 1936). For more on the star power of Shirley Temple in this era, see Kasson, *The Little Girl Who Fought the Great Depression.*

5. Kasson, *The Little Girl Who Fought the Great Depression*; Copland quoted in "Lincoln Portrait Is Presented Here," *New York Times,* April 2, 1943; Kazin, "What Have the 30s Done to Our Literature?," *New York Herald Tribune,* December 31, 1939; R. Griffey, "Marsden Hartley's Lincoln Portraits," 35.

6. Sandburg, *Abraham Lincoln: The Prairie Years*; Schwartz, *Abraham Lincoln and the Forge of National Memory,* 165, 159.

7. Filene, *Romancing the Folk,* 64–65. For more on the rediscovery of folk culture in the 1930s, see Susman, *Culture as History,* 150–83. Sandburg, *Abraham Lincoln: The Prairie Years,* 1:49; Carl Sandburg to Alfred Harcourt, March 5, 1934, in Mitgang, *The Letters of Carl Sandburg,* 303. Excerpt from Carl Sandburg letter reprinted by arrangement with John Steichen, Paula Steichen Polega, and the Barbara Hogenson Agency, Inc. All rights reserved. For more information about Carl Sandburg, please go to www.nps.gov/carl.

8. Sandburg quoted in Callahan, *Carl Sandburg,* 52; Sandburg, *Mary Lincoln*; Duffus, "Mary Todd's Part in the Making of Abraham Lincoln," *New York Times,* December 4, 1932; Sandburg, *The People, Yes.* Charles Poore, Review of *The War Years,* in *New York Times,* December 1, 1939; Sandburg, *Abraham Lincoln: The War Years.* For more on Sandburg's work in the context of the 1930s, see Hurt, "Sandburg's Lincoln within History," and Jones, *Roosevelt's Image Brokers.*

9. Republican quoted in Donald, "Getting Right with Lincoln," 78; "Taft Presents Memorial," *Washington Post,* May 31, 1922; *Address of President Hoover at Gettysburg Battle Field,*" 2; review of *Abraham Lincoln* in *National Indorses Photoplays: Their Monthly Publication* (October 1930), reel 18, DWG/MOMA; telegram of DWG to Sandburg, October 30, 1928, reel 16, DWG/MOMA; Lennig, "'There Is a Tragedy Going on Here Which I Will Tell You Later'"; *Abraham Lincoln* (film).

10. Scholarship on post–Civil War reconciliation and its narrative of fraternal unity includes Blight, *Race and Reunion*; Nina Silber, *The Romance of Reunion*; and Buck, *The Road to Reunion, 1865–1900.* Recent scholarship has challenged the pervasiveness of the "reconciliation narrative." For more on this see Janney, *Remembering the Civil War.*

11. Federal Writers' Project of the Works Progress Administration, *These Are Our Lives,* 242; Schwartz, *Lincoln and the Forge,* 56; Robertson, *Red Hills and Cotton,* 29; Dorothy Hankins to Carl Sandburg, May 26, 1941, box-folder 390a-012, SAND/ILL; Rubin, "General Longstreet and Me," 28.

12. Stokes, *D. W. Griffith's The Birth of a Nation,* 187–90; *Birth of a Nation* (film). For more on the changing nature of the Lincoln image see, among others, Peterson, *Lincoln in American Memory*; Schwartz, *Lincoln and the Forge* and *Abraham Lincoln in the Post-Heroic Era.* While I draw on this scholarship regarding the Lincoln image, I depart from Peterson's more descriptive presentation of the different Lincoln images over time and differ from Schwartz, who objects to the idea that social and political conflict is mediated through memory. Likewise, where Schwartz sees certain themes persisting, over time, in depictions of Lincoln, I see those themes being reshaped in different historical moments.

13. Sherwood, *Abe Lincoln in Illinois,* 166–68; *Young Mr. Lincoln* (film). One of the most widely cited pieces of film criticism is the Marxist critique of *Young Mr. Lincoln* published, in 1970, by

the editors of the French film journal, *Cahiers du Cinema*. Although I do not agree with all of the editors' points, I find their argument regarding the way the film creates a strong, patriarchal Lincoln to be particularly compelling. For the English translation of this article see Editors of *Cahiers du Cinema*, "A Collective Text by the Editors of Cahiers du Cinema."

14. The notion of Dos Passos's work as a chronicle of the "decline and fall of the Lincoln republic" is developed in Denning, *The Cultural Front*, 163–99. Sandburg, *War Years*, 1:21.

15. For more on the celebration of Ulysses Grant in the postwar era see Waugh, *U. S. Grant*, 216–308; letter of Stuart Henry, *New York Times*, June 23, 1935.

16. Koch, *The Lonely Man*; Sandburg, "Lincoln-Roosevelt," 5; Sebold, "The Emancipation Proclamation"; "A Tribute to Abraham Lincoln to Be Read on His Birthday," in Rosenman, *The Public Papers and Addresses of Franklin D. Roosevelt*, 5:68. Sandburg's role in linking the work of Lincoln and FDR can also be seen in letters he wrote to FDR and others in Roosevelt's administration. See, for example, Sandburg to Raymond Moley, October 20, 1933, and to Franklin Roosevelt, March 29, 1935, both in Mitgang, *The Letters of Carl Sandburg*, 298, 318. For more on FDR's use of the Lincoln image see Jividen, *Claiming Lincoln*, 97–133; Jones, *Roosevelt's Image Brokers*.

17. Undated essay, box-folder 350-006, SAND/ILL; Brooks Atkinson, review of *Prologue to Glory*, in *New York Times*, March 18, 1938; FDR quoted in Jones, *Roosevelt's Image Brokers*, 67.

18. Letter of Martha Prins, December 9, 1940, in box-folder 390b-020, SAND/ILL; Representative John Murdock quoted in 76 Cong. Rec. 6627 (1939); Representative Frank Dorsey quoted in 74 Cong. Rec. 1940 (1936). For more on the changing attitudes about "humanitarianism" see Barnett, *Empire of Humanity*.

19. Gerstle, *American Crucible*, 168; Wall, *Inventing the "American Way,"* 45; Sherwood, *Abe Lincoln in Illinois*, 137. For more on the whiteness, and maleness, of the New Deal's "common man" imagery see Gerstle, *American Crucible*, 176–82.

20. Malcolm Bingay, "The Lincoln Mystery," clipping from the *Detroit Free Press*, December 8, 1939, box-folder 363b-006, SAND/ILL; *New York Times*, February 13, 1939; obituary of James A. Ross, *New York Times*, April 28, 1949; Roosevelt quoted in Novick, *The Holocaust in American Life*, 33.

21. On the developing political coalition in the Democratic Party see Kennedy, *Freedom from Fear*, 216; Katznelson, *Fear Itself*, 166–68. FDR quoted in Chadwick, *The Reel Civil War*, 179; Sherwood, *Abe Lincoln in Illinois*, 234 (this is not part of the script but Sherwood's notes at the end).

22. For more on the complicated twists and turns of FDR's administration regarding African Americans see Sullivan, *Days of Hope*. In noting Lincoln's appeal to white immigrants in the 1930s, I depart from Gary Gerstle's argument that suggests Lincoln was a figure with "Nordic" appeal. See Gerstle, *American Crucible*, 168.

23. Gilmore, *Defying Dixie*, 19; Katznelson, *Fear Itself*, 139.

24. Douglass, *Oration in Memory of Abraham Lincoln*, delivered at the unveiling of the Freedmen's Monument in Memory of Abraham Lincoln, in Lincoln Park, Washington, DC, April 14, 1876; Robert Vann, "This Year I See Millions of Negroes Turning the Picture of Abraham Lincoln to the Wall," *Pittsburgh Courier*, September 17, 1932; Woodson quoted in Barr, *Loathing Lincoln*, 193; Gaines, "Lincoln in Africa," 260. For more on black Americans and the memory of Lincoln see Barr, "African American Memory and the Great Emancipator."

25. Vann, "This Year I See"; Earl Brown quoted in Sklaroff, *Black Culture and the New Deal*, 19; letter of Mrs. Redmond Garrett, *Pittsburgh Courier*, January 30, 1937; Baltimore newspaper quoted in McElvaine, *The Great Depression*, 192; Representative Arthur Mitchell quoted in 74 Cong. Rec. 5887 (1936).

26. Barr, "African American Memory and the Great Emancipator"; "To Open Lynch War on

Lincoln, Douglass Day," *Chicago Defender*, February 7, 1931; "Rebel Patriotism," *Chicago Defender*, May 25, 1929.

27. Representative Arthur Mitchell quoted in 74 Cong. Rec. 5887 (1936); Representative John Robsion quoted in 74 Cong. Rec. 8542 (1936).

28. Representative Arthur Mitchell quoted in 74 Cong. Rec. 8551 (1936); Davis, "The Emancipation Moment"; Sandage, "A Marble House Divided," 148–49; "Slaves Freed Twice as New Deal Blooms," *New York Amsterdam News*, October 31, 1936.

29. "Slaves Freed Twice as New Deal Blooms," *New York Amsterdam News*, October 31, 1936; "Author Tells How Abe Lincoln Opposed Race Hatred," *Chicago Defender*, February 13, 1937.

30. Scott Sandage provides a particularly compelling reading of Marian Anderson's Lincoln Memorial concert in Sandage, "A Marble House Divided." NAACP quoted in ibid., 144.

31. Ickes quoted in Sandage, "A Marble House Divided," 145; poem quoted in Kelley, *Hammer and Hoe*, 211–12.

32. On interest in Douglass see, for example, "Frederick Douglass," *The Crisis*, February 1939; letter from NAACP Field Secretary William Pickens to the *New York Herald*, February 12, 1931, box 19, folder 17, BUL/BU.

33. *Young Mr. Lincoln* (film); Anderson's performance in Springfield is noted in Arsenault, *The Sound of Freedom*, 175.

34. Robert F. Bradford, "Lincoln and the New Deal," An Address before the Lincoln Night Dinner at the Middlesex Club, Boston, February 11, 1939, in box 3, file 29, BUL/BU; E. P. Conkle, *Prologue to Glory*; Thomas quoted in Jones, *Roosevelt's Image Brokers*, 37; and in Flanagan, *Arena*, 173.

35. Flanagan quoted in Bentley, *Thirty Years of Treason*, 19.

36. Chapman quoted in "Southern Intolerance Years Ago Inspiration for Anderson Recital," *Chicago Defender*, April 15, 1939.

37. Masters, *Lincoln the Man*; Sandburg, *Storm Over the Land*, 44; Sandburg, "Abraham Lincoln, 1809–1865," 226.

38. Sandburg, *People, Yes*, 134; Sandburg, *War Years*, 3:615, 2:592; Malcolm Bingay, "The Lincoln Mystery," *Detroit Free Press*, December 8, 1939; Herzberg, "A Guide to the Study of the Historical Photoplay, Young Mr. Lincoln," 4.

39. John Malcolm Brinnin to Kimon Friar, August 20, 1939, box 3, folder 12, in John Malcolm Brinnin–Kimon Friar Correspondence, University of Delaware Library; speech of T. V. Smith at the First Annual Abraham Lincoln Lecture at Cooper Union, NY, February 11, 1940, box-folder 229a-020, SAND/ILL; Sandburg, *War Years*, 2:25.

40. Max Lerner, "Lincoln as War Leader," in *The Lincoln of Carl Sandburg*, 33. On concerns about FDR taking on dictatorial powers, specifically over his 1937 proposal to reorganize the Supreme Court, see, for example, Kennedy, *Freedom from Fear*, 332; Benét quoted in Jones, *Roosevelt's Image Brokers*, 79; Robert Sherwood to FDR, July 12, 1941, in MS Am 1947–1947.1, SHER/HARV.

Chapter 5

1. On Mitchell's voluminous correspondence, including her commitment to writing careful and sometimes lengthy responses, see Pyron, *Southern Daughter*, 338–48. Pyron estimates that between 1936 and 1949 Mitchell composed "at least ten thousand letters" (340). While most inquiries about movie parts went to the film's producer, David Selznick, and others in his company, some were directed to Mitchell, including one white woman who, as Pyron explains, put in a personal appearance at Mitchell's home to show her how well she could play the part of Mammy (351). Fan letters to Mitchell can be found in the Margaret Mitchell Family Papers, MS

905, Hargrett Rare Book and Manuscript Library, University of Georgia Libraries. Fan letters to Selznick and other members of his staff regarding the production of the film version of *Gone with the Wind* can be found at the web exhibition *Producing "Gone with the Wind,"* created by the Harry Ransom Center.

2. Margaret Mitchell to Anne Equen, December 11, 1939, in *Gone with the Wind* Literary Estate Papers, MS 3366, Hargrett Rare Book and Manuscript Library, University of Georgia Libraries (reprinted by arrangement with Paul H. Anderson Jr.).

3. Dowdey quoted in Harwell, *"Gone with the Wind" as Book and Film*, 86; Odum, *Southern Regions of the United States*, 499; Cason, "Middle Class and Bourbon," 492–93; Dollard, *Caste and Class in a Southern Town*, 187; Kendrick, *The South Looks at Its Past*, 7. For more on the merging of a geographic frame ("the South") with a temporal frame (the South as a premodern region) see Duck, *The Nation's Region*; and Dyen, "I'll Never Be Hungry Again.'"

4. For more on twentieth-century creations, especially through popular culture, of "the South," see Cox, *Dreaming of Dixie*.

5. There is a vast literature on "the Lost Cause" in post–Civil War southern thought. See, for example, *Ghosts of the Confederacy*; Gallagher and Nolan, *The Myth of the Lost Cause and Civil War History*; Brundage, *The Southern Past*; and Janney, *Burying the Dead but Not the Past*. On adapting Lost Cause thinking to include the "victory narrative" over Reconstruction, see Blight, *Race and Reunion*, 264.

6. Freeman, *The South to Posterity*, x, 204; Freeman quoted in Kammen, *Mystic Chords of Memory*, 387.

7. Robertson, *Red Hills and Cotton*, 28, 71; Phillip B. Arnold to Margaret Mitchell, December 14, 1939, in box 3, MS 905, MM/UGA; Cornelia Arvanti to George Cukor, March 31, 1938, and Burnett to David O. Selznick and Louis B. Mayer, June 27, 1938, in *Producing GWTW*.

8. UDC, *Minutes of the Thirty-Seventh Annual Meeting, Held in Asheville, North Carolina* (1930), 262; UDC, *Minutes of Forty-Fifth Annual Meeting, Held in Tulsa, Oklahoma* (1938), 166; UDC, *Minutes of Thirty-Ninth Annual Meeting, Held in Memphis, Tennessee* (1932), 135; UDC, *Minutes of the Forty-Third Annual Meeting, Held in Dallas, Texas* (1936), 47.

9. UDC, *Minutes of the Fortieth Annual Meeting, Held in Baltimore, Maryland* (1933), 190; UDC, *Minutes of the Forty-First Annual Meeting, Held in New York, New York* (1934), 63–65; UDC, *Minutes of the Forty-Fourth Annual Meeting, Held in Richmond, Virginia* (1937), 230; "Theatre: Double-Jeopardy," *Time*, March 2, 1936.

10. Robertson, *Red Hills and Cotton*, 28; Freeman quoted in Connelly and Bellows, *God and General Longstreet*, 125.

11. Margaret Mitchell interview with Medora Perkerson from July 3, 1936, PBS American Masters, http://www.pbs.org/wnet/americanmasters/margaret-mitchell-american-rebel-interview-with-margaret-mitchell-from-1936/2011/ (accessed February 24, 2017); Marion Fritz to Margaret Mitchell, December 14, 1936, box 96, MM/UGA; M. M. Miller to Selznick, September 19, 1938, *Producing GWTW*; reviewer quoted in Pyron, *Southern Daughter*, 325.

12. For an insightful analysis of Mitchell's divided mind in her portrayal of Scarlett see, for example, Faust, "Clutching the Chains That Bind"; Marian Anderson to Selznick, August 17, 1938, *Producing GWTW*.

13. Edwin Granberry, "The Private Life of Margaret Mitchell," *Collier's*, March 13, 1937, in Harwell, *"Gone with the Wind" as Book and Film*, 51; Gordon, *None Shall Look Back*, 331.

14. Cameron Shipp, review of Gordon's *None Shall Look Back*, 12; "Monument to the Memory of Thomas J. (Stonewall) Jackson," July 28, 1939, from the Committee on the Library, Report No. 1384, 76th Cong., sess. 1, 6. Agrarian writing on Confederate history includes Allen Tate's books on Stonewall Jackson, Jefferson Davis, and Robert E. Lee.

15. Percy, *Lanterns on the Levee*, 275; on Hickok's encounters see, for example, Beasley and Lowitt, *One Third of a Nation*, 148; Daniels, *A Southerner Discovers the South*, 211. Points regarding white southerners', and white Americans', appropriation of black suffering were discussed in chapter 3 of this volume. Robertson, *Red Hills and Cotton*, 264.

16. Davidson quoted in Noggle, "With Pen and Camera," 191–92; Noggle's essay also discusses the way the South became the object of more intense national scrutiny during the 1930s. As Natalie Ring notes, there was a long-standing tendency, especially in northern circles, to designate the South as "a problem." See Ring, *The Problem South*; and Marszalek, "Philatelic Pugilists," 132, 133.

17. *Pseudopodia* 1 (spring 1936): 6; Lumpkin, *The Making of a Southerner*, 225.

18. Jonathan Daniels quoted in Ritterhouse, *Discovering the South*, 236, 222–40. Ritterhouse notes that Daniels's visit with Mitchell did not appear in his published volume, *A Southerner Discovers the South*, due to Mitchell's objections.

19. Perceptive analysis on *The Unvanquished*, both the serialized and unserialized sections, appears in Donaldson, "Dismantling the *Saturday Evening Post Reader.*"

20. For more on southern workers' responses to the New Deal, including the way it promoted a new faith in the federal government, see Simon, *Fabric of Defeat*, 57–61; Pepper, "A New Deal in Reconstruction." As Bruce Baker suggests, positive views of FDR's administration among southern liberal politicians could even encourage some to rethink the history of Reconstruction, putting a positive spin on black participation. See Baker, *What Reconstruction Meant*, 97.

21. Daniels, *A Southerner Discovers*, 282.

22. National Emergency Council, *Report on Economic Conditions of the South*. For more on southern Democrats' complicated responses to FDR's policies see Schulman, *From Cotton Belt to Sunbelt*, 3–38.

23. National Emergency Council, *Report on Economic Conditions of the South*, 2, 21.

24. FDR speech in Roy, *Pennsylvania at Gettysburg*, 4:260; "At the Unveiling of the Robert E. Lee Memorial Statue, Dallas, Texas," in Rosenman, *The Public Papers and Addresses of Franklin D. Roosevelt*, 5:214; "A Greeting from the President on the Occasion of the Dedication of Stratford," ibid., 4:421; "On Visiting the Birthplace of Abraham Lincoln," June 14, 1936, ibid., 5:222.

25. National Emergency Council, *Report on Economic Conditions of the South*, 1.

26. Dowdey and Mitchell quoted in Harwell, *"Gone with the Wind" as Book and Film*, 87, 85–86.

27. Undated newspaper clipping found in box 95, MM/UGA; Senator Bailey quoted in 76 Cong. Rec. 2711 (1940).

28. On the congressional battles over antilynching legislation see Katznelson, *Fear Itself*, 166–68, 179–82.

29. Senator Andrews quoted in 75 Cong. Rec. 1181 (1938); Senator Claude Pepper quoted in 75 Cong. Rec. 974 (1938); Senator Smith quoted in 75 Cong. Rec. 229 (1938); Smith quoted in Simon, *Fabric of Defeat*, 204.

30. For more on John Long's actions see Coski, *The Confederate Battle Flag*, 82, and Prince, *Rally 'Round the Flag, Boys!*, 29; Senator Borah quoted in 75 Cong. Rec. 138 (1938); Senator Smith quoted in 75 Cong. Rec. 228 (1938).

31. More on Communist Party work in the 1930s South can be found in Gilmore, *Defying Dixie*; Kelley, *Hammer and Hoe*.

32. James Goodman analyzes the way historical memories of reconstruction informed southern white responses to communist involvement in the Scottsboro case. For more, including the quote from the *Jackson County Sentinel*, see Goodman, *Stories of Scottsboro*, 115.

33. Owsley, "Scottsboro, the Third Crusade," 258, 259, 271.

34. Ibid., 278, 275.

35. Robertson, *Red Hills and Cotton*, 281; Daniels, *A Southerner Discovers*, 24–27, 84–85; this analysis of Joanna Burden's role in *Light in August* comes from Meyerson and Neilson, "Pulp Fiction."

36. Margaret Mitchell to Harold Latham, June 7, 1937, reel 2, Macmillan Company Records, Margaret Mitchell Files, New York Public Library (reprinted by arrangement with Paul H. Anderson Jr.); Mitchell quoted in Harwell, *"Gone with the Wind" as Book and Film*, 156; more on Mitchell's anticommunist leanings can be found in Pyron, *Southern Daughter*, 441–42.

37. *The Santa Fe Trail* (film).

38. Brinkmeyer, *Fourth Ghost*, 28; R. Alexander Bate, "A Confederate Major and Two Presidents" (Louisville, KY, 1932), file in box 618, FTP/LC; UDC, *Minutes of the Forty-Sixth Annual Meeting Held in Charleston, South Carolina* (1939), 88.

39. Boothe, *Kiss the Boys Good-bye*, 91; Cecil Smith, "It Seems 'Kiss the Boys Good-bye' Has a Social Meaning: But Play Critic Prefers Just to Enjoy Gags," *Chicago Tribune*, March 26, 1939; Boothe, *Kiss the Boys*, 173.

40. Boothe, *Kiss the Boys*, vii, x; Cecil Smith, "It Seems," *Chicago Tribune*; Harwell, *Margaret Mitchell's "Gone with the Wind" Letters, 1936–1949*, 233n3.

41. Massey quoted in Vaughan, "Ronald Reagan and the Struggle for Black Dignity in Cinema, 1937–1953," 85; Boothe, *Kiss the Boys*, xi.

42. Gilmore, *Defying Dixie*, 157–200; quotation on 160.

43. For more on white southerners discovering "fascist" tendencies in southern culture see Gilmore, *Defying Dixie*, 159; Cobb, *Away Down South*, 165–66; and Brinkmeyer, *Fourth Ghost*; Cason, *Ninety Degrees in the Shade*, 89; Cash, *The Mind of the South*; David O. Selznick to Sidney Howard, January 6, 1937, in *Memo from David O. Selznick*, 152; Mike Gold, "New Escapes from the Soviets," in Gold, *Change the World!*, 38.

44. Schuyler, "Not Gone with the Wind," 205; Pittsburgh civil rights group quoted in Leff, *"Gone with the Wind* and Hollywood's Racial Politics," 108; quoted in Reddick, "Education Programs for the Improvement of Race Relations," 377; Los Angeles *Sentinel* clipping, contained in Victor Shapiro to DOS, February 9, 1939, SELZ/UT.

45. Jane Cobb, "Living and Leisure," *New York Times*, January 7, 1940.

46. *Gone with the Wind* (film).

47. An excellent review of Selznick's handling of the "Negro problem" as it related to *GWTW* can be found in Leff, "*Gone with the Wind* and Hollywood's Racial Politics"; more detailed information can be found in the file labeled "Negro Problem," folder 16, box 185, SELZ/UT.

48. Roy Wilkins to Alfred Dackett, January 31, 1940, in Records of the National Association for the Advancement of Colored People, Group II, Series A, box 277, Library of Congress.

49. Gilmore, *Defying Dixie*, 301; "Ben Davis Calls 'Gone with the Wind' Insidious Glorification of the Slave Market," *Cleveland Call and Post*, January 4, 1940; "Daily Worker Critic Forced Out of Job on Refusal to Attack 'Gone With the Wind,'" *New York Times*, December 22, 1939; DOS to John Wharton, January 19, 1940, SELZ/UT.

50. Reddick, "Education Programs for the Improvement of Race Relations," 377.

Chapter 6

1. Some brief observations about the similarities between *Virginia City* and *Casablanca* can be found in the blog *The Blonde at the Film*, https://theblondeatthefilm.com/2014/06/09/virginia -city-1940/ (accessed April 21, 2017). *Casablanca* (film); *Virginia City* (film).

2. For more on how the Civil War framework was used in the build-up to World War II see Takayoshi, *American Writers and the Approach of World War II, 1935–1941*, 99–123.

3. *Casablanca* (film). Excellent analysis of Sam's character in Casablanca can be found in Cripps, "Sam the Piano Player." On Koch and the Casablanca screenplay, see Isenberg, *We'll Always Have Casablanca*, 28.

4. Takayoshi, *American Writers and the Approach of World War II*, 99–123.

5. Collins, "Confederate Identity and the Southern Myth since the Civil War," 228n11; MacKinlay Kantor, "Back to Gettysburg," *Saturday Evening Post* (July 2, 1938); on *GWTW* and antiwar feelings see Collins, "Confederate Identity," 35.

6. Craven, *The Repressible Conflict, 1830–1861*; Randall, "The Blundering Generation," 27–28.

7. Markowitz and Rosner, *"Slaves of the Depression,"* 187, 214, 213. It seems likely that the last letter writer was a woman because she is identified as a first-time industrial worker at a shop that likely began tapping women for employment as men were becoming unavailable due to wartime enlistment.

8. Foner, *The Story of American Freedom*, 224; William Allen White, "The Freedom That Has Made America Great," speech delivered June 22, 1940, in *Vital Speeches of the Day*, 6:642–44, http://www.ibiblio.org/pha/policy/1940/1940-06-22c.html (accessed April 21, 2017).

9. Takayoshi, *American Writers*, 99–123; "Speech for Abe Lincoln in Illinois Benefit Performance," November 1938, in MS Am 1947–1947.1, SHER/HARV; Massey quoted in Theodore Strauss, "Abe Lincoln of 45th Street," *New York Times*, October 30, 1938.

10. Franklin D. Roosevelt, "A Greeting on the Anniversary Celebration of the Thirteenth Amendment," October 16, 1940, in Rosenman, *The Public Papers and Addresses of Franklin D. Roosevelt*, 9:472.

11. On Copland and Lincoln see Elizabeth Crist, "The Sound of Freedom: Copland Composes the Lincoln Portrait," http://www.neh.gov/news/humanities/2007-07/Sound_of_Freedom .htm (accessed May 5, 2010); Sherwood to Archibald MacLeish, May 24, 1940, SHER/HARV; Takayoshi, *American Writers*, 99–123; Sherwood, *Abe Lincoln in Illinois*, 248–49.

12. Sandburg, *Lincoln: The War Years*, 4:371; Robert Sherwood, "The Lincoln of Carl Sandburg: His Monumental Work Has the Character of Folk Biography," *New York Times*, December 3, 1939; Sandburg, "Abraham Lincoln," 241–42.

13. Frank Riddleberger to Carl Sandburg, December 15, 1941, box-folder 390b-022; L. C. Burch to Carl Sandburg, November 7, 1946, box-folder 349-004; John Hulston to Carl Sandburg, March 11, 1942, box-folder 390a-012; F. E. Bredouw to Carl Sandburg, November 9, 1940, box-folder 390a-004; all in SAND/ILL.

14. Jones, *Roosevelt's Image Brokers*, 80; August 19, 1941, press conference proceedings, FDR Library, http://www.fdrlibrary.marist.edu/_resources/images/pc/pc0121.pdf (accessed April 3, 2017); "These Dead . . . Shall Not Have Died in Vain," *New York Times Magazine*, February 8, 1942; "Address to the White House Correspondents' Association," in Rosenman, *The Public Papers and Addresses of Franklin D. Roosevelt*, 12:80.

15. Churchill quoted, along with the UDC president's response, in UDC, *Minutes of the Forty-Sixth Annual Meeting, Held in Charleston, South Carolina* (1939), 88; "War in Spain: Rightist Revolution," *Time*, May 2, 1938, 16; Cash, *The Mind of the South*, 143.

16. UDC, *Minutes of the Forty-Seventh Annual Meeting, Held in Montgomery, Alabama* (1940), 228; Collins, "Confederate Identity," 43; Coski, *The Confederate Battle Flag*, 91; Robert Sherwood to Walter Winchell, October 26, 1938, SHER/HARV.

17. *There Were Giants in the Land*.

18. "General Lee's Spokesman," *Time*, April 1, 1940; Douglas Freeman, "Robert E. Lee," in *There Were Giants in the Land*, 146, 148.

19. *Santa Fe Trail* (film); *Virginia City* (film); *Dixie* (film).

20. "Billy Rowe's Note Book," *Pittsburgh Courier*, September 4, 1943; on the "Double V" campaign see Kennedy, *Freedom from Fear*, 766–68.

21. Lucius Harper, "Dustin' Off the News," *Chicago Defender*, January 24, 1942; A. C. MacNeal, "Under the Lash," *Chicago Defender*, June 27, 1942.

22. Angelo Herndon, "Frederick Douglass: Symbol of Freedom," in *There Were Giants in the Land*, 138, 143.

23. Wright, "Not My People's War," *New Masses*, June 17, 1940; Theophilus Lewis, "Plays and a Point of View," reprinted from the *Interracial Review*, in *Chicago Defender*, April 19, 1941; Carl Murphy, "F.D.R.'s Opportunity," reprinted from the *Baltimore Afro-American* in *Chicago Defender*, April 18, 1942; A. C. MacNeal, "Under the Lash," *Chicago Defender*, April 11, 1942.

24. For more on the NAACP campaign to influence Hollywood and its negotiations with the black community and with the Office of War Information see Koppes and Black, "Blacks, Loyalty, and Motion Picture Propaganda in World War II."

25. Du Bois, *Black Reconstruction*; Allen, *Reconstruction*; Lawson quoted in Bruce Baker, *What Reconstruction Meant*, 131; Fast, *Freedom Road*; Baker, *What Reconstruction Meant*, 130–34; "Brief Dawn for Negroes," *Hartford Courant*, August 27, 1944; Fast, *Being Red*, 83–84.

26. Walter White to Lowell Mellett, August 17, 1942, "The Man on America's Conscience" file in NAACP Papers in ProQuest History Vault, http://cisupa.proquest.com/ksc_assets /history_vault/naacppapers.pdf (accessed April 24, 2017); "Act to Halt Distribution of MGM Anti-Negro Film; U.S. Aroused," *California Eagle*, September 3, 1942; *Daily Worker*, August 28, 1942; Mellett quoted in "Notes" section for *Tennessee Johnson* at the Turner Classic Movies website at http://www.tcm.com/tcmdb/title/92547/Tennessee-Johnson/notes.html (accessed April 24, 2017). Excellent analysis of the controversy over *Tennessee Johnson* can be found in Koppes and Black, "Blacks, Loyalty, and Motion Picture Propaganda in World War II," and Cripps, "Movies, Race and World War II."

27. *Tennessee Johnson* (film); OWI report quoted in Cripps, "Movies, Race and World War II," 65.

28. Nelson Poynter to Walter White, August 25, 1942, in "The Man on America's Conscience" file in NAACP Papers in the ProQuest History Vault; quotes from OWI in Koppes and Black, "Blacks, Loyalty, and Motion Picture Propaganda," 141; letter of E. Franklin Frazier, February 22, 1943, in "The Man on America's Conscience" file in the NAACP Papers in the ProQuest History Vault. Bruce Baker, in *What Reconstruction Meant*, also argues that anticommunism in the 1940s sabotaged films and novels, including plans for the movie version of *Freedom Road*, that offered a revisionist interpretation of Reconstruction. See Baker, *What Reconstruction Meant*, 141.

29. Cripps and Culbert, "The Negro Soldier (1944)."

30. *The Negro Soldier* (film).

31. Schwartz, *Abraham Lincoln in the Post-Heroic Age*, 56 and Appendix B; Warren, *The Legacy of the Civil War*, 79, 80.

32. Schlesinger, "Lincoln in 1944."

33. "American Bias Endangers 'Good Neighbor Policy,'" *Chicago Defender*, March 21, 1942; Keppel, introduction to Myrdal, *An American Dilemma*; Myrdal, *American Dilemma*, 671–72. Excellent analysis on the writing of *American Dilemma* can be found in Jackson, *Gunnar Myrdal and America's Conscience*.

34. Dudziak, *Cold War Civil Rights*, 50–51.

35. Bosley Crowther, "Spanking Disney," *New York Times*, December 8, 1946; Jane Cobb, "Living and Leisure," *New York Times*, January 7, 1940; "Red Paper Condemns 'Gone with the

Wind,'" *New York Times*, December 24, 1939; letter from DOS to John Wharton, January 19, 1940, SELZ/UT.

36. Coski, *The Confederate Battle Flag*, 100–101, 110–31.

37. Koch, *As Time Goes By*, 169; Niven, *Carl Sandburg*, 559–92, 573–604.

38. Pyron, *Southern Daughter*, 440–43; Mitchell quoted on 442.

39. Stewart, *Long Past Slavery*, 235–36; "Sterling A. Brown Chronology" and "'On This I Stand': A Bibliography" in Tidwell and Tracy, *After Winter*; Federal Bureau of Investigation, file on Sterling Brown, https://archive.org/details/SterlingBrownFBIFile (accessed May 16, 2017).

40. Baker, *What Reconstruction Meant*, 134; Fast, *Being Red*, 269–300, 286, 293.

Conclusion

1. Thomas L. Friedman, "Finishing Our Work," *New York Times*, November 4, 2008; on the Obama-Lincoln connections see C. Wyatt Evans, "The Lincoln-Obama Moment," in Brown, *Remixing the Civil War*, 17–36.

2. Jason Kessler quoted in Khwaja Khusro Tariq, "Charlottesville Is a Moment of Reckoning—Especially for Fence-Sitting Liberals," *Huffington Post*, August 12, 2017.

3. George Schuyler, "Not Gone with the Wind," *The Crisis*, July 1937, 205; UDC, *Minutes of the Forty-Sixth Annual Meeting, Held in Charleston, South Carolina* (1939), 88.

4. Alfred Kazin, "What Have the 30s Done to Our Literature?," *New York Herald Tribune*, December 31, 1939.

5. Franklin D. Roosevelt, "Address at Gainesville, Georgia," March 23, 1938, American Presidency Project, http://www.presidency.ucsb.edu/ws/index.php?pid=15613.

6. Gaines, "From Colonization to Anti-colonialism," in Carwardine and Sexton, *The Global Lincoln*, 259–69; Sandage, "A Marble House Divided."

7. Coski, *The Confederate Battle Flag*, 154–55; Greg Grandin, "How Endless War Helps Old Dixie Stay New," *TomDispatch.com*, July 7, 2015, http://www.tomdispatch.com/post/176020/tomgram%3A_greg_grandin,_how_endless_war_helps_old_dixie_stay_new/.

8. Blight, *Race and Reunion*, 4.

[BIBLIOGRAPHY]

Primary Sources

MANUSCRIPT COLLECTIONS

Athens, GA
  Hargrett Rare Book and Manuscript Library, University of Georgia
    Gone with the Wind Literary Estate Papers, MS 3366
    Margaret Mitchell Family Papers, MS 905

Austin, TX
  Harry Ransom Center, University of Texas at Austin
    David O. Selznick Papers

Boston, MA
  Howard Gotlieb Archival Research Center, Boston University
    Frederick Lauriston Bullard Collection

Cambridge, MA
  Houghton Library, Harvard University
    Robert E. Sherwood Papers

College Park, MD
  National Archives
    Federal Writers' Project Papers
    Record Group 69
    Records of the National Park Service

Gettysburg, PA
  Gettysburg National Military Park
    Park Main Files, 1916–54
    Paul L. Roy Papers

Newark, DE
  Special Collections, University of Delaware
    John Malcolm Brinnin–Kimon Friar Correspondence

New York, NY
  Museum of Modern Art
    D. W. Griffith Papers
  New York Public Library
    Macmillan Company Records, Margaret Mitchell Files
  New York Public Library for the Performing Arts, Billy Rose Theatre Division
    Various clippings files

Pierpont Morgan Library, Department of Literary and Historical Manuscripts
    Young Collection
Schomburg Center for Research in Black Culture
    Armstead-Johnson Miscellaneous Theatre Collection

Urbana, IL
    Rare Book and Manuscript Library, University of Illinois at Urbana-Champaign
        Carl Sandburg Papers

Washington, DC
    Library of Congress
        Federal Writers' Project: Slave Narrative Project, WPA Records
        Federal Theatre Project Collection

NEWSPAPERS AND PERIODICALS

Boston Globe
California Eagle
Chicago Daily Tribune
Chicago Defender
Cleveland Call and Post
The Crisis
Daily Worker (NY)
Detroit Free Press
Hartford Courant (CT)
Journal of Negro History
Los Angeles Sentinel
Los Angeles Times
Motion Picture Herald
New York Amsterdam News
New York Herald Tribune
New York Times
New York Times Magazine
North Georgia Review (preceded by *Pseudopodia*)
Pittsburgh Courier
Time Magazine
Variety
Washington Post

PUBLISHED PRIMARY SOURCES

Allen, Hervey. *Action at Aquila*. New York: Farrar & Rinehart, 1938.
Allen, James. *Reconstruction: The Battle for Democracy*. New York: International, 1937.
Armitage, Merle. *Martha Graham*. Los Angeles: Merle Armitage, 1937.
Arnett, Alex M., and Benjamin B. Kendrick. *The South Looks at Its Past*. Chapel Hill:
    University of North Carolina Press, 1935. Reprint, New York: Russell & Russell, 1971.
Barden, Thomas E., Charles L. Perdue Jr., and Robert K. Phillips, eds. *Weevils in the Wheat:
    Interviews with Virginia Ex-Slaves*. Charlottesville: University of Virginia Press, 1976.
Barton, Bruce. "The Faith of Abraham Lincoln." *Vital Speeches of the Day* 6 (March 1, 1940):
    291–94.

Beasley, Maurine, and Richard Lowitt, eds. *One Third of a Nation: Lorena Hickok Reports on the Great Depression.* Urbana: University of Illinois Press, 1981.

Benét, Stephen Vincent. *John Brown's Body.* New York: Rinehart & Company, 1927. Reprint, New York: Rinehart & Company, 1958.

Bentley, Eric, ed. *Thirty Years of Treason: Excerpts from Hearings before the House Committee on Un-American Activities.* New York: Viking, 1971.

Bond, Horace Mann. "A Negro Looks at His South." *Harper's Magazine,* June 1931, 98–108.

Bontemps, Arna. *Black Thunder.* New York: Macmillan, 1936. Reprint, Boston: Beacon, 1968.

Boothe, Clare. *Kiss the Boys Good-bye: A Comedy.* Foreword by Heywood Broun. New York: Random House, 1939.

Botkin, B. A. *Lay My Burden Down: A Folk History of Slavery.* Chicago: University of Chicago Press, 1945.

Bowers, Claude G. *The Tragic Era: The Revolution after Lincoln.* Cambridge, MA: Houghton Mifflin, 1929.

Buck, Paul H. *The Road to Reunion, 1865–1900.* Boston: Little, Brown, 1937.

Bulletin for the Society for Correct Civil War Information. 1935–41.

Caldwell, Erskine, and Margaret Bourke-White. *You Have Seen Their Faces.* New York: Viking, 1937. Reprint, Athens: University of Georgia Press, 1995.

Carpenter, Charles. "John Brown in Harper's Ferry." *National Republic* 19 (August 1931): 24–25.

Cash, W. J. *The Mind of the South.* New York: Vintage, 1941.

Cason, Clarence. "Middle Class and Bourbon." In *Culture in the South,* edited by William T. Couch. Chapel Hill: University of North Carolina Press, 1934.

———. *Ninety Degrees in the Shade.* 1935. Reprint, Tuscaloosa: University of Alabama Press, 1983.

Conkle, E. P. *Prologue to Glory: A Play in Eight Scenes Based on the New Salem Years of Abraham Lincoln.* New York: Samuel French, 1938.

Couch, William T. "The Agrarian Romance." *South Atlantic Quarterly* 36 (October 1937): 419–30.

———. "Reflections on the Southern Tradition." *South Atlantic Quarterly* 35 (July 1936): 284–97.

Craven, Avery. "Coming of the War between the States: An Interpretation." *Journal of Southern History* 2 (August 1936): 303–22.

———. *The Repressible Conflict, 1830–1861.* Baton Rouge: Louisiana State University Press, 1939.

Daniels, Jonathan. *A Southerner Discovers the South.* New York: Macmillan, 1938.

DeVoto, Bernard. "Gettysburg." *Harper's Magazine,* August 1937, 333.

Dollard, John. *Caste and Class in a Southern Town.* New Haven, CT: Yale University Press, 1937.

Dowdey, Clifford. *Bugles Blow No More.* Boston: Little, Brown, 1937.

Draper, Arthur. "Uncle Tom, Will You Never Die?" *New Theatre and Film Magazine* (January 1936): 30–31.

Du Bois, W. E. B. *Black Reconstruction: An Essay toward a History of the Part Which Black Folk Played in the Attempt to Reconstruct Democracy in America.* New York: Harcourt, Brace, 1935.

———. *The Oxford W. E. B. Du Bois Reader.* Edited by Eric J. Sundquist. New York: Oxford University Press, 1996.

Eisenschiml, Otto. *Why Was Lincoln Murdered?* New York: Little, Brown, 1937.

Fast, Howard. *Being Red.* Boston: Houghton Mifflin, 1990.

———. *Freedom Road.* New York: Duell, Sloan and Pearce, 1944.

Faulkner, William. *Absalom, Absalom!* New York: Vintage, 1990.

———. *Light in August.* New York: Vintage International/Random House, 1990.

———. *The Unvanquished.* New York: Vintage, 1991.

Federal Writers' Project. *These Are Our Lives.* Written by members of the Federal Writers' Project, Works Progress Administration. Chapel Hill: University of North Carolina Press, 1939.

Federal Writers' Project of the Works Progress Administration. *Mississippi: The WPA Guide to the Magnolia State.* New York: Viking, 1938.

Fenton, Charles A., ed. *Selected Letters of Stephen Vincent Benet.* New Haven, CT: Yale University Press, 1960.

Flanagan, Hallie. *Arena: The History of the Federal Theatre.* New York: Duell, Sloan and Pearce, 1940.

Ford, John. *John Ford: Interviews.* Edited by Gerald Peary and Jenny Lefcourt. Jackson: University Press of Mississippi, 2001.

Freeman, Douglas Southall. *R. E. Lee.* 4 vols. New York: Charles Scribner's Sons, 1935.

———. *The South to Posterity: An Introduction to the Writing of Confederate History.* New York: Charles Scribner's Sons, 1939.

Gold, Mike. *Change the World!* New York: International, 1936.

———. *Jews without Money.* New York: Horace Liveright, 1930.

Gordon, Caroline. *None Shall Look Back.* New York: Charles Scribner's Sons, 1937. Reprint, Nashville, TN: J. S. Sanders, 1992.

Graham, Martha. "American Document." *Theatre Arts Magazine* 26 (September 1942): 566–74.

Gruening, Martha. "'Fiddle Faddle' to the Old South." *Brooklyn Daily Eagle,* May 16, 1937.

Harwell, Richard Barksdale, ed. *Margaret Mitchell's "Gone with the Wind" Letters, 1936–1949.* New York: Macmillan, 1976.

Herzberg, Max. "A Guide to the Study of the Historical Photoplay, Young Mr. Lincoln." *Photoplay Studies* 5 (June 1939): 4–12.

Hoover, Herbert. *Address of President Hoover at Gettysburg Battle Field: Friday, May 30, 1930.* Washington, DC: Government Printing Office, 1930.

Howard, Sidney. *Gone with the Wind: The Screenplay.* Edited by Herb Bridges and Terryl C. Boodman. New York: Delta, 1989.

Hudson, Hosea, and Nell Irvin Painter. *The Narrative of Hosea Hudson: His Life as a Negro Communist in the South.* Cambridge, MA: Harvard University Press, 1979.

Hughes, Langston. *The Ways of White Folks.* New York: Alfred Knopf, 1934.

John Brown Memorial Association. *John Brown in Bronze, 1850–1859.* Lake Placid, NY: John Brown Memorial Association, 1935.

Johnson, Charles. *The Shadow of the Plantation.* Chicago: University of Chicago Press, 1934.

Kantor, MacKinlay. *Arouse and Beware: A Novel.* London: Gollance, 1937.

———. "Back to Gettysburg." *Saturday Evening Post,* July 2, 1938, 18–19, 74–78.

———. *Long Remember.* New York: Coward-McCann, 1934.

Kazin, Alfred. *On Native Grounds: An Interpretation of Modern American Prose Literature.* New York: Reynal and Hitchcock, 1942.

Koch, Howard. *As Time Goes By.* New York: Harcourt Brace Jovanovich, 1979.

———. *The Lonely Man.* Washington, DC: National Service Bureau, 1937.

La Touche, John, and Earl Robinson. "Ballad for Americans." Federal Theatre Project, 1939.

Levine, Lawrence W., and Cornelia R. Levine, eds. *The People and the President: America's Conversation with FDR.* Boston: Beacon, 2002.

Lilly, William E. *Set My People Free: A Negro's Life of Lincoln.* New York: Farrar & Rinehart, 1932.

The Lincoln of Carl Sandburg: Some Reviews of "Abraham Lincoln: The War Years" Which, for the Authority of Their Judgments and the Grace of Their Style, Deserve at Least the Permanence of This Pamphlet. New York: Harcourt, Brace, 1940.

Locke, Alain, ed. *The New Negro.* New York: Simon and Schuster, 1925. Reprint, New York: Atheneum, 1977.

Lumpkin, Katherine Du Pre. *The Making of a Southerner.* New York: Alfred A. Knopf, 1947.

Manchel, Frank. *Every Step a Struggle: Interviews with Seven Who Shaped the African American Image in Movies.* Washington, DC: New Academia, 2007.

Markowitz, Gerald, and David Rosner, eds. *"Slaves of the Depression": Workers' Letters about Life on the Job.* Ithaca, NY: Cornell University Press, 1987.

Masters, Edgar Lee. *Lincoln, the Man.* New York: Dodd, Mead, 1931.

McElvaine, Robert S., ed. *Down and Out in the Great Depression: Letters from the "Forgotten Man."* Chapel Hill: University of North Carolina Press, 1983.

McMurtry, Gerald. *Lincoln Log Cabin Almanac.* Harrogate, TN: Lincoln Memorial University, 1940.

Mitchell, Margaret. *Gone with the Wind.* New York: Macmillan, 1936.

Mitgang, Herbert, ed. *The Letters of Carl Sandburg.* New York: Harcourt, Brace and World, 1968.

Myrdal, Gunnar. *An American Dilemma: The Negro Problem and Modern Democracy.* New York: Harper & Brothers, 1944.

Odum, Howard. *Southern Regions of the United States.* Chapel Hill: University of North Carolina Press, 1936.

Owsley, Frank L. "Scottsboro, the Third Crusade: The Sequel to Abolition and Reconstruction." *American Review* 1 (June 1933): 257–85.

Partington, Richard O. *My Reminiscences of the GAR.* Bowie, MD: Heritage, 2004.

Pepper, Claude. "A New Deal in Reconstruction." *Virginia Quarterly Review* 15 (Autumn 1939): 551–60.

Percy, William. *Lanterns on the Levee: Recollections of a Planter's Son.* New York: Knopf, 1941.

Pilkington, John, ed. *Stark Young: A Life in the Arts: Letters, 1900–1962.* Baton Rouge: Louisiana State University Press, 1975.

Randall, James G. "The Blundering Generation." *Mississippi Valley Historical Review* 27 (June 1940): 3–28.

———. *The Civil War and Reconstruction.* Boston: D. C. Heath, 1937.

Raper, Arthur, and Ira De A. Reid. *Sharecroppers All.* Chapel Hill: University of North Carolina Press, 1941.

Rawick, George. *The American Slave: Georgia Narratives.* Vol. 12, parts 1 and 2. Westport, CT: Greenwood, 1976.

Reddick, Lawrence D. "Racial Attitudes in American History Textbooks of the South." *Journal of Negro History* 19 (July 1934): 225–65.

———. "Education Programs for the Improvement of Race Relations: Motion Pictures, Radio, the Press, and Libraries." *Journal of Negro Education* 13 (Summer 1944): 367–89.

Robertson, Ben. *Red Hills and Cotton: An Upcountry Memory.* New York: Knopf, 1940. Reprint, Columbia: University of South Carolina Press, 1960.

Rosenbach Company. *The Surrender of Lee and the Assassination of Lincoln, April 1865: An Exhibit of Historical Documents Commemorating the Seventy-Fifth Anniversary*. Philadelphia: Rosenbach, 1940.

Rosenman, Samuel Irving, ed. *The Public Papers and Addresses of Franklin D. Roosevelt*. 13 vols. New York: various publishers, 1938–50.

Roy, Paul F. "Gettysburg as It Is Today." *National Republic* 19 (April 1932): 20–22.

———, ed. *Pennsylvania at Gettysburg: The Seventy-Fifth Anniversary of the Battle of Gettysburg: Report of the Pennsylvania Commission*. 4 vols. Gettysburg: Pennsylvania Commission, 1939.

Sandburg, Carl. *Abraham Lincoln: The Prairie Years*. 2 vols. New York: Harcourt, Brace, 1926.

———. *Abraham Lincoln: The War Years*. 4 vols. New York: Harcourt, Brace, 1939.

———. *Home Front Memo*. New York: Harcourt, Brace, 1943.

———. "Lincoln-Roosevelt: How Two Presidents Sought Solutions of Similar Problems." *Today* 10 (February 10, 1934): 5.

———. *Mary Lincoln: Wife and Widow*. New York: Harcourt, Brace, 1932.

———. *The People, Yes*. New York: Harcourt, Brace, 1936.

———. *Storm over the Land: A Profile of the Civil War Taken Mainly from Abraham Lincoln: The War Years*. New York: Harcourt, Brace, 1942.

Schlesinger, Arthur M. "Lincoln in 1944." *New Republic*, February 14, 1944, 207–8.

Sebold, Charles E. "The Emancipation Proclamation: A Precedent for the Recovery Program." *World Tomorrow*, July 21, 1934, 364–68.

Selznick, David O. *Memo from David O. Selznick*. New York: Viking, 1972.

Sherwood, Robert E. *Abe Lincoln in Illinois: A Play in Twelve Scenes*. Foreword written by Carl Sandburg. New York: Charles Scribner's Sons, 1939.

Silber, Irwin, and Jerry Silverman, eds. *Songs of the Civil War*. New York: Columbia University Press, 1960.

Stern, Philip Van Doren. *The Man Who Killed Lincoln*. New York: World, 1942.

Tate, Allen. *Jefferson Davis: His Rise and Fall*. New York: Minton, Balch, 1929.

———. *Selected Poems*. New York: Charles Scribner's Sons, 1937.

———. *Stonewall Jackson: The Good Soldier*. New York: Minton, Balch, 1928.

Terkel, Studs. *Hard Times: An Oral History of the Great Depression*. New York: Pantheon, 1970.

Terrill, Tom E., and Jerrold Hirsch, eds. *Such as Us: Southern Voices of the Thirties*. Chapel Hill: University of North Carolina Press, 1978.

There Were Giants in the Land: Twenty-Eight Historic Americans as Seen by Twenty-Eight Contemporary Americans. New York: Farrar & Rinehart, 1942.

Twelve Southerners. *I'll Take My Stand: The South and the Agrarian Tradition*. New York: Harper & Bros., 1930.

United Daughters of the Confederacy. *Minutes of the Annual Convention*. Opelika, AL: Post and dates vary.

Wright, Richard. "Not My People's War." *New Masses* 39 (June 17, 1940): 8–12.

———. *Twelve Million Black Voices: A Folk History of the Negro in the United States*. New York: Viking, 1941.

Writers' Program of the Work Projects Administration in the State of Alabama. *Alabama: A Guide to the Deep South*. New York: R. R. Smith, 1941.

Young, Stark. *So Red the Rose*. New York: Charles Scribner's Sons, 1934.

FILMS

Abe Lincoln in Illinois. Directed by John Cromwell. Produced by Max Gordon. RKO Radio Pictures, 1940.

Abraham Lincoln. Directed by D. W. Griffith. Produced by D. W. Griffith and Joseph M. Schenck. United Artists, 1930.

The Birth of a Nation. Directed by D. W. Griffith. Produced by D. W. Griffith and Harry Aitken. Epoch Producing Co., 1915.

Casablanca. Directed by Michael Curtiz. Produced by Hal B. Wallis. Warner Brothers, 1942.

Dixie. Directed by A. Edward Sutherland. Produced by Paul Jones. Paramount Pictures, 1943.

Gone with the Wind. Directed by Victor Fleming. Produced by David O. Selznick. Metro-Goldwyn-Mayer, 1939.

I Am a Fugitive from a Chain Gang. Directed by Mervyn LeRoy. Produced by Hal B. Wallis. Warner Brothers, 1932.

Jezebel. Directed and produced by William Wyler. Warner Brothers, 1938.

Judge Priest. Directed by John Ford. Produced by Sol M. Wurtzel. Fox Film Corporation, 1934.

The Little Colonel. Directed by David Butler. Produced by Buddy G. DeSylva. Fox Film Corporation, 1935.

The Littlest Rebel. Directed by David Butler. Produced by Darryl F. Zanuck. Twentieth Century Fox Film Corporation, 1935.

Mr. Smith Goes to Washington. Directed and produced by Frank Capra. Columbia Pictures Corporation, 1939.

The Negro Soldier. Directed by Stuart Heisler. Produced by Frank Capra and the US War Department. War Activities Committee of the Motion Pictures Industry, 1944.

Prisoner of Shark Island. Directed by John Ford. Produced by Nunnally Johnson and Darryl F. Zanuck. Twentieth Century Fox Film Corporation, 1936.

The Santa Fe Trail. Directed by Michael Curtiz. Produced by Hal B. Wallis. Warner Brothers, 1940.

So Red the Rose. Directed by King Vidor. Produced by Douglas MacLean. Paramount Pictures, 1935.

Steamboat Round the Bend. Directed by John Ford. Produced by Sol M. Wurtzel. Fox Film Corporation, 1935.

Tennessee Johnson. Directed by William Dieterle. Produced by J. Walter Ruben. Metro-Goldwyn-Mayer, 1943.

Virginia City. Directed by Michael Curtiz. Produced by Robert Fellows. Warner Brothers, 1940.

Young Mr. Lincoln. Directed by John Ford. Produced by Darryl F. Zanuck and Kenneth Macgowan. Twentieth Century Fox Film Corporation, 1939.

GOVERNMENT PUBLICATIONS

National Emergency Council. *Report on Economic Conditions of the South.* Washington, DC: Government Printing Office, 1938.

US Congress. House of Representatives. Committee on the Library. *Monument to the Memory of Thomas J. (Stonewall) Jackson.* 76th Cong., 1st sess., July 28, 1939.

———. *Statue of Gen. Robert E. Lee.* 75th Cong., 1st sess., June 29, 1937.

US Congress. House of Representatives. Committee on Military Affairs. *Hearings before the Committee on Military Affairs.* 75th Cong., 3rd sess. Washington, DC: Government Printing Office, 1938.

US Congress. Senate. *The Reports of the Committees of the Senate of the United States for the Seventy-Sixth Congress.* 76th Cong., 1st sess. Washington, DC: Government Printing Office, 1939.

ONLINE SOURCE MATERIAL

Adams, Don, and Arlene Goldbard. *New Deal Cultural Programs: Experiments in Cultural Democracy* (1986, 1995). http://www.wwcd.org/policy/US/newdeal.html.

The Blonde at the Film. Digital blog. https://theblondeatthefilm.com/2014/06/09/virginia-city-1940/. Accessed April 21, 2017.

Cowan, Effie, and Ernestine Weiss Faudie. *Mrs. Ernestine Weiss Faudie.* Texas. Manuscript/Mixed Material. Library of Congress. https://www.loc.gov/item/wpalh002243/. Accessed May 4, 2017.

Crist, Elizabeth B. "The Sound of Freedom: Copland Composes the *Lincoln Portrait.*" *Humanities 28* (July–August 2007), http://www.neh.gov/news/humanities/2007-07/Sound_of_Freedom.htm. Accessed May 5, 2010.

Doug, G. B., and Josiah Waddle. *Josiah Waddle.* Nebraska, 1936. Manuscript/Mixed Material. Library of Congress. https://www.loc.gov/item/wpalh001093/. Accessed May 4, 2017.

Douglass, Frederick. *Oration in Memory of Abraham Lincoln.* Washington, DC, April 14, 1876. http://teachingamericanhistory.org/library/document/oration-in-memory-of-abraham-lincoln/. Accessed June 8, 2017.

Federal Bureau of Investigation. File on Sterling Brown. https://archive.org/details/Sterling-BrownFBIFile. Accessed May 16, 2017.

Gettysburg Sculptures. Digital blog. http://gettysburgsculptures.com/soldiers_sailors_of_the_confederacy_monument/the_1941_proposed_location_of_the_longstreet_memorial. Accessed May 4, 2017.

Green, Paul. Interview by Jacqueline Hall. May 30, 1975. Southern Oral History Project at Documenting the American South, University of North Carolina. http://docsouth.unc.edu/sohp/B-0005-3/B-0005-3.html. Accessed December 29, 2016.

Herndon, Angelo. "You Cannot Kill the Working Class." Pamphlet, 1937. http://www.historyisaweapon.com/defcon1/herndoncannotkill.html. Accessed December 30, 2016.

"Jezebel (1938) Official Trailer." Video. https://www.youtube.com/watch?v=TxXUbXhN7Ho.

Mellett quoted in "Notes" section for *Tennessee Johnson* at the Turner Classic Movies website. http://www.tcm.com/tcmdb/title/92547/Tennessee-Johnson/notes.html. Accessed April 24, 2017.

Mintz, Steven, and Sara McNeil. "The Farmer's Plight." *Digital History* (2016), http://www.digitalhistory.uh.edu/disp_textbook.cfm?smtid=2&psid=3441. Accessed June 8, 2017.

Mitchell, Margaret. Interview by Medora Perkerson. Radio, Atlanta, GA, July 3, 1936. http://www.pbs.org/wnet/americanmasters/episodes/margaret-mitchell-american-rebel/interview-with-margaret-mitchell-from-1936/2011/. Accessed May 8, 2017.

NAACP Papers. Library of Congress. Accessed via the ProQuest History Vault.

"Press Conference #762." August 19, 1941. http://www.fdrlibrary.marist.edu/_resources/images/pc/pc0121.pdf. Accessed April 3, 2017.

Producing "Gone with the Wind." Web exhibition. The Harry Ransom Center at the University of Texas at Austin. http://www.hrc.utexas.edu/exhibitions/web/gonewiththewind/. Accessed May 17, 2017.

Roosevelt, Franklin D. "The Forgotten Man." Radio address, Albany, NY, April 7, 1932. http://newdeal.feri.org/speeches/1932c.htm. Accessed August 13, 2012.

Rosiecki, Casimer. *The Blog of Gettysburg National Military Park.* March 26, 2015. https://

npsgnmp.wordpress.com/2015/03/26/fighting-today-for-a-better-tomorrow-the-civilian
-conservation-corps-at-gettysburg/#_ftn32. Accessed May 2, 2017.

Unrau, Harlan D., and G. Frank Williss. *Administrative History: Expansion of the National
Park Service in the 1930s* (September 1983). https://www.nps.gov/parkhistory/online_books
/unrau-williss/adhi.htm.

White, William Allen. "The Freedom That Has Made America Great." Speech, Holland
House, NY, June 22, 1940. Published in *Vital Speeches of the Day* 6:642–44. http://www
.ibiblio.org/pha/policy/1940/1940-06-22c.html. Accessed April 21, 2017.

WPA Slave Narrative Project. Accessed through "Born in Slavery: Slaves Narratives from the
Federal Writers' Project, 1936–1938." http://memory.loc.gov/ammem/snhtml.

Wright, Capt. H. C. *Capt. H. C. Wright*. Texas. Manuscript/Mixed Material. Library of Congress. https://www.loc.gov/item/wpalh002444/. Accessed May 4, 2017.

Secondary Sources

Adams, Jessica. "Local Color: The Southern Plantation in Popular Culture." *Cultural Critique*
42 (Spring 1999): 163–87.

Albright, Horace M. *Origins of National Park Service Administration of Historic Sites*. Philadelphia: Eastern Parks and Monument Association, 1971.

Alston, Lee J. "Farm Foreclosures in the United States during the Interwar Period." *Journal
of Economic History* 43 (December 1983): 885–903.

Anderson, Jack. *Art without Boundaries: The World of Modern Dance*. Iowa City: University
of Iowa Press, 1997.

Arsenault, Raymond. *The Sound of Freedom: Marian Anderson, the Lincoln Memorial, and
the Concert That Awakened America*. New York: Bloomsbury, 2009.

Baker, Bruce E. *What Reconstruction Meant: Historical Memory in the American South*.
Charlottesville: University of Virginia Press, 2007.

Barnett, Michael. *Empire of Humanity: A History of Humanitarianism*. Ithaca, NY: Cornell
University Press, 2011.

Barr, John. "African American Memory and the Great Emancipator." In *Lincoln's Enduring
Legacy: Perspectives from Great Thinkers, Great Leaders and the American Experiment*, edited
by Robert P. Watson, William D. Pedersen, and Frank J. Williams, 133–64. Lanham, MD:
Lexington Books, 2011.

Barr, John McKee. *Loathing Lincoln: An American Tradition from the Civil War to the Present*.
Baton Rouge: Louisiana State University Press, 2014.

Berlin, Ira, Marc Favreau, and Steven F. Miller, eds. *Remembering Slavery: African Americans
Talk about Their Personal Experiences of Slavery and Freedom*. New York: New Press, 1998.

Bernstein, Matthew. "A 'Professional Southerner' in the Hollywood Studio System: Lamar
Trotti at Work, 1925–1952." In *American Cinema and the Southern Imaginary*, edited by Deborah E. Barker and Kathryn B. McKee, 122–48. Athens: University of Georgia Press, 2011.

Blair, William A. "Celebrating Freedom: The Problem of Emancipation in Public Commemoration." In *Lincoln's Proclamation: Emancipation Reconsidered*, edited by William A. Blair
and Karen Fisher Younger, 195–220. Chapel Hill: University of North Carolina Press,
2009.

———. *Cities of the Dead: Contesting the Memory of the Civil War in the South, 1865–1914*.
Chapel Hill: University of North Carolina Press, 2004.

Blight, David W. *American Oracle: The Civil War in the Civil Rights Era*. Cambridge, MA:
Harvard University Press, 2013.

————. *Race and Reunion: The Civil War in American Memory.* Cambridge, MA: Harvard University Press, 2001.

Bodnar, John. "The Memory Debate: An Introduction." In *Remaking America: Public Memory, Commemoration, and Patriotism in the Twentieth Century,* edited by John Bodnar, 13–20. Princeton, NJ: Princeton University Press, 1992.

Bonner, Thomas N. "Civil War Historians and the 'Needless War' Doctrine." *Journal of the History of Ideas* 17 (April 1956): 193–216.

Brinkmeyer, Robert H., Jr. *The Fourth Ghost: White Southern Writers and European Fascism, 1930–1950.* Baton Rouge: Louisiana State University Press, 2009.

Brown, Thomas J. *Civil War Canon: Sites of Confederate Memory in South Carolina.* Chapel Hill: University of North Carolina Press, 2015.

————. *The Public Art of Civil War Commemoration: A Brief History with Documents.* Boston: Bedford/St. Martin's, 2004.

————. *Reconstructions: New Perspectives on the Postbellum United States.* New York: Oxford University Press, 2006.

————. *Remixing the Civil War: Meditations on the Sesquicentennial.* Baltimore, MD: Johns Hopkins University Press, 2011.

Brundage, W. Fitzhugh. *The Southern Past: A Clash of Race and Memory.* Cambridge, MA: Harvard University Press, 2005.

Callahan, North. *Carl Sandburg: His Life and Works.* University Park: Pennsylvania State University Press, 1987.

Carroll, Peter. *The Odyssey of the Abraham Lincoln Brigade: Americans in the Spanish Civil War.* Stanford, CA: Stanford University Press, 1994.

Carton, Evan. "Crossing Harpers Ferry: Liberal Education and John Brown's Corpus." *American Literature* 73 (December 2001): 837–63.

Carwardine, Richard, and Jay Sexton. *The Global Lincoln.* New York: Oxford University Press, 2011.

Chadwick, Bruce. *The Reel Civil War: Mythmaking in American Film.* New York: Vintage, 2001.

Cobb, James C. *Away Down South: A History of Southern Identity.* New York: Oxford University Press, 2005.

Collins, Bruce. "Confederate Identity and the Southern Myth since the Civil War." In *The Legacy of Disunion: The Enduring Significance of the American Civil War,* edited by Susan-Mary Grant and Peter J. Parish, 30–47. Baton Rouge: Louisiana State University Press, 2003.

Connelly, Thomas L., and Barbara L. Bellows. *God and General Longstreet: The Lost Cause and the Southern Mind.* Baton Rouge: Louisiana State University Press, 1995.

Cook, Robert. *Troubled Commemoration: The American Civil War Centennial, 1961–1965.* Baton Rouge: Louisiana State University Press, 2007.

Coski, John M. *The Confederate Battle Flag: America's Most Embattled Emblem.* Cambridge, MA: Harvard University Press, 2005.

Costonis, Maureen. "Martha Graham's American Document: A Minstrel Show in Modern Dance Dress." *American Music* 9 (Autumn 1991): 297–310.

Cox, Karen L. *Dreaming of Dixie: How the South Was Created in American Popular Culture.* Chapel Hill: University of North Carolina Press, 2011.

Cripps, Thomas. "Langston Hughes and the Movies: The Case of *Way Down South.*" In *Montage of a Dream: The Art and Life of Langston Hughes,* edited by John Edgar Tidwell and Cheryl R. Ragar, 305–17. Columbia: University of Missouri Press, 2007.

————. "Movies, Race and World War II: Tennessee Johnson as an Anticipation of the Strategies of the Civil Rights Movement." *Prologue* 14 (Summer 1982): 49–67.

————. "The Myth of the Southern Box Office: A Factor in Racial Stereotyping in American Movies, 1929–1940." In *The Black Experience in America*, edited by James Curtis and Lewis Gould, 116–44. Austin: University of Texas Press, 1970.

————. "Sam the Piano Player: The Man Between." *Journal of Popular Film and Television* 27 (Winter 2000): 16–23.

————. "Winds of Change: *Gone with the Wind* and Racism as a National Issue." In *Recasting: Gone with the Wind in American Culture*, edited by Darden A. Pyron, 137–52. Miami: University Presses of Florida, 1983.

Cripps, Thomas, and David Culbert. "The Negro Soldier (1944): Film Propaganda in Black and White." *American Quarterly* 31 (Winter 1979): 616–40.

Cullen, Jim. *The Civil War in Popular Culture: A Reusable Past*. Washington, DC: Smithsonian Institution Press, 1995.

cummings, e. e. "Poem, or Beauty Hurts Mr. Vinal." *S4N*, no. 23 (December 1922): 13–15.

Davis, David Brion. "The Emancipation Moment." In *Lincoln, the War President: The Gettysburg Lectures*, edited by Gabor S. Boritt, 63–88. New York: Oxford University Press, 1992.

Denning, Michael. *The Cultural Front: The Laboring of America in the Twentieth Century*. New York: Verso 1996.

Dickstein, Morris. *Dancing in the Dark: A Cultural History of the Great Depression*. New York: W. W. Norton, 2010.

Donald, David. "Getting Right with Lincoln." *Harper's Magazine*, April 1, 1951, 74–80.

Donaldson, Susan. "Dismantling the *Saturday Evening Post Reader*: The *Unvanquished* and Changing 'Horizons of Expectations.'" In *Faulkner and Popular Culture: Faulkner and Yoknapatawpha, 1988*, edited by Doreen Fowler and Ann J. Abadie, 179–95. Jackson: University Press of Mississippi, 1990.

DuCille, Ann. "The Shirley Temple of My Familiar." *Transition* 73 (1997): 10–32.

Duck, Leigh Anne. "Bodies and Expectations: Chain Gang Discipline." In *American Cinema and the Southern Imaginary*, edited by Deborah E. Barker and Kathryn B. McKee, 79–103. Athens: University of Georgia Press, 2011.

————. *The Nation's Region: Southern Modernism, Segregation, and U.S. Nationalism*. Athens: University of Georgia Press, 2006.

Dudziak, Mary L. *Cold War Civil Rights: Race and the Image of American Democracy*. Princeton, NJ: Princeton University Press, 2000.

Dumenil, Lynn. *The Modern Temper*. New York: Hill & Wang, 1995.

Dyen, Jonathan. "'I'll Never Be Hungry Again': Sectionalism, Economic Resistance, and the Trope of the Civil War in American Fiction, 1894–2010." PhD diss., Boston University, 2011.

Editors of *Cahiers du Cinema*. "A Collective Text by the Editors of *Cahiers du Cinema*: John Ford's Young Mr. Lincoln." *Screen* 13 (Autumn 1972): 5–44.

Egerton, John. *Speak Now against the Day: The Generation before the Civil Rights Movement in the South*. Chapel Hill: University of North Carolina Press, 1995.

Evans, C. Wyatt. *The Legend of John Wilkes Booth: Myth, Memory, and a Mummy*. Lawrence: University Press of Kansas, 2004.

Faust, Drew. "Clutching the Chains That Bind: Margaret Mitchell and *Gone with the Wind*." *Southern Cultures* 5 (Spring 1999): 5–20.

Filene, Benjamin. *Romancing the Folk: Public Memory and American Roots Music*. Chapel Hill: University of North Carolina Press, 2000.

Foner, Eric. *The Story of American Freedom*. New York: W. W. Norton, 1998.

Foster, Gaines M. *Ghosts of the Confederacy: Defeat, the Lost Cause, and the Emergence of the New South*. New York: Oxford University Press, 1987.

Fox-Genovese, Elizabeth. "Scarlett O'Hara: The Southern Lady as New Woman." *American Quarterly* 33 (Autumn 1981): 391–411.

Fraden, Rena. *Blueprints for a Black Federal Theater, 1935–1939*. Cambridge: Cambridge University Press, 1994.

Fraser, Steve. "The 'Labor Question.'" In *The Rise and Fall of the New Deal Order, 1930–1980*, edited by Steve Fraser and Gary Gerstle, 55–84. Princeton, NJ: Princeton University Press, 1989.

Fraser, Steve, and Gary Gerstle, eds. *The Rise and Fall of the New Deal Order, 1930–1980*. Princeton, NJ: Princeton University Press, 1990.

French, Scot. *The Rebellious Slave: Nat Turner in American Memory*. Boston: Houghton Mifflin, 2004.

Gaines, Kevin. "Lincoln in Africa." In *The Global Lincoln*, edited by Richard Carwardine and Jay Sexton, 259–71. New York: Oxford University Press, 2011.

Gallagher, Gary, and Alan T. Nolan, eds. *The Myth of the Lost Cause and Civil War History*. Bloomington: Indiana University Press, 2000.

Gallagher, Tag. *John Ford: The Man and His Films*. Berkeley: University of California Press, 1986.

Gannon, Barbara. *The Won Cause: Black and White Comradeship in the Grand Army of the Republic*. Chapel Hill: University of North Carolina Press, 2011.

Gardner, Sarah. *Reviewing the South: The Literary Marketplace and the Southern Renaissance, 1920–1941*. Cambridge: Cambridge University Press, 2017.

Gerstle, Gary. *American Crucible: Race and Nation in the Twentieth Century*. Princeton, NJ: Princeton University Press, 2001.

Gilmore, Glenda. *Defying Dixie: The Radical Roots of Civil Rights, 1919–1950*. New York: W. W. Norton, 2008.

Goggin, Jacqueline. *Carter G. Woodson: A Life in Black History*. Baton Rouge: Louisiana State University Press, 1997.

Goodman, James. *Stories of Scottsboro*. New York: Vintage, 1995.

Green, Harvey. *The Uncertainty of Everyday Life, 1915–1945*. New York: HarperCollins, 1992.

Griffey, Randall R. "Marsden Hartley's Lincoln Portraits." *American Art* 15 (Summer 2001): 34–51.

Halbwachs, Maurice. *On Collective Memory*. Edited and translated by Lewis A. Coser. Chicago: University of Chicago Press, 1992.

Hall, Jacquelyn Dowd, James Leloudis, Robert Korstad, Mary Murphy, Lu Ann Jones, and Christopher B. Daly. *Like a Family: The Making of a Southern Cotton Mill World*. Chapel Hill: University of North Carolina Press, 1988.

Harwell, Richard, ed. *"Gone with the Wind" as Book and Film*. Columbia: University of South Carolina Press, 1983.

Haskell, Molly. *Frankly My Dear: "Gone with the Wind" Revisited*. New Haven, CT: Yale University Press, 2009.

Hemingway, Ernest. *The Sun Also Rises*. New York: Scribner's, 1926.

Hirsch, Jerrold. *Portrait of America: A Cultural History of the Federal Writers' Project*. Chapel Hill: University of North Carolina Press, 2003.

Houseman, John. Introduction to Howard Koch, *As Time Goes By: Memoirs of a Writer*. New York: Harcourt Brace Jovanovich, 1979.

Hurt, James. "Sandburg's Lincoln within History." *Journal of the Abraham Lincoln Association* 20 (Winter 1999): 55–65.

Isenberg, Noah. *We'll Always Have Casablanca: The Life, Legend, and Afterlife of Hollywood's Most Beloved Movie*. New York: W. W. Norton, 2017.

Jackson, Carlton. *Hattie: The Life of Hattie McDaniel*. Lanham, MD: Madison Books, 1990.

Jackson, Robert. *Fade In, Crossroads: A History of the Southern Cinema*. New York: Oxford University Press, 2017.

Jackson, Walter A. *Gunnar Myrdal and America's Conscience: Social Engineering and Racial Liberalism, 1938–1987*. Chapel Hill: University of North Carolina Press, 1990.

Janney, Caroline E. *Burying the Dead but Not the Past: Ladies' Memorial Associations and the Lost Cause*. Chapel Hill: University of North Carolina Press, 2008.

———. *Remembering the Civil War: Reunion and the Limits of Reconciliation*. Chapel Hill: University of North Carolina Press, 2013.

———. "Written in Stone: Gender, Race and the Heyward Shepherd Memorial." *Civil War History* 52 (June 2006): 117–41.

Jividen, Jason. *Claiming Lincoln: Progressivism, Equality, and the Battle for Lincoln's Legacy in Presidential Rhetoric*. DeKalb: Northern Illinois University Press, 2011.

Jones, Alfred Haworth. *Roosevelt's Image Brokers: Poets, Playwrights, and the Use of the Lincoln Symbol*. Port Washington, NY: Kennikat, 1974.

Kammen, Michael G. *Mystic Chords of Memory: The Transformation of Tradition in American Culture*. New York: Vintage, 1993.

Kasson, John F. *The Little Girl Who Fought the Great Depression: Shirley Temple and 1930s America*. New York: W. W. Norton, 2014.

Katznelson, Ira. *Fear Itself: The New Deal and the Origins of Our Time*. New York: W. W. Norton, 2013.

Kazin, Michael. *American Dreamers: How the Left Changed a Nation*. New York: Knopf, 2011.

Kelley, Robin D. G. *Hammer and Hoe: Alabama Communists during the Great Depression*. Chapel Hill: University of North Carolina Press, 1990.

Kennedy, David M. *Freedom from Fear: The American People in Depression and War, 1929–1945*. New York: Oxford University Press, 1999.

Kessler-Harris, Alice. *Out to Work: A History of Wage-Earning Women in the United States*. New York: Oxford University Press, 1982.

Kirby, Jack Temple. *Media-Made Dixie: The South in the American Imagination*. Athens: University of Georgia Press, 1978.

Koppes, Clayton R., and Gregory D. Black. "Blacks, Loyalty, and Motion Picture Propaganda in World War II." In *Controlling Hollywood: Censorship and Regulation in the Studio Era*, edited by Matthew Bernstein, 130–56. New Brunswick, NJ: Rutgers University Press, 1999.

Kyvig, David E. "History as Present Politics: Claude Bowers' *The Tragic Era*." *Indiana Magazine of History* 73 (March 1977): 17–31.

Leff, Leonard. "*Gone with the Wind* and Hollywood's Racial Politics." *Atlantic Monthly* 284 (December 1999): 106–14.

Lennig, Arthur. "'There Is a Tragedy Going on Here Which I Will Tell You Later': D. W. Griffith and Abraham Lincoln." *Film History* 22 (2010): 41–72.

Leuchtenburg, William E. *Franklin D. Roosevelt and the New Deal*. New York: Harper & Row, 1963.

———. *The Perils of Prosperity, 1914–1932*. Chicago: University of Chicago Press, 1958.

Lichtenstein, Alex. "Chain Gangs, Communism, and the 'Negro Question': John L. Spivak's *Georgia Nigger*." *Georgia Historical Quarterly* 79 (Fall 1995): 633–58.

Long, Lisa A. *Rehabilitating Bodies: Health, History, and the American Civil War.* Philadelphia: University of Pennsylvania Press, 2004.

Marling, Karal Ann. *Wall to Wall America: A Cultural History of Post-Office Murals in the Great Depression.* Minneapolis: University of Minnesota Press, 1982.

Marszalek, John F. "Philatelic Pugilists." In *The Ongoing Civil War: New Versions of Old Stories*, edited by Herman Hattaway and Ethan Sepp Rafuse, 127–38. Columbia: University of Missouri Press, 2004.

Masters, Edgar Lee. *Lincoln the Man.* New York: Dodd, Mead, 1931.

Matthews, Jane DeHart. *The Federal Theatre, 1935–1939: Plays, Relief, and Politics.* Princeton, NJ: Princeton University Press, 1967.

May, Larry. *The Big Tomorrow: Hollywood and the Politics of the American Way.* Chicago: University of Chicago Press, 2002.

McElvaine, Robert S. *The Great Depression: America, 1929–1941.* New York: Times Books, 1993.

McElya, Micki. *Clinging to Mammy: The Faithful Slave in Twentieth-Century America.* Cambridge, MA: Harvard University Press, 2007.

McPherson, Tara. *Reconstructing Dixie: Race, Gender, and Nostalgia in the Imagined South.* Durham, NC: Duke University Press, 2003.

Meyerson, Gregory, and Jim Neilson. "Pulp Fiction: The Aesthetics of Anti-Radicalism in William Faulkner's *Light in August.*" *Science and Society* 72 (January 2008): 11–42.

Murray, Jennifer M. *On a Great Battlefield: The Making, Management, and Memory of Gettysburg National Military Park, 1933–2013.* Knoxville: University of Tennessee Press, 2014.

Musher, Sharon Ann. "Contesting 'The Way the Almighty Wants It': Crafting Memories of Ex-Slaves in the Slave Narrative Collection." *American Quarterly* 53 (March 2001): 1–31.

Naison, Mark. *Communists in Harlem during the Depression.* Urbana: University of Illinois Press, 1983.

Nguyen, Viet Thahn. *Nothing Ever Dies: Vietnam and the Memory of War.* Cambridge, MA: Harvard University Press, 2016.

Niven, Penelope. *Carl Sandburg: A Biography.* New York: Charles Scribner's Sons, 1991.

Noggle, Burl F. "With Pen and Camera: In Quest of the American South in the 1930s." In *The South Is Another Land: Essays on the Twentieth-Century South*, edited by Bruce Clayton and John A. Salmond, 187–204. Westport, CT: Greenwood, 1987.

Novick, Peter. *The Holocaust in American Life.* Boston: Houghton Mifflin, 2000.

———. *That Noble Dream: The "Objectivity Question" and the American Historical Profession.* Cambridge: Cambridge University Press, 1988.

O'Brien, Michael. *The Idea of the American South, 1920–1941.* Baltimore, MD: Johns Hopkins University Press, 1979.

Osterweil, Ara. "Reconstructing Shirley: Pedophilia and Interracial Romance in Hollywood's Age of Innocence." *Camera Obscura* 72 (2009): 1–39.

Paige, John C. *Civil Conservation Corps and the National Park Service, 1933–1942: An Administrative History.* Washington, DC: National Park Service, 1985.

Peterson, Merrill D. *John Brown: The Legend Revisited.* Charlottesville: University of Virginia Press, 2002.

———. *Lincoln in American Memory.* New York: Oxford University Press, 1994.

Prince, K. Michael. *Rally 'Round the Flag, Boys! South Carolina and the Confederate Flag.* Columbia: University of South Carolina Press, 2004.

Pyron, Darden Asbury. *Southern Daughter: The Life of Margaret Mitchell.* New York: Oxford University Press, 1991.

Rauchway, Eric. *The Great Depression and the New Deal: A Very Short Introduction.* New York: Oxford University Press, 2008.

Reardon, Carol. *Pickett's Charge in History and Memory.* Chapel Hill: University of North Carolina Press, 1997.

Ring, Natalie. *The Problem South: Region, Empire, and the New Liberal State, 1880–1930.* Athens: University of Georgia Press, 2012.

Ritterhouse, Jennifer Lynn. *Discovering the South: One Man's Travels through a Changing America in the 1930s.* Chapel Hill: University of North Carolina Press, 2017.

Rodimtseva, Irina V. "On the Hollywood Chain Gang: The Screen Version of Robert E. Burns' *I Am a Fugitive from a Georgia Chain Gang!* and Penal Reform of the 1930s–40s." *Arizona Quarterly* 66 (Autumn 2010): 123–46.

Roediger, David R. *The Wages of Whiteness: Race and the Making of the American Working Class.* New York: Verso, 1991.

Rogin, Michael. *Blackface, White Noise: Jewish Immigrants in the Hollywood Melting Pot.* Berkeley: University of California Press, 1998.

Ronda, Bruce. *Reading the Old Man: John Brown in American Culture.* Knoxville: University of Tennessee Press, 2008.

Rubin, Louis D., Jr. "General Longstreet and Me: Refighting the Civil War." *Southern Cultures* 8 (Spring 2002): 21–46.

Sandage, Scott A. "A Marble House Divided: The Lincoln Memorial, the Civil Rights Movement, and the Politics of Memory, 1939–1963." *Journal of American History* 80 (June 1993): 135–67.

Schulman, Bruce J. *From Cotton Belt to Sunbelt: Federal Policy, Economic Development, and the Transformation of the South, 1938–1980.* Durham, NC: Duke University Press, 1994.

Schwartz, Barry. *Abraham Lincoln and the Forge of National Memory.* Chicago: University of Chicago Press, 2000.

———. *Abraham Lincoln in the Post-Heroic Era: History and Memory in Late Twentieth-Century America.* Chicago: University of Chicago Press, 2009.

Scott, Ellen. "Regulating 'Nigger': Racial Offense, African American Activists, and the MPPDA, 1928–1961." *Film History* 26 (2014): 1–31.

Scott, Robert L. "Diego Rivera at Rockefeller Center: Fresco Painting and Rhetoric." *Western Journal of Speech Communication* 41 (Spring 1977): 70–82.

Silber, Nina. "Reunion and Reconciliation, Reviewed and Reconsidered." *Journal of American History* 103 (June 2016): 59–83.

———. *The Romance of Reunion: Northerners and the South, 1865–1900.* Chapel Hill: University of North Carolina Press, 1993.

———. "When Charles Francis Adams Met Robert E. Lee: A Southern Gentleman in History and Memory." In *Inside the Confederate Nation*, edited by Lesley J. Gordon and John C. Inscoe, 349–60. Baton Rouge: Louisiana State University Press, 2005.

Simon, Bryant. *A Fabric of Defeat: The Politics of South Carolina Millhands, 1910–1948.* Chapel Hill: University of North Carolina Press, 1998.

Sitkoff, Harvard. *A New Deal for Blacks: The Emergence of Civil Rights as a National Issue: The Depression Decade.* New York: Oxford University Press, 1978.

Sklaroff, Lauren Rebecca. *Black Culture and the New Deal: The Quest for Civil Rights in the Roosevelt Era.* Chapel Hill: University of North Carolina Press, 2014.

Smith, Timothy B. *The Golden Age of Battlefield Preservation: The Decade of the 1890s and the Establishment of America's First Five Military Parks.* Knoxville: University of Tennessee Press, 2008.

Stanley, Amy Dru. *From Bondage to Contract: Wage Labor, Marriage, and the Market in the Age of Slave Emancipation*. Cambridge: Cambridge University Press, 1998.

Stewart, Catherine A. *Long Past Slavery: Representing Race in the Federal Writers' Project*. Chapel Hill: University of North Carolina Press, 2016.

Stokes, Melvyn. "The Civil War in the Movies." In *The Legacy of Disunion: The Enduring Significance of the American Civil War*, edited by Susan-Mary Grant and Peter Parish, 65–78. Baton Rouge: Louisiana State University Press, 2003.

———. *D. W. Griffith's "The Birth of a Nation": A History of "the Most Controversial Motion Picture of All Time."* New York: Oxford University Press, 2008.

Sullivan, Patricia. *Days of Hope: Race and Democracy in the New Deal Era*. Chapel Hill: University of North Carolina Press, 1996.

Susman, Warren I. *Culture as History: The Transformation of American Society in the Twentieth Century*. New York: Pantheon, 1973.

Takayoshi, Ichiro. *American Writers and the Approach of World War II, 1935–1941: A Literary History*. Cambridge: Cambridge University Press, 2015.

Telotte, J. P. "The Human Landscape of John Ford's South." *Southern Quarterly* 19 (Spring–Summer 1981): 117–33.

Thelen, David. "Memory and American History." *Journal of American History* 75 (Spring 1989): 1117–29.

Tidwell, John Edgar, and Steven C. Tracy. *After Winter: The Art and Life of Sterling A. Brown*. New York: Oxford University Press, 2009.

Tindall, George. *The Emergence of the New South, 1913–1945*. Baton Rouge: Louisiana State University Press, 1967.

Vaughan, Stephen. "Ronald Reagan and the Struggle for Black Dignity in Cinema, 1937–1953." *Journal of African American History* 87 (Winter 2002): 83–97.

Wald, Alan M. *Exiles from a Future Time: The Forging of the Mid-Twentieth-Century Literary Left*. Chapel Hill: University of North Carolina Press, 2002.

Wall, Wendy L. *Inventing the "American Way": The Politics of Consensus from the New Deal to the Civil Rights Movement*. New York: Oxford University Press, 2008.

Warren, Robert Penn. *The Legacy of the Civil War*. 1961. Reprint, Cambridge, MA: Harvard University Press, 1983.

Waugh, Joan. *U. S. Grant: American Hero, American Myth*. Chapel Hill: University of North Carolina Press, 2009.

Wiggins, William H., Jr. *O Freedom: Afro-American Emancipation Celebrations*. Knoxville: University of Tennessee Press, 1987.

Williams, Linda. *Playing the Race Card: Melodramas of Black and White from Uncle Tom to O. J. Simpson*. Princeton, NJ: Princeton University Press, 2001.

Wilson, Steve. *The Making of "Gone with the Wind."* Austin: University of Texas Press, 2014.

Woodward, C. Vann. "History from Slave Sources: A Review Article." *American Historical Review* 79 (April 1974): 470–81.

———. "The Mississippi Horrors." *New York Review of Books*, June 29, 1989, 15–17.

Yetman, Norman. "The Background of the Slave Narrative Collection." *American Quarterly* 19 (Autumn 1967): 534–53.

Zenzen, Joan M. *Battling for Manassas: The Fifty-Year Preservation Struggle at Manassas National Battlefield Park*. University Park: Pennsylvania State University Press, 1998.

INDEX

Page numbers in italics refer to illustrations.

Abe Lincoln in Illinois (Cromwell) (movie),
101
Abe Lincoln in Illinois (Sherwood) (play), 106,
110, 160, *161*, 162
abolitionism: compared to communism,
144–45, 148
Abraham Lincoln (Griffith), 23–25, *24*, 29,
101, 104
Absalom, Absalom! (Faulkner), 68, 136
Adams, Charles Francis, 17–18
African Americans: as actors, 59–61; Civil
War memory of, 18–19; communism and,
142, 144; Depression and enslavement
and, 70–72, 75–76, 79, 85, 88, *89*; Harlem
Renaissance and, 29–30; Lincoln and,
110–17; movie criticisms of, 150–51, 168–69,
172–76; Nazi oppression comparison to,
148, 160, 165, 177; political parties and,
111–14, 141; World War II and, 160, 165,
168–73, 177. *See also* NAACP; *specific
African Americans*
Agrarians, 16–17, 54, 68, 133, 143–44, 149. *See
also specific Agrarians*
Alabama State Guide, 68
Alexander, Will, 111
Allen, James, 77, 173
American Dilemma, An (Myrdal), 178–79
American Document (Graham), 79
American Guide series, 40, 42–43, 68, 83
American Historical Association, 143, 158
Anderson, Marian, 111, 115, *116*, 117
Andrews, Charles, 140–41
anticommunism, 6–7, 80, 141–48, 181–82, 185
antifascism, 76, 147–48, 151
antilynching legislation, 4, 110, 113, 140–41,
151–52, 173
antiwar attitudes, 157–58

Armah, Kwesi, 186
Arnet, Alex, 124
Arnold, Philip, 127
Arvanti, Cornelia, 127
Association for the Study of Negro Life and
History (ASNLH), 70
Aswell, James, 41
Atkinson, Brooks, 108
Austin, Hannah, 83

Baker, Ella, 71, 86
"Ballad for Americans," 76
Baltimore Afro American, 171
Barber, Max, 19, 32–33
Bashinsky, Elizabeth, 32–33
battlefields, Civil War, 45–53; Bull Run/
Manassas, 45, 52–53; federal government
preservation of, 45–47; Fredericksburg, 53;
Gettysburg, 46–51; narrative change on,
51–53
Battle Hymn (Gold and Blankfort), 39–40,
44, 78–79
"Battles and Leaders of the Civil War," 21
Baxter, Warner, *96*
Belasco, David, 24
Benét, Stephen Vincent, 27–29, 32, 122
Bilbo, Theodore, 135
Birth of a Nation, The (Griffith), 21–22, *22*, 23,
54, 93, 105–6, 151
Black Reconstruction (Du Bois), 70, 87, 173
Black Thunder (Bontemps), 30
Blankfort, Michael, 39, 78–79
Blight, David, 187
blundering generation, 158, 178
"Blundering Generation" address (Randall),
158
BMP (Bureau of Motion Pictures), 172, 174
Bontemps, Arna, 30
Bonus March, 11

Booth, John Wilkes, 95, 105

Boothe, Clare, 146–48, 166

Borah, William, 141

Boston Globe, 101

Bourke-White, Margaret, 79, 88, 134

Bowers, Claude, 26–27, 29

Bradford, Robert, 118

Bredouw, F. E., 163–64

Brinnin, John Malcolm, 121

"Bronx Slave Market," 71

Brown, Earl, 112

Brown, John: African Americans and, 31–33; *Battle Hymn* and, 39–40, 78–79; *John Brown's Body* and, 27–28; *Santa Fe Trail* and, 145–46, 168

Brown, Sterling, 40, 42–43, 44, 70, 82, 83, 181

Bugles Blow No More (Dowdey), 69

Bullock, Rufus, 181

Bull Run/Manassas battlefield, 45, 52–53

Bureau of Motion Pictures (BMP), 172, 174

Burns, Robert Eliot, 88–89

Caldwell, Erskine, 79, 80, 88, 134, 135

California Eagle, 174

capitalism, 17, 87, 132–33, 143–44

Capra, Frank, 176

Carnegie Corporation, 178

carpetbaggers: compared to left-wingers and communists, 142–43, 144; in Reconstruction and Lost Cause narratives, 4, 56, 69, 95, 140

Casablanca (Curtiz), 80, 145, 155–57, 180

Cash, Wilber J., 148–49, 166

Cason, Clarence, 124, 148–49, 166

CCC (Civilian Conservation Corps), 46–47, 49, 128

Century magazine, 21

chain gangs, 71, 88–91, 94, 95

Chapman, Oscar, 120

Chicago Defender, 18, 71, 72, 113, 115, 169, 171, 187

Churchill, Winston, 165–66

Cindy Lou Bethany (character), 146–47

CIO (Committee/Congress for Industrial Organization), 74, 109

Civilian Conservation Corps (CCC), 46–47, 49, 128

civil rights, 5, 114–18, 149, 180, 186–87

Civil Works Administration (CWA), 128

Claassen, Helen S., 55

Clansman, The (Dixon), 21

Clark, Ruth, 41

Clay Wingate (character), 27–28

coal miners, 66, 80

Cobb, Irvin, 94

Code, the, 54, 90, 92

Cold War, 179, 180–81, 186

commemoration. *See* memorialization; monuments, Civil War

Committee for Industrial Organization (CIO), 74, 109

communism: compared to abolitionism, 144–45, 148; fascism and, 148–49; Lost Cause and, 141–48. *See also* anticommunism; Communist Party USA

Communist Manifesto (Marx and Engels), 73

Communist Party in Soviet Union, 76

Communist Party USA (CPUSA): African Americans and, 142, 144; Depression-era "slavery" and, 73–74, 76–79; fascism and, 148; Federal One and, 44; Lincoln and, 100; movies and, 149, 151–52, 171, 173, 174, 179–81; Reconstruction attitudes and, 175; Scottsboro boys and, 30

Confederate flag, 141, 166, 180, 183–84, 186–87

Confederate Memorial Day, 14

Confederate Veteran, 35

Congress of Industrial Organization (CIO), 74, 109

Conkle, E. P., 40, 44, 118, *119*

Connery, William, 86

conservatives, 4, 44, 118–19, 122, 139, 142–43, 180

Cooke, Marvel, 71

Copland, Aaron, 102, 162

Coski, John, 186–87

Costigan-Wagner Bill, 140–41. *See also* anti-lynching legislation

Couch, W. T., 111

CPUSA (Communist Party USA). *See* Communist Party USA

Craven, Avery, 51, 88, 158

Cret, Paul, 48

Crisis, The, 30, 149

Cromwell, John, 101

Crowther, Bowsley, 179, 180
cultural pluralism, 37–40, 85, 110
culture, folk. *See* folk culture
cummings, e. e., 25
Curtiz, Michael, 145; *Casablanca*, 80, 145,
    155–57, 180; *Santa Fe Trail*, 145–46, 168;
    Virginia City, 155–57, 168
CWA (Civil Works Administration), 128

Daily Worker, 78, 151–52, 174, 180
dance, emancipation, 79–80
Daniels, Jonathan, 133–34, 135–36, 144
Daughters of Dixie (play), 39
Daughters of the American Revolution, 115
Davidson, Donald, 16, 134
Davis, Ben, 151–52
Davis, Bette, 95
Davis, David Brion, 114
Davis, Jefferson, 25, 39, 184, 185
De Caux, Len, 109
Delano, Jack, *84*
Delany, Hubert, 75–76
Democrats: African Americans and, 114,
    137, 141; Bowers and, 26–27; Lincoln and,
    100, 113–14, 118; Lost Cause and, 15, 166;
    Roosevelt and, 5, 85, 110, 135, 137, 166. *See
    also specific Democrats*
Denning, Michael, 76
Depression, the. *See* Great Depression
DePriest, Oscar, 19, 113
Dewey, John, 13, 33
Dieterle, William, 174
Dixie (Sutherland), 168
Dixiecrats, 180
Dixon, Thomas, 21
documentary impulse, 81, 85, 103
Dollard, John, 17, 124
Donald, David, 100
Dorsey, Frank, 86, 108–9
Dos Passos, John, 106
Double V campaign, 169
Douglas, Jimmy, 105
Douglas, Stephen, 109
Douglass, Frederick, 111, 113, 117, 167, 170
Dowdey, Clifford, 69, 124, 139
Du Bois, W. E. B., 29–30, 31, 33, 43; *Black
    Reconstruction*, 70, 87, 173
Dudziak, Mary, 179

Edmonds, James, 74
Elmore, Mary, 59
emancipation: memory and, 6–7, 18–19;
    Roosevelt and, 86–87, 114, 161; white, 67,
    92–93, 94; working conditions and, 72,
    73, 109
emancipation dance, 79–80
Emancipation Day celebrations, 18, 19, 75–76,
    85
Emancipation Moment, 114
Emancipation Proclamation (Lincoln), 16,
    18, 107, 111
Emmett, Daniel, 168
Engels, Friedrich, 73
enslavement and the Depression, 65–97;
    African Americans and, 70–72, 75–76, 79,
    85, 88, *89*; in art and writing, 79–81, 87–89;
    communism and Popular Front and, 76–
    79, 80, 81; elevation of white over black
    and, 85–88; in movies, 89–97; New Deal
    politics and, 67, 72, 85–88, 94; overview of,
    13, 65–67, 81; slave interview program and,
    81–85, *84*; white southerners and, 67–70,
    158–59, 175; working class and, 72–76, 85–
    87, 159
Eternal Light Peace Memorial, 47, *47*–48, 52

"Faithful Slave Memorial Committee," 15–16
fascism: antifascism, 76, 147–48, 151; Lincoln
    and, 120, 177; southernism as, 147–49, 151,
    166, 170, 185
Fast, Howard, 173, 181–82
Faudie, Ernestine, 41
Faulkner, William, 68, 136, 144
Federal Art Project, 37
federalism, 27, 128
Federal One, 37–45; congressional scrutiny
    of, 43–44; Federal Art Project, 37; Federal
    Theatre Project, 37, 38–40, 43–44, 118–19,
    119, 128, *129*; Federal Writers' Project, 37,
    40–44, 68, 81–85, *84*, 181; overview of, 37–
    38, 44–45. *See also specific works of*
Federal Theatre Project (FTP), 37, 38–40,
    43–44, 118–19, *119*, 128, *129*. *See also specific
    works of*
Federal Writers' Project (FWP), 37, 40–44,
    68, 81–85, 181. *See also specific works of*
female enslavement, 65, 75, 86–87, 95–96

flag, Confederate, 141, 166, 180, 183–84, 186–87

Flanagan, Hallie, 118–19

folk culture: enslavement and, 5, 81, 82–85, 88, 92; New Deal and, 37, 38, 39, 42, 43, 110; Sandburg and, 103; Silber and, 1–2, 7

Fonda, Henry, 117

Ford, John, 58, 93–95; *Judge Priest*, 58, 94, 97; *Prisoner of Shark Island*, 58, 95, 96, 158, 184; *Steamboat Round the Bend*, 58; *Young Mr. Lincoln*, 101, 106, 117–18, 121

"forgotten man, the," 12, 74, 90, 93, 97

Fort Worth Morning Star, 52

Franco, Francisco, 166

Frazier, E. Franklin, 175–76

"Frederick Douglass: Symbol of Freedom" (Herndon), 170

Fredricksburg battlefield, 53

Freedom Road (Fast), 173, 181–82

Freeman, Douglas Southall, 68, 126, 130, 132, 167–68

Friedman, Thomas, 183

Fritz, Marion, 130

FTP (Federal Theatre Project). *See* Federal Theatre Project

Fugitive, The, 16

FWP (Federal Writers' Project). *See* Federal Writers' Project

Gaines, Kevin, 186

Gallup Polls, 157, 166

Georgia Nigger (Spivak), 88

Gettysburg, battle of: memorialization of battlefield for, 46–51, 52, 53; seventy-fifth anniversary of, 47, 47–50, 50, 138, 157

Gilham, Robert, 55

Gilmore, Glenda, 76–77, 111, 148

Gold, Mike, 2, 77–80, 149, 166; *Battle Hymn*, 39–40, 44, 78–79; *Jews Without Money*, 78

Gone with the Wind (Mitchell) (novel): background and overview of, 2, 3, 15, 25; criticism of, 70, 144–45; fan response to, 123–24, 127, 130–31; Lost Cause and, 139–40, 149–53; slavery references in, 69–70; UDC and, 127–28

Gone with the Wind (Fleming) (movie), *131*; antiwar attitudes and, 158; authenticity

and, 56, 57, 59, 60–62; background and overview of, 2, 3, 36; Communists and, 149–50, 151–52, 179–80, 181; Lost Cause and, 152–53; NAACP and, 149–51, 152, 172; premiere of, 61–62; UDC and, 57

Gordon, Caroline, 68–69, 132

Graham, Martha, 79–80

Granberry, Edwin, 132

Grand Army of the Republic, 18, 35

Granich, Itzok. *See* Gold, Mike

Grant, Ulysses S., 107

Great Depression: about, 9–11, 12–13; Civil War comparison to, 3–4, 9, 13; Civil War memory and, 35–37; economic systems and, 143, 148; enslavement and (*see* enslavement and the Depression); impact of, 10–11; Lost Cause narrative and, 125, 128–34; New Deal and (*see* New Deal)

Great Good Man, The (Hartley), 162

Great War, 35, 157, 164

Green, Paul, 65–66

Griffith, D. W.: *Abraham Lincoln*, 23–25, *24*, 29, 101, 104; *Birth of a Nation*, 21–22, *22*, 23, 54, 94, 105–6

Hankins, Dorothy, 105

Harlem Renaissance, 29–30

Harpers Ferry memorialization, 31–33

Harris, Joel Chandler, 179

Harrow, Carolyn, 99

Hart, Albert Bushnell, 14

Hartford Courant, 51, 173

Hartley, Marsden, 102, 162

Hays, Will, 54

Heisler, Stuart, 176

Heline, Oscar, 10

Hemingway, Ernest, 25

Henry, Stuart, 107

Herndon, Angelo, 77, 78, 170, 177–78

Hickok, Lorena, 65–67, 133

historians and Civil War interpretation, 51, 158, 167. *See also specific historians*

historical reflection of Americans, 12–13

Hitler, Adolf, 148, 160

Hitler-Stalin Nonaggression Pact, 151, 152, 172

Hollywood: African American participation in, 59–61, 172; enslavement vision of, 88,

90–93, 95–97, 173–75; memory creation and, 36, 53, 55–59, 61–62; production code of, 54, 90, 91
Holmes, "Parson Bill," 41
Holt, Rush, 44
Hoover, Herbert, 9–10, 12, 26, 99, 104
Hopkins, Harry, 65
House Un-American Activities Committee, 7, 44, 118, 172, 182
"How a Great Leader Met Adversity" (Freeman), 130
Hudson, Hosea, 77
Hughes, Langston, 61
Hull, Cordell, 171
Hulston, John, 163
humanitarianism, 100, 108, 110, 158
Huston, Walter, 23

I Am a Fugitive from a Chain Gang (LeRoy) (movie), 89–91
I Am a Fugitive from a Georgia Chain Gang (Burns) (novel), 88–89
Ickes, Harold, 115
I'll Take My Stand: The South and the Agrarian Tradition, 16–17, 146
immigrants, 11, 78, 109–10
industrialism, 143–44
industrializing memory, 36, 53
Information Agency, US, 179, 186
isolationism, 157–58

Jackson, Stonewall, 53, 133
Jackson County Sentinel, 142–43
Jefferson Davis (McGee), 39, 44, 128, 129
Jefferson Davis National Highway, 15, 55, 127
Jefferson Davis National Highway (UDC) (play), 39
Jews Without Money (Gold), 78
Jezebel (Wyler), 59, 95–96
Jim Allard (character), 132
Jim Crow: compared to Nazism, 148, 160; FDR and, 110, 111, 112
JMG, 75
John Brown's Body (Benét), 27–29
Johnson, Andrew, 172–73, 174–76
Johnson, Gerald, 13
Johnson, Guy, 33
Johnson, James Weldon, 148

Johnson, Nunnally, 58
Johnson, Oscar, 16
Journal of Negro History, 29, 96
Judge Priest (Ford), 58, 94, 97

Kansas City Star, 52
Kantor, MacKinlay, 157–58
Kasson, John, 101–2
Katznelson, Ira, 110
Kazin, Alfred, 4, 102, 185
Kazin, Michael, 76
Kendrick, Benjamin, 124
Keppel, F. P., 178–79
Keyes, Evelyn, 131
Kimberly, William, 49
King, Martin Luther, Jr., 186
Kiss the Boys Good-Bye (Boothe), 146–47
KKK, 22, 106, 148, 149, 150, 180
Know Nothing Party, 110
Koch, Howard, 38, 80–81, 100, 107, 156, 180
Kosciuszko, Thaddeus, 109
Kostelanetz, Andrew, 162
Ku Klux Klan, 22, 106, 148, 149, 150, 180
Kurtz, Wilbur, 56

labor: in Federal Theatre works, 80; language of slavery for, 66–67, 71–76, 87, 159; Popular Front and communists and, 76–79
labor unions, 74–76, 85–87, 109, 159
Lange, Dorothea, 89
Lanier, Sidney, 128
Lawrie, Lee, 48
Lawson, Elizabeth, 173
Lee, Robert E., 17–18, 68, 105, 107, 126–27, 138, 167
Leigh, Vivian, 60
Leopard's Spots, The (Dixon), 21
Lerner, Max, 121–22
LeRoy, Mervyn, 89–91
Lesser, Sol, 61
Lewis, John, 109, 144
Lewis, Leon, 85
Lewis, Theophilus, 171
liberals, southern, 77, 111, 137, 139
Light in August (Faulkner), 136, 144
Lilly, William, 115
Lincoln, Abraham: African Americans and civil rights and, 110–18, 116, 176–77, 179,

Lincoln, Abraham (*continued*)
186; Bowers and, 26–27; Cold War and, 186; as a common man, 102–4; conservatives and, 118–19, 122; cultural imperialism and, 163, 187; dictatorship and, 100, 120, 122; Emancipation Proclamation and, 16; fascism and, 120, 121–22; federal power and, 5, 106–8, 158; in film, 21–25, 23, 92, 101, *101*, 104–6, 117, 121, 183; as a global figure in World War II, 160–64, *165*, 177–78, 185–86; as the Great Emancipator, 7, 107, 115; as a humanitarian, 108–10; immigrants and, 109–10; as masculine and feminine figures, 105–6; memorial for (*see* Lincoln Memorial); mysteriousness of, 120–22, 163; New Deal link to, 86, 100, 106–7, 109–11, 115, 122, 164; Obama presidency and, 183; overview of twentieth-century addiction to, 3–4, 6, 99–102, 122; Popular Front and communism and, 115–17, 118–19; reconciliation theme and, 104–5; in theater, 40, 100, 102, 106, 107, 118–19, *119*, 160; white southerners and, 105–6, 185; in writings, 25, 28, 102–4, 120–22
Lincoln, Mary Todd, 103
Lincoln Lyrics (Brinnin), 121
Lincoln Memorial, 104, 186; Anderson concert at, 111, 115, *116*; construction and unveiling of, 23
Lincoln Portrait (Copland), 102
Lincoln (Spielberg), 183
Little Colonel, The (Butler), 36
Littlest Rebel, The (Butler), 36, 92–93, 97, 101, *101*, 126, 158
Locke, Alain, 29
Lomax, Alan, 7, 82
Lomax, Elizabeth, 82
Lomax, John, 7, 82
Lonely Man, The (Koch), 80–81, 100, 107
Long, John, 141
Longstreet, James, 53
Los Angeles Times, 101
Lost Cause: anticommunism and, 141–48; antilynching legislation and, 140–41; battlefields and, 45; blame on North and, 133–35, 136, 139, 140; criticism of, 135–36; fascism and, 147–49; *Gone with the Wind* and, 139–40, 149–53; movies and, 21–22,

55–56, 58, 61, 126, 139–40, 149–53; post-World War II revival of, 180; southern connection to past and, 6–7, 124–27; southern poverty and, 133–35, 137–39; sympathy for, 139–40; tie to the Depression, 14–15, 128–33, *131*; UDC and, 127–28
loyalty, slave, 15, 19, 30, 31–32, 42, 67–68, 127
Luce, Henry, 147
Lucy Churchill (character), 68–69
Lumpkin, Grace, 149
Lumpkin, Katharine, 135
lynchings, 94, 117, 140–41, 148. *See also* antilynching legislation

MacLeish, Archibald, 178
MacNeal, A. C., 169, 171
mammies: in movies, 93, 127, 151; UDC and, 15, 30, 31, 32
Manassas battlefield, 45, 52–53
Man on America's Conscience, The. See Tennessee Johnson
Margaret Mitchell legend, 124
Marx, Karl, 73, 78
Massey, Raymond, 145, 147–48, 160, *161*
Masters, Edgar Lee, 120
McConaghie, James, 46
McDaniel, Hattie, 150–51
McGee, John, 39, 44, *129*
McGlynn, Frank, *101*
McQueen, Butterfly, 60–61
Mellett, Lowell, 174
memorialization: African Americans and, 18–19; battlefields and, 45, 46–48, 47, 52–53; Confederate, 14, 18; at Harpers Ferry, 31–33; UDC and, 15–16, 30, 31–33. *See also* monuments, Civil War
memory, Civil War, 35–63; African American, 18–19; battlefields and, 45–53; Federal One programs and, 37–45; Lost Cause as, 14–15; movies and, 53–62; overview of, 2–3, 6–7, 35–36, 62–63; white northern, 17
MGM (Metro-Goldwyn-Meyer), 172, 174, 175, 180
migration, black, 11–12
Milton, George, 51
Milwaukee Social Democratic Herald, 103
Mind of the South, The (Cash), 166
miners, 66, 80

Mitchell, Arthur, 112–14

Mitchell, Margaret, 29; as an anticommunist, 144–45, 181; criticism of, 184; Daniels and, 135–36; Lost Cause and, 139; as movie adviser, 56. See also *Gone with the Wind* (Mitchell) (novel)

monuments, Civil War: Confederate Memorial at Arlington, 18; Eternal Light Peace Memorial at Gettysburg, 47, 47–48, 52; at Harpers Ferry, 31–33; at National Parks, 46–48, 47, 51, 52

Moore, J. K., 49

Morgenthau, Henry, 167

Moss, Carlton, 176

Motion Picture Producers and Distributors of America, 54

movies: authenticity and, 58–61; enslavement and, 89–97; memory making and, 36; overview of 1930s, 53–54; set in post–Civil War era, 57–58. *See also* Hollywood; *specific movies*

Mudd, Samuel, 58, 95, 97

Muni, Paul, 89, 90

Murdock, John, 108

Murphy, Carl, 171

Muse, Clarence, 60, 61

Myrdal, Gunnar, 178–79, 180

Myrick, Susan, 56, 57, 58

NAACP (National Association for the Advancement of Colored People): anti-lynching campaign of, 140, 148; fascism and, 148; Harpers Ferry memorialization and, 31, 33; Lincoln and, 115, 117; movies and, 22, 149–51, 152, 172, 174; slavery and, 71, 72, 149

National Equal Rights League, 113

National Industrial Recovery Act, 74, 85

National Negro Congress, 42

National Opinion Research Center, 177

National Park Service (NPS), 45–47, 48, 52–53

National Recovery Administration, 111

Nazism, 147, 148, 156, 160, 165–68, 171, 185–86

"Negro in Washington, The" (Brown), 44

Negro Looks at the South, A (Brown), 181

Negro Soldier, The (Heisler), 176–77

Negro Writers' Units of Federal Writers' Project, 42, 44

New Deal: Civilian Conservation Corp, 46–47, 49, 128; Federal One programs of (*see* Federal One); labor and, 74; Lincoln and, 86, 100, 106–7, 109–11, 115, 122, 164; Lost Cause and, 125, 136–37, 141, 144; overview of, 4–5, 13; Popular Front and communists and, 76, 79, 81, 88; slavery theme of politics of, 67, 72, 85–88, 94; UDC and, 128

New Masses, 79, 171

New Republic, 178

New York Amsterdam News, 114

New Yorker, 183

New York Times, 55, 107, 108, 150, 152, 179, 182, 183

New York Times Magazine, 164, 165

Nguyen, Viet Thanh, 36, 53

None Shall Look Back (Gordon), 68–69, 132

NPS (National Park Service), 45–47, 48, 52–53

Obama, Barack, 183

"Ode to the Confederate Dead" (Tate), 17

Odum, Howard, 38, 111, 124

Office of War Information (OWI), 159, 172, 173, 174–75, 176–77, 178

Owsley, Frank, 143–44, 145

Owsley, Mary, 10

Paramount Studios, 54, 59–60, 168

Paulsen, Ed, 10

Pegler, Westbrook, 145, 181

People, Yes, The (Sandburg), 2, 103

People's Songs, 7

"People to Lincoln, Douglass, The," 117

Pepper, Claude, 136, 137, 141

Percy, William, 133

Pickens, William, 117

Pippin, Horace, 3

Pittsburgh Courier, 19, 32, 112, 168–69

"Poem, or Beauty Hurts Mr. Vinal" (e. e. cummings), 25

Pool, Parker, 70–71

Popular Front: Depression-era "slavery" and, 5, 76–81, 87–89, 91; Federal One programs and, 38, 78–79, 80; labor organizing and, 74, 76; Lincoln and, 115–17

postage stamps, 134–35
Poston, Ted, 112
poverty, southern, 33, 65–66, 69, 133–34,
    137–40
Poynter, Nelson, 175
Prairie Years, The (Sandburg), 102–4, 162
Prins, Martha, 108
Prisoner of Shark Island, The (Ford), 58, 95,
    96, 158, 184
production codes, 54, 90, 92
"professional southerners," 56, 57, 58
Prologue to Glory (Conkle), 40, 118–19, *119*
Prosser, Gabriel, 30

racial justice, 5, 7, 169–70, 183, 186; Lincoln
    and, 5, 100, 111, 114–18, 122, 177
Randall, James, 51, 68, 158
reconciliation narrative: battlefields and,
    47, 48–50, *50*; FDR and, 138; Lincoln and,
    104–5, 185; in popular culture, 19–24,
    27–28, 93, 157–58
Reconstruction: African American and
    communist challenges to myth of, 70, 77,
    142–44, 148; antilynching debates and,
    4, 140–41, 173; in Bowers works, 26–27;
    Depression compared to, 65–66, 67; Lost
    Cause narrative and, 14, 125–26, 136–37,
    139–44, 148, 153; in movies, 56–58, 173–76;
    politics of, 4
Reconstruction: The Battle for Democracy
    (Allen), 173
regionalism, 37–38, 39, 40
remaking of Civil War memory. *See* memory,
    Civil War
Remembrance Rock (Sandburg), 181
*Report on the Economic Conditions of the
    South*, 137–39
Republicans: Bowers and, 26–27; Lincoln
    and, 99, 100, 104, 111–14, 118. *See also spe-
    cific Republicans*
reunion over race narrative. *See* reconcilia-
    tion narrative
Rice, Elmer, *161*
Richardson, Minnie, 59
Riddleberger, Frank, 163
Ritterhouse, Jennifer, 3
Rivera, Diego, 100

Robertson, Ben, 105, 127, 129–30, 134, 144
Robinson, Earl, 76
Robsion, John, 113–14
Rogers, Will, 58, 94
Roof, Dylann, 183
Roosevelt, Franklin Delano: African Ameri-
    cans and, 112, 169; Gettysburg reunion
    and, 138; Great Depression compared to
    war and, 12–13; labor rights and, 74; Lin-
    coln and, 4–5, 99, 102, 107–10, 114, 122, 138,
    164, *165*; Lost Cause and, 136–39; race and
    suffering and, 85–86; slavery and, 161, 171;
    white southerners and, 139, 166
Ross, Minnie, 83
Roy, Paul, 50
Rubin, Louis, 9, 105
Rushmore, Howard, 152
Rutherford, Ann, *57, 131*
Rutledge, Ann, 23

Sally Dupree (character), 28
Sandage, Scott, 186
Sandburg, Carl, 25, 40, 106–8, 120–21, 163–
    64, 180–81; *People, Yes*, 2, 103; *Prairie Years*,
    102–4, 162; *Remembrance Rock*, 181; *War
    Years*, 104, 121–22, 162–63, 164
Santa Fe Trail, The (Curtiz), 145–46, 168
Saturday Evening Post, 12, 136, 157
Scarlett O'Hara (character), 69, 130–33
Schlesinger, Arthur, 178, 180
Schomburg, Arthur, 112
Schuyler, George, 70, 149, 184
Schwartz, Barry, 102
Scottsboro Boys, 30, 142–44
SCV (Sons of Confederate Veterans), 52
Selznick, David O., 61–62, 148–49, 150, 152,
    172, 179–80
sexuality in film and writings, 25–26, 28
Shepherd, Heyward, 31–32
Sherman, William, 134–35
Sherman, William, Jr., 42
Sherman's March, 42, 134–35
Sherwood, Robert: *Abe Lincoln in Illinois*,
    106, 110, 120–21, 160, *161*, 162; isolationism
    and, 157; Lincoln and, 109, 122, 163, 164;
    Nazism and, 160, 166–67
Silber, Irwin, 1–2, 7

Sims, Caldwell, 83
slave interview project, 41–43, 71, 81–85, *84*
slavery: Cold War views on, 179; conflict
    avoidance and, 51–52; Depression and (*see*
    enslavement and the Depression); erasure
    of, 175; fantasy narrative of, 20; loyalty
    memory and, 15, 19, 30, 31–32, 42, 67–68,
    127; as metaphor for fascism, 170; parallel
    to World War II of, 159–60, 164, 165–67,
    170–71, 177–78; portrayal of, 5–6
Smith, Al, 26
Smith, "Cotton Ed," 141
Smith, Lillian, 135
Smith, Thomas, 121
Society for Correct Civil War Information, 17
Song of the South (Walt Disney movie), 179
Songs of the Civil War (Silber), 1
Sons of Confederate Veterans (SCV), 52
So Red the Rose (Vidor) (movie), 54–56,
    59–60, 126, 150
So Red the Rose (Young) (novel), 17, 54
southern Democrats, 3, 5, 85, 137, 166, 180
southernism compared to fascism, 147, 148,
    185
Southern Literary Messenger, 139
Southern Negro Youth Conference, 115–17
Southern Popular Front, 77. *See also* Popular
    Front
Spanish-American War, 20
Sparks, Elizabeth, 19
Spartacus (Fast), 182
Spivak, John, 88
states' rights, 14, 15, 125, 139
Steamboat Round the Bend (Ford), 58
Stevens, Thaddeus, 26, 173, 174–76
Stokes, Melvyn, 105–6
Storer College, 31–33
stretch-out system, 67, 73, 74
Sullavan, Margaret, 60
Sumner, Charles, 26
Sun Also Rises, The (Hemingway), 25
survival and resiliency, 4, 130–31, 184
symbolism for the Confederacy, 53, 180,
    183–84, 186–87

Taft, William Howard, 23, 104
Takayoshi, Ichiro, 157, 160

Tarbell, Ida, 102
Tate, Allen, 16–17, 144
Tatten, Pearl, 32
Temple, Shirley, 54, 92, *101*, 101–2, 126
Tennessee Johnson (Dieterle), 172–76
Terrell, Harry, 10
There Were Giants in the Land (essay collec-
    tion), 167–68, 170
Thomas, J. Parnell, 44, 118
Thompson, Tony, *84*
time lag of the South, 124–25
Time magazine, 128, 166
Tragic Era, The (Bowers), 26
Trotti, Lamar, 58
Trump, Donald, 184
Tucson Star, 51
Tugwell, Rexford, 13
Turner, Nat, 30
Twentieth Century Fox, *96, 101*

UDC (United Daughters of the Confed-
    eracy). *See* United Daughters of the
    Confederacy
Uncle Tom's Cabin (Pollard) (movie), 58,
    92–93
unions, labor, 74–76, 85–87, 109, 144, 159
United Daughters of the Confederacy
    (UDC): communism and, 146, 185; Lost
    Cause and, 14–15, 38, 39, 40, 127–28, *129*,
    185; memorialization and, 30–33, 35,
    134–35; movies and, 55, 56, 57, 58, 59, 61;
    Sherman stamp and, 134–35; slave loyalty
    memory of, 15, 31, 42, 68; World War II
    and, 166
Unvanquished, The (Faulkner), 136
US Information Agency, 179, 186
US War Department, 45

Vann, Robert, 112
Variety, 55
Verri, Rocco, 99
veterans, Civil War: battlefields and, 45–46,
    48, 49–51, 52, 62; Gettysburg seventy-fifth
    anniversary and, 47, 48–50, *50*, 157; *Gone
    with the Wind* and, 62; as memory care-
    takers, 3, 17–18, 35; in movies, 94
Vidor, King, 54–55, 60

Virginia City (Curtiz), 155–57, 168
Vladeck, Baruch Charney, 162

Waddle, Josiah, 49
wage slavery, 72–73, 78, 80, 99
Wall, Wendy, 11
Walthall, Henry, 58, 94
War Department, 45
Warner Brothers, 89, 155, 180
Warren, Robert Penn, 16, 177
War Years, The (Sandburg), 104, 121–22,
     162–63, 164
Waters, Enoch, 72
Way Down South (Goodwins and Vorhaus),
     61
Wheeler Dam, 128
White, Walter, 150, 151, 152, 172, 174
White, William Allen, 159–60
white slavery, 5, 6, 73, 158–59, 174–75
white southerners: communism and fascism
     and, 144, 165–66, 185; Depression era and,
     65–66; Depression-era slavery narrative
     and, 65–70, 85–86, 134, 184; liberal, 110–11;
     Lincoln and, 105, 111, 177, 185; Lost Cause
     and, 4, 14–16, 125–27, 133–38, 141–42, 180;
     movie making and, 54, 56–62, 91–92; New
     Deal and, 5, 110, 128–30, 136–38; World
     War II and, 166, 169
white supremacy: African American and
     communist protest against, 148, 169;
     Agrarianism and, 17; confederate symbols
     and, 183–84, 187; in film, 21, 56; Lost Cause

and, 14, 15, 140, 141; Nazism and, 148;
     reconciliation and, 20, 21
"whole South slave," 69–70, 134
Wilkins, Roy, 151
women: enslavement of, 65, 71, 75, 86–87,
     95–96; in *Gone with the Wind*, 131–32; New
     Deal exclusion of, 86–87; sexuality and,
     25, 26
Women, The (Boothe), 147
Woodring, Harry, 49
Woodson, Carter, 29, 42, 70, 96, 112
Woodward, C. Vann, 2
working-class and Depression-era enslave-
     ment, 72–76, 85–87, 159
Works Progress Administration (WPA), 128;
     Federal One programs (*see* Federal One);
     Negro Writers' Units, 42, 44; Slave Inter-
     view Project, 41–43, 71, 81–85, 84
World War I, 35, 157, 164
World War II: African Americans in, 173;
     Civil War memory and, 7, 156–58, 167–68,
     177, 185–86; propaganda films of, 176–77;
     South and, 166–68
Wright, H. C., 41
Wright, Richard, 38, 44, 171
Wyler, William, 95–96

You Have Seen Their Faces (Caldwell), 80,
     134
Young, John, 49
Young, Stark, 16–17, 54–55, 56, 78, 133
Young Mr. Lincoln (Ford), 101, 106, 117–18, 121